The Greatest Sedition
is Silence

The Greatest Sedition is Silence

Four Years in America

William Rivers Pitt

Pluto Press

LONDON • STERLING, VIRGINIA

First published 2003 by Pluto Press
345 Archway Road, London N6 5AA
and 22883 Quicksilver Drive,
Sterling, VA 20166–2012, USA

www.plutobooks.com

British Library Cataloguing in Publication Data
A catalogue record for this book is available from the British Library

ISBN 0 7453 2010 4 hardback

Library of Congress Cataloging in Publication Data applied for
Pitt, William Rivers, 1971–
    The greatest sedition is silence : four years in America / William Rivers Pitt.
        p. cm.
Includes bibliographical references and index.
    ISBN 0–7453–2010–4 (HBK)
    1. Civil rights—United States. 2. United States—Politics and
government—2001– 3. War on Terrorism, 2001–   I. Title.
    JC599.U5 P48 2003
    973.931—dc21

                                                                    2002015700

Designed and produced for Pluto Press by
Chase Publishing Services, Sidmouth, England
Typeset from disk by Stanford DTP Services, Towcester
Printed and bound in the United States of America by
Phoenix Color Corp

Contents

The current flows fast and furious. It issues in a spate of words from the loudspeakers and the politicians. Every day they tell us that we are a free people fighting to defend freedom. That is the current that has whirled the young airman up into the sky and keeps him circulating there among the clouds. Down here, with a roof to cover us and a gasmask handy, it is our business to puncture gasbags and discover the seeds of truth.

Virginia Woolf

Necessity never made a good bargain.

Benjamin Franklin

This book is for my mother – a single working parent forging
a good life for her son and herself – who taught me
absolutely everything.

This book is for my father, always in the fight for the rule of law,
who taught me everything else.

This book is for my grandparents, who taught me
the definition of honor.

This book is for Cara, who loves me foolishly for reasons I could
never explain, who embodies my reason for being.

Finally, this book is for Minister Gordon Glenn,
because nobody likes him.

Introduction:
A Book of Memory

I am sitting on my porch in Boston on a perfect summer day. My CD player
has a guy named Robert Randolph spinning in it, recorded at a singularly
wonderful show I saw last winter at the 'Paradise'. My cat is curled up in
the sunshine, there is a good pot of coffee warming in the kitchen, and I
am engaged to be married come next May to a truly extraordinary woman
whom I have loved since first setting eyes on her in San Francisco back in
1995. In a month I will return once again to the joyful space that is my
classroom, where I will teach English Literature, Journalism, and Writing
to roomfuls of bright-eyed teenagers.

Life is calm and good on the surface, but there is a shadow across my
space here on the porch. It comes from the building on the other side of
the fence that borders my lawn, from the American flag that flutters in the
wind on the roof there. I sit out here often and gaze at that flag. I feel a
great swell of pride when I consider the ideals represented in it – freedom,
equality, opportunity, the just rule of law. In those moments, I also feel
an oceanic sadness at the gulf between those ideals and the reality of the
nation over which that flag flies.

It is entirely possible that this great democratic experiment has come to
a close. There is no question that it absorbed a terrible blow from a
September sky as blue as that which shelters me today. The tragic fact of
September 11, and the grievous wound we received that day, do not in any
way tell the whole story. The real tragedy lies in the wounds we have
inflicted upon ourselves in the aftermath. No terrorist, armed with all the
weapons of nightmare, could do the damage to this country that has been
done in the name of freedom by those most warmed by its light.

Perhaps the experiment is finished. It will be years before we fully
appreciate the damage we have done to the rule of law under our
Constitution and Bill of Rights. As it stands today, a man named Jose
Padilla is being held at the pleasure of the Bush administration under
suspicion of terrorist activity. He has been charged with nothing, has seen
neither judge nor jury, and will not be provided that opportunity in the
near or distant future. He sits in prison, stripped of all the rights and

privileges afforded an American citizen, because the Bush administration has decreed it must be so.

This is but one of many malodorous legal precedents being set these days. Padilla may well be a dangerous man, worthy of prison, but he is an American citizen. The simple fact of that requires that he be given the chance to defend himself against the charges that have been leveled against him. Any American would expect and demand the same quarter, and would be appalled if it were denied them. Yet that is the status of the rule of law in America today.

There is a passage in Robert Bolt's play, *A Man For All Seasons*, which aptly describes what is at stake in the matter of Jose Padilla's treatment under the new system of laws we currently endure:

> *Roper* So now you'd give the Devil benefit of law!
> *More* Yes. What would you do? Cut a great road through the law to get after the Devil?
> *Roper* I'd cut down every law in England to do that!
> *More* Oh? And when the last law was down, and the Devil turned round on you – where would you hide, Roper, the laws all being flat? This country's planted thick with laws from coast to coast – man's laws, not God's – and if you cut them down – and you're just the man to do it – d'you really think you could stand upright in the winds that would blow then? Yes, I'd give the Devil benefit of law, for my own safety's sake.

In America, you can be held indefinitely and without ever facing, or being allowed to defend yourself against, the charges that have put you in stocks. Your citizenship does not matter: if the Bush administration says you are a terrorist, then you are a terrorist and shall not see the light of day. The same new provisions that allow this – the PATRIOT Anti-Terror Act, the Homeland Security Act and Bush's own Executive Order signed November 2, 2002 – also provide for the invasion of any American home, without warrant or notification to the citizen, for a full search by Federal authorities. Again, you need only come under suspicion of terrorist activities, an accusation of dangerous elasticity in these days of super-patriotism and paranoia, for your rights as an American to be brushed aside.

We have cut that great road through the law to get at the Devil, and the winds have only just begun to blow.

Benjamin Franklin once said that those who would sacrifice freedom for security deserve neither. He never lived in days when airplanes could be used as fuel-air explosives against civilians, never knew a world filled with the tools of nuclear holocaust, never conceived of a world where an entire city block could be destroyed of all life by the biological contents of a glass vial. Yet he knew a few things, did old Ben. He knew that freedom destroyed is not easily recovered. He knew that the ideal that is America was a prize to be defended at all costs, for in the annihilation of that ideal lives the loss of the greatest hope of humanity. He knew that destroying freedom in order to save it is folly.

Were he alive today, Franklin might be forced to concede that, with all we Americans have done to damage that which is best and purest in this country, the terrorists have won a greater victory than all the bombs and fire and fear could ever bring to our shores.

The damage we have inflicted upon ourselves goes beyond that sacred graveyard in midtown Manhattan, beyond the new and ever-expanding holes that have been punched through our most fundamental rights. My television has shown the stock market trapped in a death spiral of losses. The fact of that spiral is less important than the reasons behind it. Capitalism, that great engine of innovation, has discovered a fatal cancer in its guts. Men of low morals, empowered to steal by the cowboy deregulations enacted by Republican Congresses of the late 1990s, have ripped the markets to tatters and shreds.

This cancer has metastasized itself into the highest offices of government in this land. George W. Bush and Dick Cheney stand accused, amid rafts of evidence to support those accusations, of engaging in the same foul practices while in the petroleum business. They partook in the tactics listed above as a matter of course and as a pure expression of their concept of capitalism. They are cast from the same mold as those who ran Enron, WorldCom, IMClone, and the rest, right into the ground, taking untold billions of dollars' worth of investor trust with them. The pirates have seized this ship of state, and have two of their own at the helm.

Yet Bob Dylan once sang, 'Even the President of the United States sometimes must have to stand naked.'

I am nobody of importance. At the time of this printing, I am a high school teacher. I pay my taxes every year and signed up for the Selective Service on my eighteenth birthday, on the eve of the Gulf War, like a good American. I have led a fairly unremarkable life. Yet I pay attention. On the Christmas Eve of my fifteenth year I heard my president, Ronald Wilson Reagan, tell me that my generation would likely be the one to face the Apocalypse. I have been watching like a hawk ever since. I have come to understand that the level of attention I pay to the news, and to politics in general, distinguishes me from the ranks of everyday Americans.

Most people, I think, read maybe one newspaper a day. They cruise the front page, perhaps lingering over the editorial page, before moving on to the Arts or Sports sections. They watch the local news every night, maybe the nightly national broadcast on one of the networks, and know where to find CNN or Fox News if they have cable. Some will get international news via the BBC broadcast on NPR, but the vast majority of Americans get all of their information from American media sources. This is a generalization, to be sure, but an accurate one for the most part. The narrowness of perspective engendered by this cannot be overstated and will be elaborated upon in the coming chapters.

In the last several years, thanks to the Internet, I have made it a solid habit to read through the meat of perhaps a dozen newspapers across the country and the world. The *Boston Globe*, the *New York Times*, the *Washington Post*, the *Los Angeles Times*, the *Chicago Tribune* and *Sun-Times*, the *Miami Herald* and the *Dallas Morning News* are daily stops. Augmenting these perspectives are the London *Guardian* and the BBC, along with a host of international wires and news services. Every perspective and every angle – Left, Right, and Center – are represented.

Does it sound like this takes up my entire day? It doesn't. I have carved out special times to do the work. And it is work. But I made it a priority a long time ago, and it has in many ways made me a very dangerous sort of American. I am one of We The People, regular in every way, who has made the decision to be an informed disciple of democracy. For the people who run this country and the world, I am the simplest sort of nightmare. If too many other people start doing what I do, the men behind the curtain will suddenly have an awful lot to worry about. There could be no more dangerous threat to the new status quo than a citizen army of Americans, armed to the teeth with information and the right to vote, paying active attention to the ways and means of our government and economy.

What follows is a book of memory. History happens so fast these days – stories and events that would have captivated the news media for weeks now rise and are forgotten in a matter of hours. So very much has happened in the last two years, and most people simply do not have the time and energy to keep up with it all. I have tried with this book, with my years of observation, research, and writing, to capture some of the history that has overtaken us.

The American Experiment may well be finished, gone beyond our reach forever, but I will not allow it to pass without a fight. The heart of this country still beats, and the soul of this country still glows with the optimism and strength that first birthed it. I am just one man in the watchtower, reading and scribbling and remembering. I pray you will join me on the battlements, armed with memory and with hope, so that together we may defeat all enemies – foreign and domestic – and begin to bring this great nation once more into the light.

William Rivers Pitt
Boston, Massachusetts

The Dream That Was America

There once was a dream called America.

In the beginning, it did not reside on a particular patch of earth. It had no borders, no mountains, no rivers, no forests. It had no seas, crops, roads, or cities. It claimed no army, navy, or air force. No nuclear weapons were coiled in the soil, waiting for the order to spring.

The dream that was America was born in turbulent days surrounding the final collapse of the Stuart monarchy in England. King James II believed it within his purview to dismiss, ignore, and override Parliament, who were the representatives of the people. He held citizens in prison without charging them or bringing them before a magistrate. He deigned to have them tried before secret courts. Troops loyal to him entered private homes as they pleased. Citizens who did not practice the religion of the king knew fear.

When William of Orange marched on London in 1688, trailed by an army once loyal to James and backed by the will of Parliament, the last Stuart monarch was sent across the English Channel to live in exile in France. It is believed that he threw the Great Seal of the Stuarts into the frigid waters, a final symbolic drowning for a disgraceful era.

From that day, Britain was to be ruled by the people, through their representatives in Parliament. Parliament was to rule the king, and not the reverse. A Bill of Rights was drafted, in which was enshrined the first true habeas corpus laws protecting the basic rights of citizens against the infringements of government. Troops could no longer enter private homes, citizens could not be held without charge or trial, and qualified religious freedom, with some exceptions, was at long last established.

This was the first germination of the dream that was America. The idea, realized in the wake of a tyrant, demanded that the citizens of a nation have the right to self-determination and self-rule. They were tasked to decide for themselves who would represent them in government and had the power to rescind the invitation if a particular representative did not perform as required. The days of an absolute monarchy, a single ruler whose word was law, were at an end.

There was a responsibility inherent in this: if government spun out of control, it was the people who had to set it right. In payment for this responsibility, the people knew security in home and church, in person and belief.

Over the next 300 years, the idea that was America carved out a space on the planet that became a powerful nation. It found borders and mountains, seas and rivers, crops and sky. It created an army, a navy, and an air force. It buried nuclear dragons in the soil, and rolled out great roads across it. Magnificent cities rose into the clouds, housing people rich and poor.

Underneath it all lay two sheets of paper, upon which were scrawled words straight from the heart of John Locke, who was there when the Stuarts were sent on their way. The Constitution and the Bill of Rights defined the dream that was America and codified the rights that each citizen could expect. Amendments were attached over time, a remarkable thing, that extended these rights and freedoms to places never before known in the history of humanity.

This was the dream: Americans had the right – the right! – to life, liberty, and the pursuit of happiness. They had the right to be secure from governmental searches of their homes. They were free to practice whatever religion they chose, or to practice no religion at all. They could say or write anything they wished, so long as those words did not overtly threaten or unduly frighten any other citizen.

They could not be imprisoned without charge or trial, could not be punished cruelly, and had the right to zealous representation by a lawyer in whom could be placed absolute trust, thanks to the protection endowed by privilege. With elastic restrictions, Americans even had the right to arm themselves with incredibly powerful and deadly weapons.

To be sure, the dream had never been truly realized. The birth of the dream came only after the death of another, when the people who occupied the land first were driven out and butchered. Citizens were denied many of the basic rights outlined in those tattered documents due to foul souls and wretched bigotry. Other barbarous crimes were committed within and without the borders of the nation that housed the idea. Chattel slavery was one. There were failures, and failures again.

This was the magic of the dream, the poetry and beauty of the idea: that such wrongs could and would be righted, that the idea would march ever onward to a greater perfection, that those illegitimately excluded would be brought inside the fold, because, according to the idea, that was the only right thing to do. For 300 years it was happening, and would continue to happen, unto the end of the world.

On September 11, 2001, the dream that was America died in a ball of fire, flesh, and dust.

It was not murdered by the killers who brought such hideous carnage to the land. A dream so powerful, an idea so pure and good, was too strong to be shattered by outsiders. No, such a thing can be destroyed only by those who live within it, by those who had for so long pulled the warm blanket of liberty to their chins that they came to take it for granted. The dream that was America died at the hand of those who were most warmed by it.

The dream began to die long before September 11, 2001. Cracks began to appear every election day, as more and more Americans decided they wanted no part of the responsibility that guaranteed the safety of the rights and privileges. On the night of the 2000 election, 100 million citizens – fully one half of the voting populace – did not participate in that most fundamental of obligations. The result, after a contested election and the intervention of a politically biased court, was a government that represented only the narrowest slice of the nation.

This court had been installed years before by representatives who won office through elections in which great swaths of the populace did not participate. By abdicating responsibility, the citizens guaranteed this outcome.

It is all finished now. Today, in America, it is dangerous to speak feely. Officers of the government may enter private homes without notice and perform invasive searches of personal property. Officers of the government may listen to private conversations between client and attorney, thus tearing away the veil of privilege and the guarantee of zealous representation. Individuals are being held without charge or trial, their fates to be determined by secret courts.

It was said once that the Constitution is not a suicide pact, and there is wisdom in this. The physical nation that is America endured a catastrophic attack, and there must be a response. Today in America, that response has been to murder the idea that is America. The idea is more important, far more important, than the land or the borders or the treasure, or even the people. Without the idea, the nation is worthless. In the death of the idea lies complete and total victory for those who attacked the country. They need never come here again, for their job is well and truly done.

The war to combat the evils of September 11 is not a suicide pact, either. The only hope, the last hope, for a nation based upon an idea is the simple truth that no good thing ever truly dies. Like the phoenix, it can rise in glory from the ashes of its own conflagration. Today, the dream that was America has ceased to exist. Tomorrow, it may come again. If it does, it will happen only because the citizens of the country who are the keepers of the flame decide once more to place upon their shoulders the yoke of responsibility that was for so long scorned and ignored.

The citizens of that idea must take back the government that has robbed them of their freedoms. They must snatch victory from the jaws of defeat. They must send these newly incarnated Stuarts into disgrace. They must cast the Great Seal of a corrupted, failed ruler into frigid waters, drowning it once and for all.

In the paralyzing aftermath of September 11, it stands to reason that good people stand unsure of what to do and how to act. The idea that dissent equals treason has been well promulgated. The sense that any criticism may be construed as an insult to those who died and those who grieve is ever present. The time has come, however, to shoulder these burdens and cast aside fear. So much damage has already been done. If we do not act, and soon, there will be nothing of this country worth fighting for, beyond worthless stock options and tattered flags strapped to car antennae.

If you need guidance, cast your eyes around this country. There are bright examples everywhere of what to do, and also what not to do. Too often, those who should be guiding us to righteousness and freedom instead point the way towards hate and fear. This adds to the confusion.

The Reverend Jerry Vines, senior pastor of the Jacksonville, FL, First Baptist Church, spoke to the faithful at the 2002 Southern Baptist pastors conference in St Louis. In his remarks, Vines stated that, 'Islam is not just as good as Christianity.' Vines went on to decry Mohammed, the founder of Islam, as 'a demon-possessed pedophile.'

The Reverend Jack Graham, newly elected president of the Southern Baptist Convention, seemed to speak for the congregation as a whole when questioned about Vines' remarks: 'His statement is actually a statement that can be confirmed,' said Graham. 'I believe the statement is an accurate statement.'

Vines was by no means the main event of this conference. Two days later, George W. Bush graced the pastors with his presence via satellite link. His image smiled down upon them from a huge screen. 'I want to thank all of you for your good works,' Bush told them. 'You're believers, and you're patriots, faithful followers of God and good citizens of America. And one day, I believe that it will be said of you, "Well done, good and faithful servants."'

The pastors, to make a bad pun, went into raptures as Bush spoke. The message was clear: The president stands with them. Vines' patriotic work spreading xenophobia and religious intolerance across the nation earned him the title of patriot. The Southern Baptists are already politically powerful – House Majority Leader Tom DeLay is a member of the Texas congregation – and Bush's words only reinforced the belief they hold in their own rectitude.

The simple bigotry within Vines' statements would be laughable if it were not so appalling. Imagine the outrage that would pour forth if someone were to claim that all Christians on earth are on the same moral level of belief as Jerry Falwell and Pat Robertson, who blamed the September 11 attacks on gays, feminists, and the American Civil Liberties Union. Imagine if someone called Jesus Christ a 'demon-possessed' individual who consorted with known whores.

Bush's appearance in a place where intolerance and hatred are preached by spiritual leaders of this comparatively extreme sect of Christianity underscores the central crisis facing America today. America is a great nation. The attacks of September 11 did not only take life and destroy property, however. The attacks have brought us to a place where we are unsure of the validity and sustainability of our most basic freedoms.

Due to a catastrophic failure of leadership at the highest levels, Americans are no longer sure which way is up. We have lost our sense of moral clarity. Our freedom to ask questions without fear of reprisal has been cast into a well of doubt that is made all the darker by homespun threats and intimidation.

John Ashcroft's announcement that an American named Jose Padilla had been arrested for plotting to explode a low-yield 'dirty' radioactive device in a major American city set the nation on tense edge. The White House reprimanded Ashcroft, stating that the threat was minimal and that his predictions of 'mass death and injury' were off the mark. Padilla had been arrested a month earlier. It quickly became clear that he was little more than a petty criminal who talked a good game, but lacked the resources to blow up much of anything. He is currently imprisoned without having been charged, and there are no plans to bring him before a court, as is his right as an American citizen. No dirty nuke could do the damage to the country that the precedent set by this action has done.

Bush, Rumsfeld, and Cheney were telling everyone who would listen of impending doom, inevitable biological attacks, suicide bombers on American streets, and the looming destruction of the Statue of Liberty and the Brooklyn Bridge. This spate of warnings came hot on the heels of revelations about security breakdowns before September 11, FBI agents who were starting to talk, and a Congressional inquiry into it all. Even within a badly compromised media, a sense that the administration was purposefully jarring Americans with these warnings to deflect heat and to cow the Democratic opposition began to fester openly. Ashcroft's gaffe only exacerbated this.

Americans are now subject to a government that will terrorize them in order to further whatever agenda happens to present itself at the moment. More often than not, that agenda is about protecting the Bush administration from criticism about the catastrophe that was their preparedness for September 11. The administration and its security apparatus was warned, repeatedly and in detail, by foreign intelligence services about an impending stateside attack. They failed to act, and now scare Americans into forgetting to ask the hard questions about this. There is no moral clarity here, but only a base instinct for political self-preservation.

The loss of our moral clarity has left us in such dire straits that we do not even need a fearmongering government to slap us into line. On far too many occasions of late, we do this to ourselves in the name of 'patriotism.'

When Ohio State University held its graduation ceremony for the class of 2002, George W. Bush was the commencement speaker. Students there had organized a Turn Your Back On Bush protest to signal their disregard for his war and the shredding of civil liberties at home, and had marked their mortarboards with taped-on peace symbols so each could know the other. At the moment Bush was to appear on the podium, these protesters would, simply and eloquently, turn their backs to him. Eyewitnesses at the scene state that they were unable to number the peace symbols, because there were too many to be counted.

Before the students were led into Ohio Stadium for the ceremony, however, an announcement from the school administration was made. Students who turned their backs on Bush faced expulsion from the ceremony, denial of diploma, and arrest. They were informed that school staff members, police officers, and Secret Service agents would be watching. As they entered the stadium, the students were told to 'cheer loudly for President Bush.' Despite all this, the protesters planned to go ahead with their action.

One protester whom I know personally never got the opportunity to see how it came off. When the moment arrived, he stood and turned his back on Bush. Before he could assess how many others around him were doing the same, he was hustled out of the stadium by a Columbus police officer and a Secret Service agent. He was told that if he left peacefully, he would not be arrested for 'disturbing the peace.' Because he had his daughter with him, he wisely avoided detainment.

And so it goes. Who needs a PATRIOT Act when ordinary Americans – educators, no less – will happily suppress, with threats of arrest and the denial of a hard-earned diploma, any views contrary to those espoused by the government? The Bush administration was likely more than pleased with OSU's actions on that Friday, for they govern by the same principles. This government does not lead with hope and promise, but with fear. They are the purveyors of night sweats and bad dreams. They are profiteers in the boneyard.

The boneyard they use for their gain, however, is haunted. It is haunted by Katy Soulas, who lost her husband in the World Trade Center. It is haunted by Kristen Breitweiser, who also lost her husband. It is haunted by Mary Fetchet, who lost her son. It is haunted by nearly 100 parents, brothers, sisters, and children of the September 11 victims who rallied outside Congress in June 2002 to urge an independent investigation into the attacks. They came as the congressional inquiries, which Bush believes 'understand the obligation of upholding our secrets,' met behind closed doors.

For these families, the secretive nature of the hearings was insufficient. A picture appearing alongside the *Washington Post*'s report of the rally showed one family member holding aloft a sign which read, 'Bush & Cheney Left D.C. For Over A Month, Bush in Florida 9/11, Ashcroft Stops Flying Commercial Airplanes.' Only an independent investigation, free of political influence, will suit them. They know too much.*

The moral clarity of these families is beyond question. They do not launch bigoted attacks against Islam and they do not wish to turn the deaths of their loved ones into some sort of boon. They seek to make sure that nothing like September 11 ever happens again and believe an all-inclusive, unrestrained investigation is the only way to achieve this. Beside them at the rally were Democratic Senators Charles Schumer, Hillary Clinton, and Joe Lieberman, along with former House Minority Leader Richard Gephardt. Each affirmed the demands of the families by stating that the ongoing inquiry is not enough.

Heroes are hard to come by these days. These families, however, are a beacon of light in the darkness. The Democratic Congressmen and women who stood with them deserve highest praise, as do Democratic House members Barbara Lee, Cynthia McKinney, and Dennis Kucinich, who stepped forward to question the ways and means of this terror war long ago. Those who faced down the threat of arrest at OSU on Friday are an inspiration to us all.

---

* In November 2002, Henry Kissinger was tapped by Bush to chair an investigation into September 11. Kissinger is the ultimate manifestation of covert activity and cover-ups in America. This was a telling choice by Bush.

It is a beginning. Many within the opposition still fear to speak openly of their doubts about Bush and his administration. Those who do get short shrift from the national media – CSPAN, which covers virtually every event in Washington, failed to afford coverage to the September 11 families' protest and the Democratic leaders who attended.

Bush and his people would have us believe in a black-and-white world of clear good and clear evil. Though such premises are hopelessly simplified, their actions are actually bringing about the setting of such straightforward divisions. Bush stands on one side, praising bigoted religious xenophobia, speaking of secrets while whispering of disaster. The families of September 11 victims, along with a few bold politicians and the students at OSU, stand across from them seeking the truth and demanding a country of principles. In between them lies the moral clarity that will save us all, if its imperatives are heeded.

Heeding this call to stand and be counted has traditionally been an unsure venture in America. Our history is rife with stories of FBI agents infiltrating and harassing citizen groups that would change or derail dangerous actions by our government. The CIA and COINTELPRO (the FBI's domestic counter intelligence program) are an ever-present reminder that you, yes you, can and will be watched if you step out of line.

With the arrival of the Bush administration, and after the attacks of September 11, the level of intimidation has reached unprecedented levels. Attorney-General John Ashcroft, the most powerful police official in the land, was called before Congress on December 6, 2001, to give testimony regarding the restrictions being placed upon the commonest of American liberties. With the passage of the PATRIOT Anti-Terror Bill, and through an Executive Order signed by Bush authorizing secret military tribunals for suspected terrorists (the latter of which was enacted with virtually no congressional oversight, despite the fact that it seems to violate the spirit, if not the letter, of the Posse Comitatus Act), Ashcroft had some things to answer for.

From the beginning of his testimony, Ashcroft was defiant in the face of some skeptical Democratic senators. He waved a copy of an Al Qaeda terrorism handbook in their faces as proof positive that no restriction of freedom was too severe when considering the enemy we face. In his opening remarks, Ashcroft made the following statement:

To those who scare peace-loving people with phantoms of lost liberty, my message is this: Your tactics only aid terrorists – for they erode our national unity and diminish our resolve.

There is no plainer way to say it – this is rank demagoguery of a strain so pure that it has not been heard in the political dialogue of this nation since the dark days when Richard Nixon and Joseph McCarthy made careers out of shattering innocent lives during highly publicized anti-communist congressional hearings in the 1950s.

In essence, John Ashcroft claimed that if you question the unprecedented steps he and his Justice Department are taking, if you voice doubts about the concept of destroying freedom in order to save it, if you step out of the narrow line being drawn by him and Mr Bush, you are a terrorist. If you dare to participate in that most fundamental American activity – dissent – you are aiding and abetting the murderous butchers who sent thousands of our citizens to death.

No graver an accusation can be leveled in this time. It is one thing to sit and hold your tongue for fear of being called unpatriotic, as many patriotic Americans have done in the aftermath of September 11. It is another again to be called a terrorist for defending the sanctity of the US Constitution from men who come for it with erasers and redacting tape.

Ashcroft claimed that there are people who are scaring Americans with 'phantoms of lost liberty.' Let us examine some of these phantoms, and see if there is any flesh on the bones.

The First Amendment of the Constitution reads as follows:

> Congress shall make no law respecting an establishment of religion, or prohibiting the free exercise thereof; or abridging the freedom of speech, or of the press; or the right of the people peaceably to assemble, and to petition the Government for a redress of grievances.

The idea that it was unpatriotic to question Bush in the aftermath of September 11 received wide play and acclamation in the media, and still does in many circles. This skirted the edges of free speech restrictions forbidden by the First Amendment. Ashcroft's proclamation that anyone who speaks out against his and Mr Bush's plans fairly defines the reason this Amendment was created in the first place.

Patriotic Americans now fear to speak out against the government, the first fundamental responsibility of any citizen, for fear of an accusation that will taint them forever. It is intimidation in the raw of the first principle – the right to speak your mind and to defy authority when it has gone awry.

The Fourth Amendment to the Constitution reads as follows:

The right of the people to be secure in their persons, houses, papers, and effects, against unreasonable searches and seizures, shall not be violated, and no Warrants shall issue, but upon probable cause, supported by Oath or affirmation, and particularly describing the place to be searched, and the persons or things to be seized.

Section 213 of the PATRIOT Anti-Terrorism Bill is entitled 'Authority for Delaying Notice of the Execution of a Warrant.' Legal analysts have given this provision a snappier title: the 'sneak and peek' provision. Under Section 213, Federal officers can enter your home, search your belongings, and attach devices to your personal computer that record and broadcast back to them any and all keystrokes you make while online. They can do all of this without ever letting you know they were there.

Ostensibly, this provision is aimed at true-blue terrorists. We don't want them to know we're watching. After Ashcroft's performance of December 6, however, any belief we may have that he or his department will refrain from using this provision to police ordinary Americans must be shaken to the core. If you speak out, you are a terrorist. The next logical step is that you will therefore be treated as one.

The Sixth Amendment to the Constitution reads as follows:

In all criminal prosecutions, the accused shall enjoy the right to a speedy and public trial, by an impartial jury of the State and district wherein the crime shall have been committed, which district shall have been previously ascertained by law, and to be informed of the nature and cause of the accusation; to be confronted with the witnesses against him; to have compulsory process for obtaining witnesses in his favor, and to have the Assistance of Counsel for his defense.

One of the main reasons Ashcroft was ordered to appear before Congress was because of Bush's Executive Order authorizing the use of secret military tribunals to try – and potentially order the execution of – anyone suspected of being a terrorist. This is troubling on its face: secret trials with secret evidence followed by secret judgments. It was this sort of behavior that sent the Stuart king into exile.

Read the Executive Order closely, however. The section entitled 'Definition and Policy' describes what manner of suspect would come before the tribunal:

(a) The term 'individual subject to this order' shall mean any individual who is not a United States citizen with respect to whom I determine from time to time in writing that:

(1) there is reason to believe that such individual, at the relevant times, (i) is or was a member of the organization known as al Qaida; (ii) has engaged in, aided or abetted, or conspired to commit, acts of international terrorism, or acts in preparation therefor, that have caused, threaten to cause, or have as their aim to cause, injury to or adverse effects on the United States, its citizens, national security, foreign policy, or economy; or (iii) has knowingly harbored one or more individuals described in subparagraphs (i) or (ii) of subsection 2(a)(1) of this order; and

(2) it is in the interest of the United States that such individual be subject to this order.

It is (2) that gives pause. There are some 20 million non-citizens occupying and working in the US right now. They could be arrested, detained, tried and convicted in secret if someone decides 'it is in the interest of the United States.' If John Ashcroft, whose idea of treason extends to questioning his highly questionable actions, is representative of the attitude being brought to this anti-terrorism endeavor, the precepts laid out in the Sixth Amendment have suddenly turned appallingly fragile.

Considering the lengths Ashcroft seems willing to go in order to stifle dissent, one wonders how difficult it would be to strip someone like you or me of our citizenship if we yell a bit too loudly. We would then be subject to (2) as well. Once again, the circumstances surrounding the limitless imprisonment of Padilla without charge come to the fore.

The phantoms Mr Ashcroft so arrogantly disparaged seem to have some significant substance, after all.

America is an idea, one represented and defended by the Constitution, the Bill of Rights, and the Amendments listed above. Destroy the idea and you have destroyed the nation. If we are to believe the hyperbole of the administration, those who attacked us on September 11 did so because they despise our freedoms. To destroy those freedoms in response to the attack is tantamount to surrender.

Fascism is defined as 'A system of government marked by centralization of authority under a dictator, stringent socioeconomic controls, suppression of the opposition through terror and censorship, and typically a policy of belligerent nationalism.' This definition cuts too close to the bone. The time has come to stand up and say no to this slow evisceration of the idea that is America, to say no to men like Ashcroft who hold our essential freedoms in such contempt. Never forget that it was Ashcroft, in the earliest draft of the Anti-Terrorism bill, who penciled in the suspension of habeas corpus. If there is a beating heart within the body of laws that protect our freedoms, habeas corpus is it. Thankfully, a wiser head erased Ashcroft's line from the Act, but the fact that it was ever there at all should be enough to rouse us.

The argument men like Ashcroft and Bush have put forth to defend their actions is simple: it is in the best interest of the nation that nothing controversial regarding the administration be publicly discussed. To do so would undermine all efforts currently directed towards bringing the terrorists to justice. The maintenance of this best-interest argument relies on the idea that the administration deserves total freedom of action, and the belief that everything they are doing is directed towards protecting us and capturing the butchers.

The great trust Americans are laying at the feet of George W. Bush and his administration is being horribly abused. Such abuses are being ignored in the name of unity and patriotism by much of the media.

Under this patriotic cloak of absolute faith, the Bush administration is engaged in crimes and constitutional perversions that besmirch the very essence of the American system. Their actions undermine completely and totally the premise described above. They do not deserve our trust and do not deserve the shroud of trusting silence that has enveloped them. They must be called to account for it. As Bill Moyers so eloquently stated in his speech on October 16, 2001, the greatest sedition at this point is our silence.

The betrayal began in earnest with the passage of Bush's stimulus package, which gave vast swaths of our tax dollars to massive corporations which are still turning a healthy profit in these economically trying days. They are in the black while many Americans dive headlong into the red, and yet it is the financially sound corporations who will receive 80% of the stimulus. No provision has yet been created to provide protection for the scores of Americans who are out of work.

The airline industry received a massive financial bailout. The insurance industry has come to Bush with hat in hand and will be rewarded. For working Americans there is nothing, and nothing, and nothing but the fraudulent promise of trickledown economic principles that has been proven time and again to be empty. Despite all that has happened, Bush clings yet to greedy conservative economic concepts that reward the top 1% immediately while relying on some absurd concept of financial gravity to assuage the needs of the rest of us. It did not work for Reagan and it will not work today. Still, they persist.

Then came the airline security bill. Millions of Americans need to fly for their livelihoods, and millions more require that passenger flow to maintain their businesses. Visions of aircraft slamming into buildings still dance in everyone's heads, and getting on an airplane today requires more courage than the average American ever expected to have to display on their own soil. A vast majority of these people want and need assurance that these planes are safe. The economics of the airline industry, and the cottage industries that have grown around it, demand that sense of security.

The airline industry, presumably, knows this. It was their security failure in large part that helped the terrorists attack us, because they chose for years to scrimp on security in the name of the bottom line. That bottom line apparently remains the dominant consideration, despite the Federal bailout, because the airline industry lobbied hard against the airline security legislation proposed by the Senate.

The cognitive dissonance involved in this process is baffling until the political cards are laid down. Bush wants to help the economy, wants to assuage our fears, wants us to continue living our lives with as much normalcy as possible. Yet his actions on behalf of the airline industry will not calm American fears of flying, which will make it difficult to return to normal, which will keep us off the airplanes, and further damage the economy. Never forget that when revelations appeared that Bush and his security agencies had been warned, stridently and repeatedly, of an imminent terror attack, he offered this excuse: he did not order heightened security within the airline industry because he feared it would damage their profits.

Lay those cards down and the answer comes clear. In the name of politics and cash, Bush is willing to gamble with our financial and personal security. This is a betrayal of staggering proportions. He does not deserve our silence.

This is the administration that has been handed unprecedented power after the passage of the PATRIOT Anti-Terrorism Bill of 2001. This 'sneak and peek' provision outlined in section 213 of the bill is a stake driven through the heart of the Fourth Amendment.

Have the actions of this administration to date given them the right to expect our trust in this? Absolutely not. By giving them this power, we have placed the noose around our own necks. Before we drop to our doom we must take that power back. We cannot allow Bush to have it, because he is demonstrably unworthy of it.

Bush and his administration should fear the judgment of history. By their actions, it is made clear that they already do. Yet their recent actions have been aimed at thwarting history, denying it, hiding it, burying it at midnight. On November 2, 2002, Bush signed an Executive Order sealing all presidential documentation. This Order further states that any president may seal up the papers of any former president, even if that former president wants them released.

This Order shreds the Presidential Records Act, legislated by Congress in 1978 in the wake of Watergate. Any persons who now wish to view presidential records must demonstrate a 'specific need' to see them, the gravity of that need to be decided by the administration.

Why?

68,000 pages of communications between Ronald Reagan and his advisers were due for release in January 2001. Many people in Bush's current administration were part of the Reagan cabal, and would have their names and deeds all over these papers. The most notable name that would be found within these papers is George Herbert Walker Bush. The administration managed to defer this release for months, but in the end ran out of excuses for doing so. This Executive Order was the last gasp, created in the name of 'national security.'

The audacity of the action is staggering. Even the stupefyingly naive must see through the farce for what it is: a betrayal of the Freedom of Information Act meant solely to protect members of this current administration from being called to task for their actions. The truth of the Iran/Contra scandal is likely in these papers, something that Bush Sr would just as soon see buried.

What else is in these papers? Which members of the current administration have a vested interest in seeing them buried forever? Why?

If this administration is so worthy of our trust, as we have been led to believe, how can we maintain our faith in the face of this betrayal of history? Why can't they tell us the truth? If they are indeed hiding nefarious and criminal actions taken two decades ago, what on earth should give us faith that they can be trusted today?

The act perpetrated on September 11 did not erase or recast the definition of dishonesty. In fact, it has solidified that definition as we know it. America, with all she has suffered, deserves far better than what we have in power today. We cannot allow these immoral and fraudulent robber barons to range about unchecked, unsanctioned, and uncontrolled.

The current administration has no interest or intention of responding to the will, or the dire needs, of the American people. This administration is stealing from us, undermining our safety, and lying to us with their bare faces hanging out. Our representatives in Congress are not acting vigorously enough to thwart these crimes. We must, therefore, act in our own defense and in the name of true American justice. We must begin yet another American Revolution, and we must do it within the bounds of the law.

The reasons Al Gore lost the contest in Florida were not first forged in the polling houses, or in the vicious actions of men like James Baker, or even in the Supreme Court. The reasons were first forged by the conservative Republican redirection of energies. They stopped pestering the Federal government and began running their people for low-level offices in states all across the Union.

By 2000, their people were entrenched in local Florida government, giving Bush a massive home-field advantage when push came to shove. These office-holders were able to act with partisan vigor any way they chose, and their actions killed Gore's chances before Justice Antonin Scalia ever became involved. Evidence of this redirection of energy is also evident in the conservative takeover of the House in 1994. The Republican Party (the GOP) went to the grass roots, running their people for state offices, priming the field, setting the tone locally for a push to the Federal level. This effort, in the end, yielded the administration of George W. Bush.

The people must abandon their faith in government, release the idea that simply shouting up to these representatives is enough to carry the day. We must look down into our own neighborhoods and precincts and wards and districts. We must imitate the victors. We must run our own people locally all across the country and take back the dialogue. The only effective way to do this is to work from the bottom up.

With the people more truly in power, the airline industry would not be able to steal from us with one hand while shredding our security with the other. With the people more truly in power, corporate greed can be brought to heel and real election reform can become a reality. With the people more truly in power, criminal administrations will be unable to hide behind Executive Orders forged in the wake of tragedy. They have been lying to us, and we can do nothing to stop it today. Tomorrow, however, is another matter.

This is a call to the Minutemen, to the real American patriots. Stand up and get to work. The new American Revolution is at hand and we need everyone. Run for local office or support one of us who does so. It will take time, and it will take patience, but it must be done.

Can such an effort be successful in the current climate? With absolute certainty, yes it can. The events of September 11 have awakened Americans to the realization that each and every one of us has a personal and fundamental stake in the development of justice, democracy, and human rights here and across the globe. We are the targets when these ideals fail. The current administration acts as though this awakening has not occurred. It has, and we must act upon it.

Lost amid all the death and fear that roared out of the sky on September 11, lost in the chorus of twisted words from George W. Bush, John Ashcroft, Donald Rumsfeld, and the rest, lost amid the nebulously defined War on Terror, which promises to be eternal in ways the Cold War never dreamed of, is that dream that was America. A thing so pure, so good, a thing forged in the best ideals that humanity ever conceived, deserves a better fate. It deserves to be defended, fought for, cherished, and prized. It does not deserve the fate our leaders, and our own largesse as citizens, have so callously damned it to.

Do not forget that dream. Do not let your children forget.

Twenty Pounds of Bullshit
in a Ten Pound Bag

Amidst the dust and ruin of September 11, amidst the pain and woe, amidst the remarkable unity that was demonstrated by Americans everywhere, there lurked a vein of hatred and evil that is nearly beyond description. Some Americans in the aftermath of that day leveled fingers of blame at homosexuals, at liberals, at the ACLU, at those who protect and defend a woman's legal right to reproductive freedom.

That anyone sought to smear fellow American citizens with blame for the atrocities that were visited upon us was wretched enough to make any decent human being physically ill. That those who did this were denouncing our fellow citizens in the name of God is the definition of evil and is the same kind of hate that drove those airplanes into the heart of our nation.

I am ashamed to be an American because of Jerry Falwell and Pat Robertson. This is what Mr Falwell had to say on the nationally broadcast television show, 'The 700 Club':

> The ACLU's got to take a lot of blame for this ... throwing God out successfully with the help of the federal court system, throwing God out of the public square, out of the schools. The abortionists have got to bear some burden for this because God will not be mocked. And when we destroy 40 million little innocent babies, we make God mad. I really believe that the pagans and the abortionists and the feminists and the gays and the lesbians who are actively trying to make that an alternative lifestyle ... all of them who have tried to secularize America. I point the finger in their face and say, 'You helped this happen.'

America absorbed a mighty blow. We are pulling together as best we can, even now. So much greatness was demonstrated by our firefighters, police, medical professionals, rescue workers, and ordinary citizens who lined up to give blood, because it was the best they could do. Yet, here was a religious bigot who had the unmitigated gall to lay blame upon some of our citizens because he does not agree with the way they live. He did this in the name of his vicious, hateful, bloody God. His God is not my God.

His America is not my America. Mr Falwell should have turned that finger of blame towards his own miserable face. Religious zealotry and intolerance – on both sides – lies at the root of this disaster.

No worse fate could ever befall America than to have it to come under the sway of demagogues like Jerry Falwell.

Gay? To the wall.

Pro-choice? To the wall.

ACLU, defender of the Constitution? To the wall.

Not Christian? To the rack, and then the wall.

Support any of the above, or believe those citizens who support the above have the right to do so? To the wall.

Jerry Falwell gravely injured millions of American citizens with his words. The First Amendment of the Constitution allowed him to do so, allowed him to advocate the destruction of the very rights that protect his hate and evil. I say, as an American, that these men do not represent the nation I love and would die for. They are a cancer on the soul of our country.

I say to my homosexual brothers and sisters, to those who are not Christian, to those who support the legal right of reproductive choice, that I am with you. I stand with my fellow American citizens in this time of trial.

Mr Bush, I denounce you for failing adequately to castigate these men, loudly and publicly, when they spewed their hateful words. Once upon a time you gave your soul to Jesus in the presence of Falwell. Your silence whispered agreement with their statements, further proving to me that you are indeed a minority leader and no president.

Mr Bush promised to bring honor and integrity back to the White House during his campaign. For the sake of clarity, let's get some definitions out on the table. According to my dictionary, the word 'honor' is defined as:

High respect, as that shown for special merit; Esteem; Good name; Reputation; A source or cause of credit; Glory or recognition; Distinction; A mark, token, or gesture of respect or distinction; Nobility of mind.

The word 'integrity' is defined as:

Steadfast adherence to a strict moral or ethical code; The state of being unimpaired; Soundness; The quality or condition of being whole or undivided; Completeness.

Focus on one aspect of the above-captioned definition of integrity: 'The state of being unimpaired.' I take this to mean that a person of integrity is not encumbered by nefarious or illegitimate attachments. An unimpaired person of integrity stands alone and acts from an independent core of being that is not dictated or swayed by outside considerations.

I require a barnload of salt in order to swallow this definition as applied to George W. Bush. It is perhaps the worst kept secret in America that Bush is dominated and directed by outside considerations, primarily those corporations dealing in oil. One could almost see the puppet strings attached to his sleeves and shoulders as he campaigned across the country before November, and in choosing Dick 'Halliburton' Cheney as his prime minister – the semi-useless connotations attached to the position of vice president simply do not apply here – it became clear to all that Bush's administration would be steeped in unrefined petroleum.

I assumed, as did many others, that Bush would at least make some attempt to conceal the fact that he was where he was to make rich people richer and to undo environmental regulations for the benefit of corporations. After all, Bush would not be the first president who belonged to those who cared little for the well-being of the American people, and woefully will not be the last. But presidents before him, Reagan being the most prominent, had at least the acumen to disguise this fact as best they could. In politics, after all, what is not said out loud does not actually exist.

And then, like a bolt of lightning from a smog-filled sky, George W. Bush opened his mouth and spoke out loud the dark truth of where his loyalties actually lie, and the myth of his integrity was exposed for all to see. On May 11, 2001, George W. Bush stood before a battery of cameras and reporters to speak the following lines:

> I am deeply concerned about consumers, I am deeply concerned about high gas prices. To anybody who wants to figure out how to help the consumers, pass the tax relief package as quickly as possible ... It will be good for the economy, and will be a real way to deal with high energy prices.

There it was, from the horse's mouth. The reason for shoveling our tax money into the coffers of the already rich was at last made clear: whatever crumbs fall from that gilded plate can be used to purchase the product sold by Bush's best friends in business. It was perhaps the most remarkable thing I have ever heard from the mouth of a politician.

In gambling, there is something known as a 'middle.' A gambler who achieves a 'middle' knows he will get paid no matter who wins the big game, because he has taken bets in both directions and is covered in every way possible. George W. Bush could give lessons in Vegas because, with this tax-cuts for gas gamble, he reached for the biggest 'middle' ever made.

According to the Center for Public Integrity, the petroleum corporation Enron was number one on the list of lifetime contributors to Bush's political career, having given $572,350.00 to his various campaigns. The Houston law firm Vinson & Elkins has contributed $322,700.00 to Bush's political future, placing them at number four on this roll of honor. Vinson & Elkins enjoyed Enron Corporation as one of their most lucrative clients. The Sterling Group, also out of Houston, is another petroleum corporation. They are number seven on this list, having given Bush $262,000.00.

According to Bush's theory that people needed this tax break for gas, these energy corporations scored a double-whammy: the rich board members and stockholders of these companies profited personally from the tax-cut, and their companies enjoyed higher profits from their inflated prices because average citizens spent their refunds tanking up their SUVs. Either way, Bush's biggest contributors received the long-anticipated payback for their investment.

Bush has often claimed to stand for the people, but this tax-cuts for gas scam illuminated for all time who actually makes up his constituency. That Bush gave his soul to Jerry Falwell and Jesus does not make him a Christian – more on that in a bit – and his lip-service to the citizens his economic policies have screwed does not make him a leader of the people.

Bush stands for that 1% Gore spoke of in the debates – rich businessmen like Ken Lay, whose scruples so neatly mirror his own. The tax-cut, and virtually every economic policy he has since lobbed, established this for all time. Most Americans seemed to accept this without much complaint for a time – eight years of peace and prosperity under Clinton dulled their wits, and anything that did not center on illicit sex was not widely discussed. The people took their $300 checks and banked them, and that was that.

300 bucks only buys so much loyalty though. It is not enough of a payoff to ensure hard-core, do-or-die support. One must look into some truly dark corners to find the folks who think Bush is a paragon of honor and integrity. I found one such corner and it shook me up. It was like finding a rattlesnake coiled beneath a stone. My discovery began with a striking moment during the Florida madness of 2001, which has stayed with me ever since.

'Inside Politics' was running 24 hours a day on CNN, you will recall. I was watching one evening, several days into the thing, and there was Judy Woodruff interviewing conservative columnist Bob Novak. The question of the hour was whether Al Gore should quit and go home.

On that night, Novak was pointing to a public poll that had been running on CNN.com. You know these polls. Log on to a news site and you can vote your opinion on whatever happens to be the headline of the day. The poll Novak referred to asked the question: 'Should Al Gore concede?'

The results showed that some 89% of the American population who found their way onto CNN.com voted 'Yes' to this question. The count of those who voted numbered in the tens of thousands. Novak flapped this poll all around the studio as indisputable proof that a large majority of the American people saw Gore as a thief and a usurper, a sore loser who should just go away. Soon enough, Gore did.

I never forgot that night and never lost the sneaking suspicion that something shady had occurred. Somehow, someone had flooded that poll with 'Yes' votes to skew the results. I had no proof, and the theme song to the 'X-Files' was sounding in my head … but I was mortally sure that something was rotten in the state of Denmark.

Not long after that night, I figured out what happened that night. That CNN.com poll was 'Freeped'.

What does it mean when something gets 'Freeped'? Aim your browser to http://www.FreeRepublic.com, join the conversations in the forums, and you will find out.

FreeRepublic.com is a website which describes its cause thus: 'We're working to roll back decades of governmental largesse, to root out political fraud and corruption, and to champion causes which further conservatism in America.'

This seems innocent enough. I am a particular fan of governmental largesse, for those who have need of it, but respect coherent arguments against it. I believe my work against Bush proves my dedication to rooting out political fraud and corruption. And while I am no conservative, I have met many conservatives whom I admire for their intellect, ability to articulate a message, and integrity in the truest definition of that word: 'Steadfast adherence to a strict moral or ethical code.'

My grandfather was a conservative of great integrity from the old school, and I never once found cause to look down on him, even when we disagreed on a principle, which we often did. My grandfather was the ideal conservative, in my opinion. A part of me is glad he died before I could tell him about the Freepers.

A Freeper is a member of FreeRepublic.com. Freepers speak to each other on the forums of this website, discussing all varieties of topic. Purportedly, they support the ideals espoused above. In reality, there is a yawning chasm between word and deed.

Take the CNN.com poll, for example. A common Freeper tactic is to post on the FreeRepublic forums a notice that a poll exists somewhere which asks a question dear to the conservative heart: 'Should the Congress pass more gun control legislation?' or 'Is Bill Clinton the illegitimate spawn of Satan and Baal?' The URL to this poll is provided, and the Freeper legions swarm to vote ... say, 'No' on the first and 'Yes' on the second. There are a lot of Freepers, and many of them will vote multiple times. This obviously skews the result. And that is how a poll is 'Freeped.'

Novak and CNN used the 'Freeped' CNN.com poll to convince the public that 89% of them wanted Al Gore to quit before the votes were counted. This helped to swell the rising tidewater that allowed the Supreme Court to get away with stealing the election.

Is this not political corruption? Does such a disruption skew information that is provided to the public via the media? Does this not pervert the truth? Of course, there are liberals out there who organize the same kind of coordinated mugging of public Internet polls. It can be argued that such things are no more than political gamesmanship.

Dig a little deeper into the Freeper phenomenon, however, and you will find a darkness where true morality dares not show its face.

As we all know, Jenna Bush was busted for attempting to purchase booze at a restaurant named Chuy's in Austin, Texas. The manager of the establishment, named Mia Lawrence, called 911 when she saw what was happening. The Freepers took this personally, believing the Jenna fiasco to be part of some liberal conspiracy to humiliate Bush and the daughters. They called for a 'Freeping' of Chuy's restaurant.

Anthony York of Salon.com wrote a story about the Freeper reaction to the situation entitled 'The jihad against Chuy's.' I quote it in part below:

The attacks against Mia Lawrence, the bar manager, are being orchestrated on the Internet. Her address, date of birth, driver's license and registration information, physical description, and even birth information about her infant child have been posted on Freerepublic.com, along with calls for punitive actions. Freerepublic.com Web site's sysop pulled some of the information as it was called to his attention – to his credit

– but the info has circulated and been posted to other Internet forums to spread the 'Get Lawrence' frenzy.

I felt a chill in my spine when I first read these words. Mia Lawrence was, in all likelihood, seeking to save her restaurant from breaking Texas's punitive underage drinking laws, signed by then Governor George W. Bush, which would have cost Chuy's its liquor license. She earned for her trouble a legion of stalkers who speak openly of loving guns. Her personal information, along with maps providing driving directions to her home, were posted on FreeRepublic. I am confident in my prediction that she did not sleep for days after dialing 911.

I did some research regarding this topic on FreeRepublic. Entering the word 'Chuy' into the search engine provided, I found the following Freeper commentary:

The manager, (aka 'Mia the Liberal DemonRat'), tried to cause as much trouble for the Bush twins and their dad as possible and now might get it returned back on her own head in spades!!! This is sweet! – Truth_Eagle

Hell! Surround Chuy's with tanks and set the place on fire while fully occupied. – olustee

Let's turn that TEXMEX joint into a BARBECUE! – makoman

I read comments, quickly removed by the moderators of FreeRepublic, which suggested that someone should go into Chuy's and smear butyric acid on the tables.

To be fair, a fellow Freeper posted the following dissent:

Every thread that had Mia's addy posted on it got pulled. Every one. *It's NOT OK*. Printing a map to the house, and having the addy on the map, is arguably worse. – CyberLiberty

CyberLiberty is proof positive that not all Freepers are violent psychopaths. Still, there were far more posts in the vein of olustee's.

I am forced to wonder how posting the name, address, and physical description of a restaurant manager from Austin, as well as the description of her infant child, furthers the conservative cause in America. I am reminded of the words of art critic and author Harold Rosenberg: 'The values to which the conservative appeals are inevitably caricatured by the individuals designated to put them into practice.'

Clearly, the purported targeting of the daughter of the president was mortally offensive to the average Freeper. I decided to do a search using the words 'Chelsea Clinton.' I found the following:

(question asked) I really do wonder what perversions Chelsea partici-pates in. (response) THAT is something I would rather NOT wonder about. Animals, plants, the elderly ... echh. The girl is a walking STD. – AntiChris

If people didnt know that hillary was an ugly assed dyke – they must have been blind – she just put up with old dumb ass so she could run the white house – just look at the bizarre bunch she put in office – the female version of frankenstein – which is janet reno – and this could go on and on – halfbright looks just like broomhilda – weirdest looking bunch ever to defile any government – and all courtesy of mr hillary – and then she supported all the fags in hollywood and along with her fat assed dyke buddy rosie – they all look like something from a sideshow at a circus – everyone of them has the coyote rating. – candyman34

In these two short entries, the daughter of the president was accused of carnal knowledge of animals and plants. She was accused of spreading sexually transmitted diseases. Senator Hillary Clinton was called a 'dyke.' The very notion of balance or fair play was conspicuously absent here. The hatred was palpable.

Hatred ... which brings me to yet another favorite Freeper topic.

A singular characteristic of the average Freeper is an abiding love and respect for Jesus Christ of Nazareth. Many Freepers use Christ as the shield with which they defend their views. Sometimes, they use him as their sword. If I remember my Sunday School classes, Jesus said in John 15:12, 'This is my commandment, that ye love one another.'

I entered the word 'homosexual' into the FreeRepublic search engine and found the following. Keep the Bible quote I provided in mind as you read:

The spread of infectious diseases ... oral and anal cancer ... death from HIV infections ... Just some of the ways GOD gets even with the queers and faggots. – upchuck

In another time, and in another place, they burned people like this ... –
East Bay Patriot

I will tell you that the Lord God has at least 7000 righteous in the USA
that have not bowed their knee to baal = and these flames of fire are
going to rise up soon and speak the Living Word of a Holy God to these
frog-demon-freaks and ban them from our land. I will NOT let this
country be over-run by Communist/Socialist/Globalist/Abortionist/
Feminist Sodomites. – jdhmichigan

That last comment from jdhmichigan sounds for all the world like it was
spoken by a dedicated member of Al Qaeda. I have been a Christian all my
life. My understanding of the teachings of Jesus directs me to love my
enemies and accept everyone – Christian, Jew, Muslim, Buddhist – as a
child of God. Jesus was the son of God, but was also a revolutionary seeking
freedom from Roman persecution. Therefore, as a Christian and a freedom-
loving American, I respect and love those who do not bend a knee to any
religion.

I do not pretend, as a card-carrying heterosexual, to understand fully
how one man can look with lust upon another man. But after being
friends, and after sharing apartment space, with a number of homosexual
men and women, I know in my heart that such things exist for a reason
and are not wrong. God loves everyone equally, as He sees the smallest
sparrow fall. I love everyone, too. Perhaps, like gay men and women, I was
born that way.

I have never espoused the burning at the stake of any human being, be
they gay or conservative. How such a statement falls within the yardstick
of Christianity or true conservatism is a mystery which I may never solve.
I do know this, however: were Jesus to log on to FreeRepublic and read the
perversion His message has undergone in 2,000 years, He would beg to be
crucified again, to be spared exposure to such hatred.

I suppose it is easy for the average Freeper to post such virulent messages
on a public forum. After all, they dare not use their real names. Names like
Truth_Eagle, upchuck and AntiChris are masks behind which cowards
hide. It is easy to speak when no one can see your face. A veteran of many
email flame wars, I know well how brave a person can be when shielded
by the anonymity of a computer keyboard. Those who sexually stalk
teenage girls in Internet chat rooms use similar tactics. It is very effective.

The glaring fact of the cowardice of the average Freeper should not in
any way diminish the effectiveness of their actions. They pervert public
polls. The call and email congressional representatives *en masse*, thus

creating the illusion of massive public pressure that twists the actions of elected officials who seek only to respond to the legitimate concerns of constituents. They bombard media outlets with prurient stories to discredit respectable Democratic officeholders. They are the bedrock base of the entity we know as the GOP.

Keep these things in mind when you find yourself shocked by the results of a poll on MSNBC, or when a senator refuses to support reasonable gun control laws, or when the press decides to spend two years covering a consensual sex act between adults.

Robert Kennedy described Richard Nixon as being a symbol of 'the dark side of the American Dream.' Were he alive today, he would describe FreeRepublic in the same terms. This is all the more disturbing when you recognize that this army of Freepers stand as the unbending spine of support for Bush and the GOP.

Reading the way they craft their words, you get the sense that these people believe themselves to be an average slice of our American population. Most of them profess to be Christians. Yet somehow they have dedicated themselves to furthering the fortune of the corporatist stooge Bush, who would see all of them completely screwed over if he was granted even half of the items on his wish-list. The root of their support is religious – Bush claims to be Christian, and therefore must be pure and good. I've done some looking into that aspect of this phenomenon.

It is written in the Bible that the rock shall not hide, nor shall the dead tree give shelter, on the Day of Judgment. This is a piece of news that someone ought to give Bush before those four horsemen take to their saddles. I have been studying the Book of Luke. It contains many important truths that seem to have eluded the man in the White House, which is troubling when one remembers his wide and varied claims of devotion to the Christian faith.

I'm not sure what version of the Good Book Mr Bush has been reading, but if it is anything like my copy, it is apparent that his lack of intellectual depth includes a deficit in the area of reading comprehension. Take, for example, Luke 12:15: 'Take care to guard against all greed, for though one may be rich, one's life does not consist of possessions.'

This seems to be the basis for the more folksy saying, 'You can't take it with you.' When you die, all you have is your soul, the actions of your life, and the memories those who live after you keep. All the cars and houses and bank accounts and money you may have accumulated do not make the trip to the Other Side.

By all reports, Bush gave himself to Jesus in the presence of Jerry Falwell not long after he reportedly surrendered the bottle. It can be assumed that he was given Luke to read so as to edify his newly minted soul. It would seem, though, that this passage left no impression upon him.

Had it done so, Bush would not be dedicating his entire administration to the advancement of the wealthy. Had Luke resonated within him, he would not have shattered Social Security and Medicare with a tax-cut that gave billions of dollars to rich people who don't need the cash and who won't be able to take it with them.

Had Luke found a purchase, Bush would not be molding environmental policy in favor of polluters who don't wish to spend any profit on the safeguarding of our air and water, thus solidifying a bottom line to produce money that won't help a whit when they face their Maker. The same could be said for his energy plans, meant to engorge the wallets of petroleum barons who have not evidenced a single iota of compassion for the people they gouge or the planet they rape.

There is more in Luke that Bush should have paid some attention to. Consider Luke 3:11: 'Whoever has two cloaks should share with the person who has none. And whoever has food should do likewise.'

It can be argued that this is the essence of Social Security. It is a safety net for citizens who, due to age or infirmity, are not able to enjoy the capitalist fruits those who are able to be productive enjoy. Social Security takes something from you and me and the fellow in the cubicle next door to make sure that those who have no cloak are sheltered, and that those who would otherwise go hungry can eat.

Medicare makes sure that the sick who cannot afford insurance are healed and cared for by the marvels of modern medicine that put the healing power of Jesus in deep shade. Combined, these two programs provide a margin of safety for millions of Americans. The fiscal program put forth by George W. Bush has all but destroyed this margin of safety. This is, for lack of a better word, an act of violence perpetrated against scores of our weakest and most needy citizens. If I came into your home and turned you out, stripped you of your coat so you had to face the cold wind, and stole the food from your mouth, I would be arrested and imprisoned. This is what Bush has done.

That he has done this at all is bad enough. That the rich have been allowed to feast upon funds designed to protect the weak is worse by orders of magnitude. That he intends to use whatever is left to make weapons of war stretches the very definition of evil. That he lied in order to achieve this nefarious goal is the worst truth of all.

Consider his campaign promises. Al Gore has borne the brunt of many *Saturday Night Live* jokes about the phrase 'lock box.' This word was a GOP invention at the outset, meant to describe the place where Social Security funds would be protected, one that Bush seized upon in order to convince people that he was worth their trust. Simply put, he vowed and promised not to do what he is in the process of doing.

The Book of Revelation does not have happy words for liars. Consider chapter 21, verse 8: 'But for the cowardly and unbelieving and abominable and murderers and immoral persons and sorcerers and idolaters and all liars, their part will be in the lake that burns with fire and brimstone: which is the second death.'

It is a symbol of these dark and twisted times that George W. Bush has been able to finagle support from millions of decent American Christians, because they have been duped into believing that he is one of them. Bush is no Christian. He is a liar who smiles while depriving solace from the meek to fatten the rich.

It is said that there can be no peace without justice. If we are to achieve true justice in America today, those Christians on FreeRepublic and elsewhere in America who would carry Bush's banner and cross must come to see him for what he is. They must repudiate him, revile him, expose him as a wolf in sheep's clothing. They won't, because Jesus told them otherwise, and that is the saddest part of all. They will be taken down with the rest of us if Bush's plans are not held in check, and they will likely be praying as they fall.

The phenomenon of Bush can be understood only if framed in the context of the GOP as a whole and the massive changes it has undergone in the last few decades. The Republican Party has suffered its share of catastrophes in the last 50 years. Richard Nixon is the very personification of a multitude of calamities: a narrow loss to Kennedy, exposure of the Pentagon Papers, the calumny of Watergate. The Reagan administration suffered through the exposure of the Iran/Contra scandal, that Byzantine plot which funded terrorists and murderers on both sides of the globe.

The public success of the Gulf War was not enough to save the languid administration of George H. W. Bush, ushering in eight years of Clinton. The high tide of Gingrich's Contract for America broke against Clinton's political brinkmanship when the government shut down. When the waters receded, many GOP revolutionaries were washed out.

The impeachment jihad exposed many in the Republican Party as moralizing hypocrites, further eroding their majority in Congress when the people went to the polls in 1998. The madness of the 2000 election stripped George W. Bush of even the pretense of a mandate. When James Jeffords walked away from Bush's conservative program, Trent Lott was stripped of his throne in the Senate, depriving the GOP of their long-sought control over all of government.

Each of these events surely took their toll on the party. All of them combined, however, cannot compare to the disaster of 1932, when the Republican Party lost the White House to Franklin Delano Roosevelt. Today, the Republicans are working very hard to undo the results of that election. They may very well have succeeded.

The years leading up to the election of 1932 were terrible ones for America, as any schoolchild knows. The nation was mired in the Great Depression. The incumbent President, Republican Herbert Hoover, appeared unwilling or unable to help matters. Hoover ran a campaign in 1932 that seemed based upon his hurt feelings; he was being blamed unfairly for all economic pain. He lashed out at friend and foe alike, dooming his chances.

When the dust cleared on election day in 1932, Roosevelt had carried 42 states. He won the electoral college by a margin of 472 to 59. He won the popular vote by a margin of 22,809,638 to 15,758,901. By any meaningful standard, Hoover was routed.

This election ushered in the New Deal, the bringing of Big Business to heel, and the institutionalization of the idea that government can and should help the helpless to bring forth the best possible attributes of every American citizen, regardless of their economic caste.

It was an election that the Republican Party, simply put, has never recovered from. It was an election that has redefined the character of that Party, twisting it into the malignant and greedy entity that it is today.

The Republican Party was first organized in 1854 from the tattered remnants of the Whigs. The fundamental purpose of the Party was opposition to slavery, though several factions were not entirely committed to that cause. Abraham Lincoln is the most famous member of the wing of the Party that was not completely dedicated to abolition.

It is worthwhile to note that the Democratic Party, for the most part, was absolutely against abolition in any form at this time. The Confederate South was a Democratic stronghold. The Copperheads, a group committed to derailing abolition and the Civil War, were staunch Democrats. At this point in American history, the Republicans were solidly on the side of righteousness as we understand it today.

Lincoln was perhaps the most famous 'big government' president the Republican Party has ever known. He expanded the army to mind-boggling size, instituted taxes upon the populace that had never existed before, and single-handedly directed a war that spilled an ocean of blood for the purpose of keeping the whole nation under Federal rule.

The transmogrification of the Republican Party began under Lincoln, in the subjugated and ravaged South. The defeated Democratic Party, as time passed, slowly began to change. When the century turned, they became known as 'Dixiecrats,' politicians who did not want the Federal government to meddle in their business. Strom Thurmond is the most famous member of this clan.

The Republicans were once environmentally-minded, as evidenced by the policies of Theodore Roosevelt. Teddy grabbed massive swaths of land in the West and kept them in trust for the American people as national parks. Were he alive today, he could not even get elected as dog-catcher if he were to espouse such plans to the current Republican base in the West. Teddy was also a staunch foe of massive business conglomerations, breaking many during his rule and institutionalizing the idea that large corporations cannot do as they please. Once again, he'd be looking for work today with such ideas in his head.

The slow evolution of the Republican Party was surely affected by the Civil War, by Lincoln, by Teddy Roosevelt, by the explosive growth and influence of the business community in America. The election of 1932 and subsequent victory by FDR caused these changes to burst forward at a dizzying pace.

Franklin Roosevelt, working to repair the awesome damage created by the Great Depression, turned the Federal government into a means to heal America's economic wounds. He put people to work on road programs. He forced banks to open. He laid the groundwork for programs such as Social Security, Medicare, and Welfare. In doing so, he brought the nation back from the brink.

Republicans, by this time, were staunchly in the corner of Big Business. And Big Business hated Roosevelt with a passion that has seldom been seen since. They desperately wanted him out of office and worked very hard to achieve this. Their plans were foiled with the outbreak of World War II. The nation had begun to recover economically, and was now facing a terrible threat in Europe and Asia. No one was interested in changing the man at the top.

By the time the war ended, Roosevelt had died. He was at his death the closest thing we have had to a king, and the programs he instituted were cemented into the policy framework of Washington, D.C. and the nation.

My understanding of the basics of Republican Party ideology is this: they believe in self-sufficiency, in a government that does not interfere with business or with the operation of state government. They believe in capitalism, that the market will correct itself without governmental intrusion. They believe that people, not government, will help through charitable organizations those who are in need.

Much of this is admirable on the surface. Self-sufficiency is an excellent quality and charities can do great work. Unfortunately, the basics of Republicanism have been undermined by a variety of factors. The ideals have been perverted, and those who espouse them today ignore the realities of that perversion.

When the Dixiecrats became Republicans, their states-rights baggage of racism was carried into the party with them. That racism undermines the ability for the self-sufficiency argument to be effective. The market can correct itself only in an environment of equality. That quality has never existed in America. Thus, leaving the market to its own devices spreads inequality.

Franklin Delano Roosevelt's governmental programs for the poor and unemployed offended the basic premise of self-sufficient Republicanism and its business-oriented base. Business cannot run free today, because government has taken an active role since FDR in controlling a good deal of its activities. Business must bend to the common good as viewed by the government. This chafes.

More than anything, the symbiotic relationship between business and the Republicans has ravaged the better angels of that party's nature and has woefully damaged our politics as a whole. Reagan's Republicanism ended any serious taxation of corporations, and subsidized many of them with his massive military buildup, allowing them to grow to their currently bloated and powerful state. FDR's social programs lost much of the funding they needed, opening up the circular argument proffered by the GOP that these programs do not work.

What these arguments ignore is the unavoidable reality of the size of America, and the ugly underbelly of capitalism. America is a massive nation that needs a massive Federal government to function. The American Dream never worked for too many of our citizens because they were the wrong color or because too many jobs do not pay enough. The Republican ideology of capitalism ignores this. FDR believed in capitalism, but also knew that governmental programs were needed to temper some of its abuses. Charity can do only so much.

The power of corporations to affect politics through campaign contributions is something that virtually no Republican wants to change or modify. Why would they choose to cut off those who share their ideology?

Self-sufficiency works best when you are rich, after all. For the GOP, this argument is moot. For the sake of political survival, many Democrats have had to keep their snouts in this particular trough. But there is no doubting where this disease began. The Republican elephant never forgets.

The election of Roosevelt and the subsequent defection of the Dixiecrats has had a profound effect upon the Republican Party. They are the Big Money, Big Business Party now. A notable number within their ranks look back with fondness to the days when states could do as they pleased with their minority population and when business was beholden to nothing but itself.

At the bottom, modern Republican ideology, rooted deeply in capitalism, places an Ayn Randian dollar value upon each American citizen. If one cannot succeed financially, one is sick and not worth the trouble. Roosevelt's programs fly in the face of this ideology and have done much to thwart its preponderance in our culture.

Two events have transpired recently that appear to be a declaration of total war upon Roosevelt's governmental social programs. The first was Bush's massive tax-cut, and the second was his faith-based initiative. They are intimately interlinked.

The tax-cut was too large for the Federal budget to handle. In the weeks after September 11, Bush raided surplus money set aside for Medicare and Social Security. This will destroy these programs completely, erasing at long last the legacy of the 1932 election.

Bush's faith-based programs, with some Federal subsidies, are his attempt to bridge the fiscal gap created in the budget by his tax-cut. They will not be enough. No charity can provide health care coverage for the millions who need it, nor can a charity give financial security to the millions who have retired or are unable to work. The report about the Salvation Army and the Bush administration's apparent acceptance of the fact that many of these programs plan to discriminate on the basis of sexual orientation demonstrate clearly that the safety net Bush proposes is not for everyone. Essentially, Bush's faith-based programs are a sop thrown to the people after his tax-cut finishes ravaging FDR's governmental social programs. It is not a real solution and is doomed to fail.

America is an amazing country. We believe in equal rights for all our citizens. We believe that hard work will reap great benefits. We believe our vote is the greatest weapon for change. We believe this place to be the land of opportunity. For many of us, it is all these things.

For many others, however, it is not. Franklin Delano Roosevelt saw this clearly and enacted programs that help those for whom America's opportunities are not available. He believed that government can help each person become their best selves. Capitalism, charity, and the market can do only so much.

His election in 1932 wrought dark and fundamental changes upon the Republican Party. It is today a party that subsists on greed. It pointedly ignores many ugly social realities in its quest for political dominance. It exists now solely for the benefit of the rich and for corporations. The Republican Party seeks today to undo the great good that began with the election of 1932. They are well along the path to success.

The single biggest shard of evidence to support the claim that the GOP is completely lost in the pocket of Big Business is the sorry way political campaigns are financed. If you have the cash, then you have the ear of a congressman or a president. This has been a disease shared equally by both parties: who can forget the incredible talent for fundraising Clinton displayed during the 1996 campaign?

The devil, as always, is in the detail. Gore, during the 2000 campaign, pledged unequivocally to sign the McCain/Feingold Campaign Finance Reform the second it arrived on his desk if he became president. Personally, I believed him. It suited him politically, for it offered him the opportunity at last to get out from under the taint of that 1996 Buddhist Temple fundraising scandal.

He never got the chance. Bush never supported McCain/Feingold with anything more than half-hearted lip service. Even Clinton's amazing cash-grabbing in 1996 could not surmount the total Bush hauled in during the 2000 campaign. He was able to eschew spending limits because of it. It was a powerful campaign weapon, and he had no intention of surrendering it.

And then one day, along came John.

Republican Senator John McCain of Arizona wore a smile like the grille of a highballing Mack truck as he watched seven years of hard work finally come to fruition. The passage of the McCain–Feingold Campaign Finance Reform Bill secured him a place in congressional history, fulfilled a promise he made during his 2000 presidential campaign, and cemented his legacy as a reform-minded maverick with a taste for bucking his party leaders. Along the way, he may even have helped clean up an American political system in dire need of a dose of drain cleaner; but that remains to be seen.

The gleam of steel in McCain's smile was likely due to one other all-important factor. The passage of his reform bill presented an incredible dilemma for his former primary foe, George W. Bush. Bush, a man who has profited more from 'soft money' campaign contributions than any living human on Earth, did not want to sign this legislation into law.

Consider the dilemma: If he refused to sign it, he would have betrayed the wishes of a vast majority of the American people. If he did sign it, the hard-right flank of his own party, those Republican elephants who truly never forget, would raise howls of betrayed rage that might wake the dead.

It has been four years since the viciousness of the South Carolina primary, when Bush confederates publicly questioned McCain's patriotism, flagged the idea that McCain cared nothing about breast cancer, and made thousands of phone calls to South Carolina voters attacking his character. Before entering politics, McCain was a fighter pilot schooled in the art of waiting for a hard target to appear in his sights. With the ache of those old South Carolina scars beneath his skin, he finally had George in the crosshairs.

The essence of McCain's legislation centered on the avalanche of unregulated 'soft money' campaign contributions that have been cascading into politics in recent years. Ostensibly, this money is meant to build political parties via registration and get-out-the-vote drives. In fact, the money is used to attack rival candidates and purchase influence. McCain–Feingold dammed that flow. McCain's bill also put limits on those anonymous 'issue ads' that viciously slander opponents using the same soft money. The bill raised to $2,000 the limit on 'hard money' contributions that can be given directly to a campaign, increased contribution limits for those facing wealthy opponents, and tightened disclosure requirements.

It is a coin-toss as to which party benefits more from this legislation. The GOP historically has been more adept at raising hard money, and the raised ceiling on those contributions would seem to benefit them. Some said Bush should happily sign the legislation into law because it would further free him from the common practice of accepting Federal matching campaign funds. These funds, established in the wake of Watergate, give Federal money to candidates who agree to campaign spending limits. Bush eschewed those limits and funds in 2000, with demonstrable success. Now that the hard money limit is $2,000, there was little reason for him to change his tactics.

The ace up the Democrats' sleeve is union support. If the Democratic Party can dragoon union loyalists into pouring hard money campaign contributions into the 2004 nominee's coffers, they may well be able to match Bush's fundraising prowess. Added to this is the rising star of wealthy Massachusetts Senator John Kerry, considered by many to be first in line for the 2004 nomination. Kerry's personal fortune, combined with union support, could free him from the spending limits Gore was forced to accept in 2000. This fact, more than his record of service in Vietnam and in Congress, may make Kerry the most important Democrat in America today.

All this is theoretical. Bush did, in fact, sign the bill. He held no ceremony and invited none of the drafters to the Oval Office. He signed it behind closed doors and pushed it away as if it stank like a rotten fish. A blizzard of litigation followed. Senator Mitch McConnell of Kentucky hoped to be first in line at the courthouse, carrying with him the claim that McCain–Feingold violates the free speech rights outlined in the First Amendment. The connection between campaign funding and free speech was codified within the Supreme Court decision *Buckley* v. *Valeo* of 1976, and it is on the shoulders of this case that McConnell and others intend to rest their claim.

The outcome of these challenges will ride upon the court's interpretation of a line in the Buckley case. Political contributions are free speech, stated the Supreme Court, whose restriction can be justified only by overriding government interest. If supporters of McCain–Feingold can argue successfully that special interest control of government, represented vividly by the influence Enron had over the current administration, demands restrictions in the name of a cleaner democracy, the challenges offered by McConnell and others may well fail.

The cold dish of revenge McCain served up for Bush with this legislation had little to do with the vagaries of financial advantage or the survivability of the bill in court. Bush has spent years advocating reform from one corner of his mouth while attacking McCain's bill from the other. His supporters on the Far Right fervently believe that any limitation on campaign spending is a direct assault on free speech, a view cash-fattened conservative bankrollers have been careful to cultivate over the years. When Bush put ink to the bill, he joined his father in the 'Read My Lips' roll call of disfavor among those who like to call themselves 'true conservatives.'

The dunning began even before he signed the thing. Conservative talk show host Rush Limbaugh claimed in an article that, 'If the President does not veto this bill, and leaves the dirty work to the Supreme Court, he runs the risk of tarnishing his legacy, despite his outstanding leadership as commander-in-chief and war president.' Sentiments of a more venomous mien bloomed like crabgrass on conservative Internet forums where the faithful gather. On FreeRepublic, one poster summed up the anger felt by many when it was reported that Bush promised to sign the legislation into law next week: 'I regret working to get him elected, I regret voting for Bush, and I regret being my GOP precinct captain. Never again.'

Signing that bill, even in private and with all the realpolitik reasons to do so, cost Bush dearly among those who make up the backbone of his support, among those who willingly savaged McCain's reputation in South Carolina so as to put Bush where he is today. The flowers are blooming in Arizona and John McCain is smiling. The cold dish was well served.

What does all this say about Bush? September 11 gave him a veneer of political invincibility, and the kind of conservative voters that people FreeRepublic believe him second only to God in what they view as a Holy War. Yet he betrayed some core principles by signing McCain–Feingold, and a close look at the basics of Christianity seem to demonstrate that he has few core principles of his own to speak of. His personal business practices are another story entirely, and a miserable one at that.

What it all means, in short, is that Bush – for all his happy talk about Jesus and morality – is as vulnerable to the caprices of hardcore conservatives as his father was. It means he enjoys the support of a certain breed of person that most decent Americans would hesitate to share a meal with. The party he belongs to has become a bastion of extremism and vile demagoguery, as evidenced by the knee-jerk reaction of Falwell and Robertson. His party has also lost itself to a corporatist mindset that will do virtually anything to advance the fortunes of a tiny minority of wealthy Americans and be damned to the rest.

The last question, of course, is simple: Can he be beaten in 2004? A surprise defection from the White House helps to shed some light on the answer to that all-important question. George W. Bush's vaunted Iron Triangle of political advisors – Karl Rove, Joe Albaugh and Karen Hughes – lost one of its sharpest corners. Hughes, violet-eyed warrior-queen of the administration, surrendered her spear for the familiar, if dusty, environs of her home state of Texas. According to early reports, the decision was made with her son in mind. It seems the metro D.C. area did not resonate with this scion of the Hughes line, to such a degree that Karen decided to abandon one of the most powerful positions in the Executive branch, a position that marked the apex of her remarkable career.

Hughes began her professional life as a television journalist. In 1980 she was assigned to cover the elder Bush's presidential campaigns in Iowa and New Hampshire. The barb of politics sunk deep after that experience, and in 1984 she left television to become the Texas coordinator for the Reagan–Bush re-election campaign. By 1992 she had moved on, becoming executive director for the Texas Republican Party. It was in this capacity that she became closely acquainted with another political operative named Karl Rove.

Hughes began her work with George W. Bush in 1994 during his first run for the Texas gubernatorial office, serving as his communications director. She held this position again when Bush ran for re-election in 1998, the race that first delivered him to national attention. From 1995 through 1999, Hughes served Governor Bush as director of communications for his office. When Bush announced his intentions to run for president, Hughes was brought on board, again as communications director, over the strenuous objections of some who wished for a more nationally experienced hand.

During the years she worked for him, Hughes became an indispensable part of Bush's highly regimented corporate model of governance. She was, in short, the message delivery component of his cabinet. Hughes would craft, and deliver to all points on the compass, the policy or philosophy thought of the day. This disciplined approach made campaigns far smoother and less prone to verbal gaffes, and got the Bush message effectively and clearly out onto the wires. Her strengths as a partisan warrior have served Bush for years, particularly during the weeks-long street fight for the Florida vote after the 2000 election.

Hughes' departure came at an incredibly tense time for the Bush White House. After disdaining the peace process in the Middle East for much of their rule, the Bush administration fell under withering national and international criticism in the aftermath of horrific violence in that region. That criticism only escalated after Secretary of State Colin Powell was belatedly dispatched to the region, tasked with the job of reining in the combatants. Powell returned to America empty-handed from a trip many deemed a failure, darkening the cloud over the White House. Hughes' mastery of the message did not save Bush from making several contradictory statements regarding the conflict, further blurring an already scattered policy.

Hughes' abrupt resignation came on the heels of rumors that another prominent Bush administration official, Army Secretary Thomas White, would soon be leaving government service. White, a former Vice President of Enron, has come under the taint of that scandal. Accusations of insider trading by White have surfaced, claiming that he dumped his Enron stock before their value dropped because he knew of that company's impending demise. White himself has stated that he will leave if the scandal becomes a distraction to his duties.

Following the attacks of September 11, the role Hughes played in the White House did not diminish to any great degree. Purposefully excluded from National Security meetings to avoid leaving the image that politics plays a role in the prosecution of the war, Hughes nonetheless had daily meetings with Bush and still crafted the disciplined 'message' the White House delivers to the world. She had little to do with the hands-on work behind crafting Bush's foreign policy, but it fell to her to sell it to the American people.

Upon her announcement, Hughes remained, as ever, on message. Her claim that the resignation came because her son did not like Washington was a 'family-oriented' decision from a 'family-oriented' White House. If true, it represented one of the most profound professional sacrifices in modern memory. Few in government had the power of Hughes, and it would be remarkable indeed if she had in fact chosen to leave her coveted position for this reason. A more likely reason may lie in some Texas poll numbers that suggested the Democrats stood to make significant gains within that state in the 2002 midterm elections. Her talents were needed down there to help avoid an embarrassing reversal for Bush. Beyond that, perhaps, Hughes no longer felt comfortable selling a foreign policy that had endured several vividly public disasters.

Whatever the reasons for her departure may have been, the fact remains that the White House has not been the same in her absence. The void left behind will be filled by her counterpart, Karl Rove, a fact sure to increase his already formidable influence. Back in 1999, when Bush was pulling together the team that would help him gain the Oval Office, he bluntly informed Hughes that he would not run if she were not on board. Hughes accepted his offer and Bush went to Washington. Now she is gone, back in Texas and out of the loop. The Iron Triangle, always pointing towards victory for Bush, is broken.

George W. Bush has missed her well-spoken presence acutely. A White House that seemed to hover above the fray fell into disarray after she hit the road. Bush's administration has come under siege from a variety of fronts, and her absence has made an obvious difference in his ability to deal with that.

But let us get down to brass tacks. What sort of man is George W. Bush, really? American journalist Gail Sheehy once described the secret of leadership as the habit of action one develops after facing the tests of a lifetime. As a person handles whatever fate throws at them, a pattern of reaction becomes clear. It amounts to the quality of a person's integrity under the onslaught of the inevitable slings and arrows. A good leader's habit of action will carry them across rough passages. A bad leader will make those passages all the rougher. A fool will lay waste to everything with a stupid look on his face.

Even at this late hour, Americans not beholden to his bastardized view of Christianity should contemplate the habits of action displayed by George W. Bush. The voters will not be afforded the opportunity to make any substantial adjustments until 2004, and it must be duly noted that all the necessary data have been available for years. Yet here is the man they call the President, and on the shoulders of his rule tilts the fate of the world. What have we learned about him since the beginning of his movement through the crucible of leadership?

Bush often enjoyed touting himself as a leader in education reform before the necessities of war overcame him. He was fortunate enough to receive the opportunity to be educated at Harvard and Yale, thanks to the financial resources and powerful connections of his family. With this opportunity laid out before him, the Education President worked just hard enough to earn the C average he has since boasted of.

With a Harvard MBA in hand, he went on to run a number of businesses – Arbusto, Spectrum 7, Bush Exploration and Harken – straight into the ground. It seems the business school lessons absorbed by Enron and Arthur Andersen executives were the same ones Bush doodled through during his student years. He did what they did, but on a much smaller scale. Imagine what he might have accomplished had he earned straight As?

Bush described his personal politics as being located within the precepts of something called 'compassionate conservatism.' As a clear definition of this has never been forthcoming, one must extrapolate the meaning of compassion by observing how he Bush promulgates it in his work.

Certainly, compassion must encompass mercy. It is, therefore, a curious parsing of the word when mercy is not present. While Governor, Bush was presented with a plea for mercy from Karla Faye Tucker who was on Texas's death row. He refused to commute her sentence. Former Arkansas governor Clinton had acted in the same way when he was presented with a plea for mercy from Rickey Ray Rector, a mentally damaged man also on death row.

Clinton never boasted of his decision to let Rector die, nor did he mock Rector's pleas for mercy. In an interview for *Talk Magazine* in August 1999, however, Bush was more than willing to ridicule Tucker, who had aired her plea during a CNN interview. When asked by *Talk* to recount Tucker's plea, Bush pinched his face into a parody of tearful fear and whimpered, 'Please ... don't kill me.' He then smiled and chuckled to himself. The humor of the situation was lost on many.

No president since FDR has been required to address the grave concerns that face Mr Bush at this point in history. How he has dealt with current realities affords a perspective on his habits of action in this regard. After all,

3,000 civilians and soldiers died in violence on September 11, and thousands of Afghan civilians joined them in the aftermath. These are serious times, to say the least.

Mr Bush has been traveling the GOP fundraising circuit in recent months. During his frequent stops, he often recalls the promise he claims to have made during the campaign: he would not allow the Federal budget to slip into deficit unless and until the rise of war, recession or national emergency. After a great deal of research performed by a variety of journalists, it was revealed that Al Gore actually made that statement. Yet in several speeches made at these fundraisers, Bush has pointedly referred to the promise as his own.

In horse racing, a trifecta is achieved when someone placing a bet correctly chooses the first three horses to cross the finish line. Hitting the trifecta at the track is a most lucrative happenstance and is considered to be extraordinarily lucky. Mr Bush appears to have spent some time betting on the ponies, for he has parlayed war, recession, and national emergency into a trifecta joke that never fails to elicit laughter from the audiences at those Republican fundraisers.

'You know, when I was running for president, in Chicago, somebody said, would you ever have deficit spending?' commented Bush at one of these fundraisers. 'I said, only if we were at war, or only if we had a recession, or only if we had a national emergency. Never did I dream we'd get the trifecta.' Delivered with that trademark smirk twisting his features, Mr Bush made it clear to his audience that he was fishing for giggles, and he got them.

Bush repeated this joke 15 times between September 2001 and June 2002, using almost exactly the same words each time. Making a joke once about death, war, and national catastrophe could be chalked up to nothing more than a rhetorical misfire by a man famous for mangling his scripts. Fifteen repetitions, however, makes it a standing part of his routine. The fact that this joke is used while he is asking for money makes it all the more unseemly.

Habits of action become clear after a time on this ground. When presented with the opportunity to receive an expensive education available only to a select few, Bush did just enough to cross the threshold of average. When presented with business opportunities, he failed to capitalize, and in fact appeared to have committed convictable crimes. When presented with instances of woe and suffering, in the guise of Karla Faye Tucker and the murder of thousands of Americans, he resorted to crass jokes that fly in the face of any semblance of decency.

Bush's vision for America and this war can be shocking at times. Consider his solution for the sensation of horror that ripped through the populace after September 11: 'We need to counter the shock wave of the evildoer by having individual rate cuts accelerated and by thinking about tax rebates.' Delivered on October 4, less than a month after the Towers came down, Bush saw fit to exploit the national trauma by pushing more tax-cuts for companies like Enron, which hadn't paid taxes in years.

Consider his delineation of America's reasoning for making war on terror: 'One of the great goals of this nation's war is to restore public confidence in the airline industry, is to tell the traveling public: "Get on board. Do your business around the country. Fly and enjoy America's great destination spots. Go down to Disney World in Florida, take your families and enjoy life the way we want it to be enjoyed."' After revelations that our intelligence services were aware of serious terrorism threats in the months before September 11, Bush claimed that security was not stepped up because of the harm it would do to the airline industry. These comments from September 27, coupled with the massive bailout he engineered for the industry, demonstrate an odd set of priorities.

Bush heralded the passage of the PATRIOT Anti-Terror Act by proclaiming, 'We're an open society, but we're at war. The enemy has declared war on us and we must not let foreign enemies use the forms of liberty to destroy liberty itself.' Considering the manner in which the Act burns holes through our Constitution and Bill of Rights, Mr Bush seems to be right on course. The enemy cannot destroy our freedoms when we willingly destroy them ourselves.

Families of September 11 victims have been rallying on the Capitol steps for an independent investigation into how and why these attacks could have possibly taken place. They seek a hard look into the inner workings of our intelligence services to ensure that nothing like it can ever happen again. These families should have listened to promises made by Bush on September 26, 2001. 'In order to make sure that we're able to conduct a winning victory, we've got to have the best intelligence we can possibly have,' he said. 'And my report to the nation is we've got the best intelligence we can possibly have.' It is certain such strong and truthful words will help them overcome their grief and outrage, even if no one can quite understand what a 'winning victory' is.

Bush's habits of action continue to develop. There are definite patterns to be seen. One cannot entirely fault him for being unsure of what to do in a time of war. He missed a golden opportunity to learn of these things by defending his nation as a soldier. Bush was granted a slot in the Texas

Air National Guard during the Vietnam conflict, a boon delivered once again by family influence. Records indicate that he simply failed to show up for a great portion of this non-combat duty.

It is too bad. Mr Bush might have learned a thing or two about leadership in times of conflict had he seen his obligation to the military through to completion. At least he has a sense of humor about it all. Perhaps, under his leadership, America will develop similar habits of action that allow us to find it all worthy of a joke, too.

Bush has Falwell and Robertson. He has the Freepers, who believe he has Jesus. But he also has the corrupted ideology of the GOP hanging around his neck. He has an economy rocking from scandals by corporations that use the same business model he once did as a wildcatter down in Texas. Despite the ultra-conservative mob that backs him, Bush's support among average Americans is a mile wide and a centimeter deep. And never forget John McCain, who may well have a few cold dishes yet to be served.

Anyone who thinks Bush will be invincible in 2004 has not been paying attention. Honor and integrity may yet prevail in America. If the Democrats wise up and turn that disgusting trifecta crack into a campaign commercial, Bush won't be able to show his face anywhere but at Republican fundraisers. I doubt very much that Jesus gets the joke.

Enronomics

In order to make a few extra dollars during the summer gap between teaching high school, I applied for and nailed down a job at a well-known store. The store, which I won't name for obvious reasons, is part of a large chain that covers pretty much the whole country. They sell a variety of items: clothes, books, videos, high-tech gadgets, and the like. If I named the place, you'd know it.

After a few shifts, I was stunned I got the job in the first place. I quit a few weeks after I started for a number of family-oriented reasons (I needed the time again), but in the many hours I worked there, I served only a handful of people. Plenty came in to browse and to take advantage of the air conditioning, but no one was buying anything. I had conversations with the register jockeys at neighboring stores – we were all located in a popular tourist zone/shopping district – and they all sang the same tune. The wallets were not coming out.

A year ago, I was told by my manager, the store was positively booming. They did not have enough people to handle the customer volume. During my time there, the home office sent daily memos to the store cajoling the sales associates to throw a full-court-press at everyone who came through the door. Sell anything you can, we were told, and squeeze out every dollar possible. They set daily sales goals that were missed by thousands of dollars. These goals were based upon last year's sales totals. Each day, we calculated our sales and compared them to last year's. Each day, our sales were off by between 30% and 80%. Why they hired me is a mystery. They didn't need me and my meager salary was further cutting into their profits.

I had gotten myself a dog's eye view of this recession, a ground-level perspective on the spending habits of very average Americans. People were completely unwilling to part with their money. This is a cancer of the most elemental economic kind that goes by the moniker of 'consumer confidence.' From my dog's eye view behind the register, there was no confidence out there at all.

The political observer in me wants to believe all this was happening because of the disastrous stories of Enron, WorldCom, Tyco, Arthur Andersen, and the rest. The fear that every single share of stock on Wall Street had been polluted and corrupted by lies and shady profit reporting cast a long shadow across the economy. Even the good stocks – and there are plenty of them – were burdened by a sense of total mistrust.

Strangely enough, the political observer in me has to take into account that most of the people I've questioned about these companies know very little about the scurrilous details of their dirty dealings. It is almost as if all these tales of fraud and deceit are taking place in another dimension. Most people seem bored by the dry facts behind these stories and have not bothered to inform themselves on them to any great degree.

Why is it, then, that my hours as a retail sales associate were spent watching people absolutely refusing to buy anything? Something seems amiss.

Maybe consumers, like the prey they are, have begun to smell danger on the wind. There is more to consumer confidence, after all, than the desire to buy doodads at some store. A Zogby poll that came out during my tenure behind the register indicated that Bush held a 69% approval rating, but only 51% of the people questioned would vote for him in 2004. The margin of error for that last number put Mr Bush right back to where he was on November 7, 2000. The 18-point gap between those numbers suggested that the populace was not entirely comfortable with the guy in charge.

Another poll from that summer stated bluntly that some 46% of Americans didn't think Bush was in charge of anything beyond deciding what kind of sandwich meat to have for lunch. These people believed he is controlled entirely by the corporate interests that funded his campaign. This takes us back around the bend to Enron and WorldCom. Even the catastrophically uninformed know that Bush was tight with Enron's CEO, Kenneth Lay, to the point that Lay and other Enron executives basically wrote Bush's energy policy proposal.

On July 9, 2002, Bush delivered a speech to Wall Street heavy-hitters decrying a lack of integrity in the market. He promised sharper teeth for the Securities and Exchange Commission and jail time for corporate criminals. This was, of course, months before SEC Chairman Harvey Pitt resigned his post as chief watchdog because he wasn't getting the job done. Above all, said Bush, a return to decency and morality was needed to stave off investor mistrust in the aftermath of Enron, WorldCom, and the others. The Dow responded by dropping another 170 points.

From a purely objective and disinterested distance, it was a fascinating thing to watch. There was George W. Bush in Alabama on Monday, July 16, praising the economy on all the news channels while promising to get tough on evil-doing corporate thieves. Meanwhile, those same news channels had busy little numbers whirring along next to his image. They all had small red down arrows next to them. When Bush began speaking, the Dow was down 164 points. By the time he finished, it was down over 300 points.

A president cannot single-handedly revive a flagging economy, but he sure can boost consumer and investor confidence with some well-chosen words and policy suggestions. This did not happen; before the carnage was over, the Dow had lost over 439 points. The New York Stock Exchange applied program trading curbs, put into effect when the Dow rises or falls around 200 points. They were all dropping. The 'curbs' were even failing to slow the slide, a quickening downward spiral that threatened to tear the floor out from under Wall Street.

This kind of action had been happening for weeks, as investors got familiar with names like Enron, Kenny-Boy, WorldCom, and the rest. The Dow was making daily history with its posted losses. The Nasdaq took a similar pounding, and the dollar became slightly less valuable than the Euro on the international market. Bush gave two of these speeches on television. Both times, the market got clobbered after he was done.

The mantra of 'Recovery' is everywhere. Bush says it, the stock analysts say it – we've hit a bump here on our economic recovery, folks. Nothing to fear, and certainly no reason to suspect that our great economic system has developed a nasty case of pneumonia. One wonders, however, that if this is a recovery, what does a slump look like?

Here is the thing, though: we cannot look at this mess from an objective and disinterested distance. Millions of Americans are losing their futures. It used to be that stock market crashes affected only the big hitters. Now, more than half the working country – teachers, tech workers, secretaries, steelworkers – have money in the market in some form or another. According to present accounting of losses, they are looking at ten more years' work before they can even begin to think about retiring. That's how much of a disaster this is.

A lot of people treat economics like voodoo. It's arcane and mysterious, with all these obscure phrases: macroeconomics, microeconomics, leading indicators, and the rest. People go to school for years to learn how to parse it all. But so very much of it is blood simple: Americans will spend money if they trust the leadership and whatever they are looking to invest in. This we call 'consumer confidence.' If that is absent, the people keep their wallets in their pockets, and the voodoo of economics grinds to a halt.

The giant sucking sound on Wall Street was nothing more or less than the single most important poll George W. Bush has taken to date, and his numbers looked soft. He went on television to instill confidence and everything fell apart around his ears. Forget the Zogby and Pew polls – everything you need to know about how Americans feel about Bush and his people can be summed up in those busy little numbers and the tiny red arrows next to them on the news channels.

Really, there is no surprise here. Presidents can instill confidence in consumers with well-chosen words only if the consumers think he has anything to do with the process. Americans knew a while ago that Bush was a corporate puppet on some very short strings, and now the corporate puppeteers have been revealed to be Armani suit-wearing versions of the smash-and-grab thieves that plague the jewelry stores at your local mall. This does not instill confidence in the puppet.

The sense has begun to walk and talk out there that Bush is basically guilty of the same crimes and lies that crushed Enron in the first place, guilty from back in the days when he was a petroleum executive with Harken Energy. Bush's lawyers have maintained for years that he sold that Harken stock to pay off some debts. The *Washington Post* published details of a 'Hold Letter' that Bush signed two months before he sold out. The letter, with his signature, was his promise that he would not sell his stocks for six months. This begs the question: if he was planning to sell the stocks to pay off debts, why would he sign that letter?

It's just another accent in the symphony. There is a cancer on the presidency of George W. Bush. Maybe he jobbed Harken stockholders, maybe he didn't. Maybe he sold out with insider information, maybe he didn't. Maybe he was part of the Harken scheme to lie about their stock value, maybe he wasn't. But he always seems to be standing right next to the scumbags when the bad noise starts, doesn't he?

As all of this was unfolding there was, of course, a push by many within the GOP to blame Bill Clinton. It is a visceral reaction among these folks, automatic in its essence. They always manage to forget that when Bush passed his massive, ruinous tax-cut, thus gutting the Treasury, this American economy became his and his alone. But blaming Clinton for the economy, for September 11, and for anything else that may go wrong is part of the playbook that GOP legislators and media mouthpieces use when they join the club.

The facts beg to differ. The collapse in stock market value and the preponderance of corporate criminality is not Clinton's fault. The crisis we're dealing with came about through the actions of the Republican-controlled Congress in 1995, through a bill called the Private Securities Litigation Reform Act (PSLRA).

The Act basically allows corporations to wildly overstate the value of their stock. Before PSLRA, the SEC severely limited the ability of corporations to make claims about their value – such predictions are prone to exaggeration because the executives want to present their businesses in the best possible light. But along came PSLRA, passed by Congress, which basically did away with all restrictions along these lines. Corporations could promise the moon and lie without restraint about the value of their stock.

From 1935 to 1995, fewer than 100 corporations were forced to restate their earnings, *à la* Enron and WorldCom. In the last seven years, approximately 1,000 corporations have been forced to restate their earnings. The difference? PSLRA in 1995. Here is the Clintonian rub: Bill vetoed PSLRA, but the Republican Congress – with the help of some shamefully compromised Democrats – overrode his veto. In that override were sown the seeds of this mess.

So now, as you gaze at the crater that used to be your 401k, don't blame Bill. Hell, don't blame Bush – but take note of how the ethics his personal business life mirror the ethics of the thieves, and wonder at his credibility when he says he will fix it. If you are looking to lay blame, find Newt Gingrich and the cowboys his revolution brought to Congress in 1994.

Alan Greenspan came riding in the Tuesday after Bush spoke to save the markets with a rosy report about a healthy economy. The stock reporters on the news channels were fairly drooling about it. That is all well and good, but it bears notice that Big Al does not own one single, solitary share of stock in anything. Greenspan likes his Treasury Bonds, his bank accounts, and probably even has a few tin cans filled with quarters buried somewhere under his porch. Who can blame him? Wall Street has become a dangerous place to bring your paycheck. The day after Greenspan spoke, the markets were up. The following morning saw the death spiral return.

The market, it appears, knows a hypocrite when it sees one. Leaving Bush to shepherd the economy towards morally sound shores is like asking the wolf to tend the sheep. The traders must have listened to that speech while choking back chortles. This guy ran every business he touched into the ground. He played the same slick accounting games that have blown huge holes in the market, throwing in a little insider trading for good measure. His friends are among the worst offenders. He has bent his administration's policy to enrich these criminals while coddling terrorist regimes and overthrowing democracies, all in the name of oil and energy profiteering.

WorldCom declared Chapter 11 bankruptcy on July 22, buried under a $3.85 billion accounting scandal that has succeeded in doing what seemed impossible – their bankruptcy filing has managed to make the Enron implosion look small by comparison. WorldCom stock, once valued at $64 a share, was trading for nine cents a share when the markets closed the previous Friday. This is a microcosm of the disease that has rotted what was once a gloriously lucrative stock market.

Vice President Dick Cheney's health is so poor that he spends most of his time sleeping or resting. Perhaps he is hiding from reality in slumber – the thunderheads developing around his time as head of Halliburton Petroleum, which has recently earned itself an SEC investigation because of WorldComesqe accounting fudgery, led the Chicago *Sun-Times* to declare on its July 21 front page that Dick will likely not be on the ticket in 2004. The comic strip Doonsebury ran cartoons of Cheney in prison as the Judas goat for this administration.

Bush's own curious definition of business integrity earned wraparound coverage on all the news networks. The Harken story got more and more interesting by the day. Questions were pouring forth regarding what Bush knew and when he knew it as a board member for the doomstruck petroleum company. It is clear that he knew how rough the profit situation was for Harken when he sold off $850,000 worth of them, just before the bottom fell out, because Harken was forced to admit that they, too, had fudged the books. The tiny trickle of Harken documentation that the SEC has deigned to release – because Bush won't authorize a full disclosure – reveal that he was, in fact, all too aware of how badly the company was doing before he bailed out. He was in the loop for all the letters and meeting minutes describing how dire the situation was, right up until the day he left.

The *New York Times* on that same Sunday ran a front-page report describing the civilian cost for Bush's war in Afghanistan. Some 812 innocents have died as a result of erroneous bombings and strafings since Bush unleashed armed forces, a number sure to go higher as investigators continue their travels to burned-out villages. In all that blood, our actions there have failed to bring about the capture of a single Taliban leader. Most notably, of course, is the fact that Osama bin Laden still breathes free air somewhere in the world. Local Afghan officials were incensed by these civilian disasters and may break from the Bush fold if it continues.

James Carville once said 'It's the economy, stupid,' and Bush's slump in most every respected poll shows this all too clearly. The support he has been getting comes from Americans' belief that he is running the war well. This speaks more to the loyalty of the American people than anything else – after September 11, a ham sandwich would poll around 80% if it looked good in a suit and had people calling it 'Mr. President.' In Afghanistan,

812 families and 3,000 families connected to the World Trade Center, may say otherwise. Osama eludes justice and children die in the shadow of the Khyber Pass.

More ominously, Homeland Security Director Tom Ridge floated the idea that the military should be given much greater police and shoot-to-kill authority while on American soil. This further erodes the Posse Comitatus Act of 1878, a law that expressly established the fundamentally important firewall between civilian and military law enforcement. The burning of our basic liberties continues apace, one flicker of flame at a time.

Remember, millions of working Americans now face the hard reality that they will have to continue working at least ten years longer than they expected to before they can afford to retire, thanks to the shredding of their retirement portfolios at the hands of corporate brigands whose version of ethics comes right out of the Harken 'How-To' manual.

It's funny. A lot of people know Bush is in the bag for Big Business. Until recently I seemed one of only a few folks aware of the specifics. Bush's understanding of business comes directly from his own failed dalliances in the world of oil. Once upon a time, a person's ability to manage a budget effectively, whether it be personal or business-oriented, was an essential aspect of the character analysis performed if that person wished to seek political office. Financial records would be disclosed and examined by many eyes. If said person appeared unable to handle his money, or the money of others, that person stood little chance of getting elected.

Take the failed candidacy of Massachusetts Governor Michael Dukakis as a working example. His 1988 presidential run was hamstrung almost immediately by the staggering economy of Massachusetts and it reflected poorly on him throughout the campaign. A variety of other factors helped lead him to his inevitable slaughter at the polls, but the question of his fiscal abilities played no small role. The sluggish late 1980s economy of Massachusetts was not entirely Dukakis's fault, any more than the foul state of Boston Harbor was. Since he was the Governor, however, the buck stopped with him.

Somewhere between then and now, we seem to have lost the ability to effectively analyze the fiscal responsibility level of our candidates. The presidency of George W. Bush is the most recent, and perhaps most fearsome, example of this phenomenon. If the election game in 2000 had been played by 1988 rules, Bush would have never gotten out of Texas.

The sad and sorry story of Arbusto Energy provides the first of what has become a long indictment that suggests George W. Bush should on no account be allowed to handle other people's money in any capacity.

Arbusto was created by Bush in 1978 in the wake of his failed congressional campaign using start-up money collected from well-to-do family friends. All in all, he raised some $4.7 million for his enterprise between 1979 and 1982, an astounding figure when one realizes that Bush was a total neophyte in the oil business. Astounding, that is, until one considers that his father was either running for president or sitting as vice president at the time. His investors, clearly, were looking to get in good with the son of a man who would have considerable pull on their behalf in Washington, D.C.

Over the course of the next several years, Arbusto traveled a snarled trail of near-bankruptcy before finally exploding in a cloud of dry Texas dust. Before the deal went down, Arbusto had its name changed to Bush Exploration in 1982, at which point its stock value cratered. Two Bush family friends who owned an oil business called Spectrum 7 came in and bought him out, making him the third largest shareholder in that company.

In 1986, Spectrum 7 also began to sink. In the best tradition of the *deus ex machina*, however, yet another angel descended to rescue the son of the sitting Vice President. A Republican Party fundraiser named Alan Quasha swooped in and acquired Spectrum 7, incorporating it into his bizarre little oil business, Harken Oil. Bush and his partners were given $2 million in Harken stock for the deal and named as special 'consultants.'

At this point, the story gets strange. Harken was anything but a big player on the world stage. Few had heard of the company before 1990, when Harken landed an impressive deal to drill for oil in the Persian Gulf emirate of Bahrain. Petrochemical business analysts were surprised, to say the least, as Harken had never before played with the big boys on the world stage. How, then did they land this contract? The answer likely lies somewhere along the hallways of power that led to Vice President Bush's White House office.

It's nice to have friends in high places. Apparently, it's even nicer to have family members there. Several months after landing the deal, all hell broke loose in the Gulf. Iraq invaded Kuwait and the international oil community's financial situation was roiled. This did not bode well for Harken's new arrangement, but somehow George W. Bush managed once again to escape unscathed.

On June 22, 1990, Bush sold a large wad of his Harken stock for $848,560 – a 200% profit. The sale was well timed. Weeks after he sold his stock, Harken announced a $23.2 million loss in quarterly earnings and Harken stock dropped sharply, losing 60% of its value over the next six months.

Basically, Harken was guilty of the same crimes perpetrated by WorldCom and God only knows how many other huge corporations. They lied about being profitable until the lies ran out of steam. When the sunlight hit them, they died.

It seems clear that Bush knew Harken was in deep financial trouble, so he bailed out on the stock before it devalued, but failed to alert his investors of the impending calamity. Somehow he escaped SEC penalties for what appears to be nothing less than opportunistic profiteering at the expense of those who helped him get his businesses off the ground, a place they found themselves on several occasions. He avoided taint, even though he did not disclose his stock sale to the SEC until eight months after the deal went down. The SEC did investigate in 1991, but as it was part of his father's administration at the time, that inquiry went exactly nowhere.

When asked these days, Bush responds that none of the circumstances behind the demise of Arbusto, Spectrum 7, or Harken was his fault. These things happen when one chooses to go wildcatting for oil with other people's money. He should not be held responsible for it, and indeed he has not.

Yet as investigators and regulators sift through the shattered remains of the energy giant Enron Corporation, which flamed out in what will be recorded as one of the biggest business catastrophes in the history of human enterprise, fingerprints matching those of the president are being discovered in all sorts of strange places.

Enron, the *enfant terrible* of energy companies in the 1990s, spent the last several years hiding the fact that it was losing billions of dollars in revenue. They managed to obscure this by setting up a variety of hidden boxes controlled by Enron executives, into which were piled as much bad financial news as possible. This served to keep the losses off the books, until a $1.2 billion shortfall was revealed.

Apparently, Enron was ailing for quite a long time. Yet the aforementioned executives were able to maintain the mirage of financial viability by stuffing the debt into what are called 'off-balance-sheet partnerships.' In essence, each of the executives built personal banking bunkers and hid what has been revealed to be staggering Enron debts within them, keeping the fact that the company was hemorrhaging money off the publicly displayed balance sheets. This maintained the company's credit rating and allowed it to continue doing business.

This went on for four years, which means several things. It means that most of the Enron executives were aware of and/or actively participating in this criminal and highly irresponsible activity. It means the stockholders, including 4,000 loyal Enron employees, were lied to. It probably means that the executives knew the stock value was doomed when they bailed out and cashed in. It means they let their employees lose the retirement funds they believed were growing within their Enron stock portfolios. It means a lot of people got screwed by a pack of sharp operators who didn't give a damn about anyone but themselves.

Enron stock plummeted and some 4,000 Enron employees were shown the door, their pockets stuffed with stock options no longer worth the paper they were printed on. People who had depended on these stocks to fund their retirement began investigating the requirements needed to sign up for Food Stamps, while the executives parachuted to the streets of Houston with a cool $1 billion in 'bonuses' to show for their deceit. Once upon a time, people like that were called pirates.

Lawyers pursuing a civil suit against disgraced Enron CEO, Kenneth Lay, allege that he may have cashed in for as much as $184 million before his company folded. Similar charges have been levied against Army Secretary White, a former Enron executive, who sold his personal stock holdings after several suspiciously timed telephone conversations with individuals still employed by the company. The comparison between Lay and White will be difficult to avoid and will surely be an embarrassment for Bush.

Federal investigators pursuing criminal charges against Enron and its executives are squeezing a number of mid level managers who have intimate knowledge of the company's illicit dealings. They seek to nail down plea deals with these managers in exchange for testimony. If one of them decides to play John Dean in order to escape prison time, something the prosecutors view as likely, events will begin unfolding rapidly. With all the financial ties between Enron and Bush, and considering the influence that company had in crafting Bush's energy policy, the revelations that may come from these managers could be explosive.

Kenneth Lay, architect of this disaster, has for years been the single most important patron of George W. Bush. The two have been friends for years and Lay is listed prominently as one of Bush's Pioneers, a title given to anyone who raised $100,000 or more for the 2000 Bush campaign.

Bush was given the use of Enron corporate jets during the campaign. Karl Rove, *consigliere* to Bush, held as much as $250,000 in Enron stock. Harvey Pitt, Bush's chairman of the SEC, was hand-picked by Lay and Enron because of his business-friendly ideas on regulation. Bush himself was so tight with Lay that he even gave him a nickname: Kenny-Boy. This close connection led to the Bush administration's hiring of a number of influential individuals within Enron's orbit for important government positions:

- Thomas E. White, Bush's Secretary of the Army, was once Vice Chairman of Enron Energy Service, and held millions in Enron stock.
- Presidential advisor Karl Rove owned as much as $250,000 in Enron stock.
- Former economic advisor Larry Lindsay leapt straight from Enron to his current White House job.
- Federal Trade Representative Robert B. Zoellick did the same.

There are some 31 Bush administration officials who had a line item for Enron in their stock portfolio, including Defense Secretary Donald Rumsfeld. It is fair to say that the woebegone corporation held, and continues to hold, enormous influence over the day-to-day machinations of Federal government policy. One wonders if Bush's gutting of the Clean Air Act, a decision designed to improve the fortunes of companies like Enron, was the brainchild of people with deep connections to the energy industry.

The trail of influence left by Enron leads also to the scabrous heart ventricles of Vice President Dick Cheney, who admitted under duress to six meetings with Enron executives while formulating the Bush administration's energy policy. Cheney, a former executive of the Halliburton Petroleum interest, was in charge of creating this policy. Cheney refused to detail the specifics of the creation of this policy, citing – of course – the need for secrecy.

Columnist Robert Scheer referred to the Bush administration's involvement in the Enron debacle as 'Whitewater in spades.' One wonders if 'Watergate' would be a more appropriate comparison. It should be noted that Halliburton has fallen under the same harsh spotlight as WorldCom, with revelations that the company vastly overstated its profitability during Cheney's tenure.

If the worst is true, Bush will have a hard time getting out from under. This is not a situation where the illegal destruction of evidentiary documents will do the trick. The chain of evidence has names, and it will prove a messy affair if Bush tries to stuff Rove or Pitt into a document shredder. He may try at some point to resort to his favorite toy, the Executive Order, in an attempt to stuff any investigation that gets too close.

The political implications for Bush are enormous. The scandals surrounding Enron and other Wall Street corporate criminals have done their damage, and the prevailing mood on Wall Street has turned decidedly bearish. The recovery, so soon begun, turned sour in a heartbeat.

We must attend to the central truth: any time George W. Bush gets within shouting distance of a company, it collapses. This is a troubling fact when one considers that Bush is currently at the helm of the US economy.

While the September 11 attacks certainly play a part in the slowdown, Democrats will tell you that Bush's massive and ill-advised tax giveaway to rich people, an act that gutted the Clinton surplus and left little maneuvering room for the Federal budget, is a central factor. They are quite correct. The Enron, WorldCom, Arthur Andersen, Tyco, Xerox, and Martha Stewart/IMClone scandals have done their damage, as well.

Bush sees himself more as a corporate CEO than as a president. If his past and present management history holds any mirror to his soul, it can be said without qualification that he is the worst CEO in modern history, perhaps second only to his lifelong chum Ken Lay. Everything he touches turns to dust.

So, with all this in mind, we are forced to remind ourselves to look at the way a candidate handles his business. It will also pay dividends to look into the company a candidate chooses to keep. In the last several months, an angry song of betrayal and loss insinuated itself into constant rotation on the alt-pop radio stations. When the news of corporate lies and fraud becomes too maddening, flee to one of these stations and you will see what I mean. Spend ten minutes flipping the dial, and the gravelly growl of Nickelback will inevitably come pouring through your speakers: 'This is how you remind me of what I really am ...' goes the refrain.

In these days, it is difficult to listen to the meanest and most vapid song on the radio without giving it a level of context it does not deserve. The state of this nation and the world has added dazzling and disturbingly vivid color to what was once mundane and beneath notice. Music bears a heavy burden with this, and Nickelback has become my personal musical albatross. Whenever that chorus finds its way into my car speakers, I cannot help but think the same dismal thought:

Thank you, Kenny-Boy. Thank you for reminding us of what we really are.

Americans like to believe they live in a democracy, based upon their individual right to vote. Those who remember their high school civics lessons like to think of America as a constitutionally democratic republic, based upon the right to choose representatives in government. The essence of the ideal remains constant – We The People run the show, we choose the leaders, and they in turn honorably represent our interests to the best of their abilities.

The underpinnings of this ideal have been subverted by years of campaign finance chicanery on both sides of the political aisle, and this is no secret. Only benighted fools miss the influence cash-heavy donors have upon the legislative process and the formation of national policy. Yet we cling to our belief, almost in desperation, that the purity of the American democratic ideal still beats like a heart within the body of our government and the souls of our representatives.

Thank you, Kenny-Boy, for shattering that illusion forever.

The roll call of senators who have taken campaign donations from Enron reads like a Who's Who of the Washington, D.C. cocktail circuit:

Robert Bennett (R-Utah): $8,053
Christopher Bond (R-Mo): $17,000
John Breaux (D-La): $11,000
Conrad Burns (R-Mont): $23,200
Michael Crapo (R-Idaho): $18,689
Phil Gramm (R-Tx): $101,350
Ernest Hollings (D-SC): $3,500
Kay Baily Hutchison (R-Tx): $101,500
Charles Schumer (D-NY): $21,933
Gordon Smith (R-Or): $14,500

The final balance of Enron contributions to House and Senate officeholders comes to 72% for Republicans and 28% for Democrats. As political Jedi James Carville noted on *Meet The Press*, 'If the score of a game is 72–28, that is not a tie.' Of the 30 senators holding office in 2002 who have never received Enron money, only seven were Republicans. In the 2002 House, there was not one single member who has not accepted Enron money at one time or another.

While Carville made a valid political point, this does not spare us from the stark reality to be found in the disbursements above. The taint of Enron is as bipartisan a fact as has ever been found on Capitol Hill. These members, whose job it is to zealously represent our interests, have for years been ravaging the regulation of the energy industry at the behest of companies like Enron. They have done it because they were paid to do it. It is as simple as that.

Thank you, Kenny-Boy, for helping us to see where their loyalty is truly to be found.

After the election, Enron used its financial reach to better its fortunes. As the Bush administration pulled together national energy policy behind locked doors, an Enron lobbyist named Edward Gillespie was formulating plans to defang the anticipated Democratic attacks against it. 'Carterize the Democrats' was the run of his thoughts. Make them the party against sound policy, remind voters of the gas lines of the 1970s, and, above all, obscure the perception that the GOP sits snugly in the pocket of big business.

Some weeks after Gillespie crafted memos detailing his plans, television advertisements began appearing across the country comparing Democratic resistance to Bush's energy plans to Carter's request that Americans wear sweaters to defray energy costs. This obvious connection between the formulation of Bush's energy policy and Enron, including the six meetings between Enron executives and chief policy formulator Dick Cheney, is among the myriad reasons why the administration is fighting tooth and nail to keep those meetings secret.

Thank you, Kenny-Boy. You couldn't just subvert the legislative process with your all-encompassing funding. You had to roll up your sleeves and get right into the game, didn't you?

Congressman James Greenwood (R-PA), who chairs the oversight and investigation wing of the House Committee on Energy and Commerce, stated that Enron's financial practices, while uncommon, are certainly not unheard of. Mr Greenwood stated that there could be 'dozens of Enrons' lurking in the weeds, just waiting to implode. The disaster of the first Enron still echoes on Wall Street. WorldCom and the rest added to the thunder. American faith in the stock market, in the accounting industry, and in the viability of virtually every retirement portfolio in the country, has been badly shaken. Two or three more could bring our whole economy down around our ears.

Thank you, Kenny-Boy.

The media have apparently lost Enron and Kenny-Boy somewhere in the shuffle. This shouldn't be surprising; hell, there's no sex here, and figuring out the details requires actual work. This does not mean that the scandal has disappeared. Any Western smokejumper will tell you that the most dangerous kinds of forest fires aren't the ones that burn in the treetops, but the ones that burn slow and hot just below the surface of the ground. Treetop fires can be seen for miles, allowing firefighters to track them and contain them. Fires that smolder beneath the surface, fed by years' worth of fallen leaves that can lay as thick as a foot below the forest floor, can burn undetected for acres in every direction. Only when the flames explode upwards, charring everything around them to dust in the blink of an eye, does the danger become apparent.

This analogy is appropriate when considering the last two political scandals of significance that scorched the woods of Washington, D.C. The Whitewater scandal of the Clinton years was a treetop fire: visible in all directions, it spit sparks into the wind that singed but never fully burned down the President of the United States. In the end, its own lack of substance caused it to burn out. The recently released Special Counsel report codified the years and money spent investigating Whitewater as a colossal waste of time and energy.

For a long time, the Whitewater fire lit up the sky. Reading accounts by former conservative assassins like David Brock, or simply parsing the tortured language of Investigator Robert Ray, one is left with the undeniable sense that those who participated in the aggrandizement of the Whitewater scandal knew in their hearts that there was nothing to it. It was a far sharper political tool than a legal one. This explains why the fire burned so bright. The flames fanned by partisan operatives obscured the true proportions of the scandal.

The other scandal of note, involving the disgraced firms Enron and Arthur Andersen, barely glows at all. One must peruse the back pages of newspapers and the daytime television of C-SPAN to hear anything about it. The *New York Times*, which for a time carried at least two Enron stories a day on its front page, has moved on to more combustible pastures. As a scandal, it has become quite dull from a media perspective. In reality, however, the fire has moved below the surface. It burns slow, hot, and undetected. It has become dangerous.

Consider the implications of the Federal criminal conviction handed down against the accounting firm Arthur Andersen. Andersen, bookkeepers for Enron, was accused of obstruction of justice for their shredding of bales of pertinent Enron documentation. The executives of Andersen were not accused – it is the corporation itself that was been criminally charged. When the Justice Department prevailed in its case, Arthur Andersen essentially ceased to exist.

Justice had a strong case, as evidenced by the particulars of another instance where the Federal government pursued a corporation in a criminal prosecution. In the ruling for *United States* v. *Hilton Head Corp.* (467 F.2nd 1000) the judge declared:

> A corporation is responsible for the acts and statements of its agents, done or made within the scope of their employment, even though their conduct may be contrary to their actual instructions or contrary to the corporation's stated policies.

This decision was later affirmed on appeal (409 U.S. 1125, in 1973).

The legal and the political are tightly intertwined here. The fact that George W. Bush's own Justice Department pursued Arthur Andersen with such deadly intent, despite its connections to Enron and all attendant political implications, means something serious is afoot. *U.S.* v. *Andersen* erased one of the largest accounting firms on earth. This fact alone stands the Enron scandal tall in political importance.

Congress has fired out subpoenas in the Enron matter, focusing new scrutiny on connections between the energy corporation and the White House. The scope of these subpoenas covers 1992 through to the present, which means Clinton's dealings with Enron will likewise be examined. This lends a bipartisan veneer to the proceedings, a wise tactic that should serve to knock down accusations of unfairness by Republicans who feel the ground getting hot beneath their feet.

Most important to this ten-year scope is the fact that it will cover any and all dealings Bush had with Ken Lay back in his Texas gubernatorial days. It was there that the ties between these two men were forged, on both personal and policy levels, and it is there that the evident political connections within Bush's national energy policy were created. Like the Enron investigation, the focus of the Whitewater investigations was on Clinton's dealings before he arrived in Washington, D.C. Unlike Whitewater, this Enron work by Congress moves slowly and quietly, almost completely beneath the radar of the media.

The gold standard for Washington political scandals is, of course, Watergate. Before Watergate became a treetop blaze that burned Nixon's administration to the ground, it was a slow, smoldering fire that did not earn a great deal of notice. The Watergate break-in that started everything happened on June 17, 1972, when the burglars were arrested in the act. The conflagration did not truly begin until October 20, 1973, after the infamous 'Saturday Night Massacre.' The principal actors were not indicted until March 1974. Nixon did not resign until August of that year. One does not need to see a column of smoke to know a fire is burning.

Are there any specific areas where Bush's favoritism towards the petroleum people of the world has been fully on display? It is a certainty that the aforementioned energy plan is one – not since the days of the robber barons has such substantive domestic policy been written almost entirely by corporate magnates. The omission of Saudi Arabia from the Axis of Evil, despite that nation's blatant ties to international terrorism, is due entirely to the oil it has under its deserts. The fact that Bush's security agencies failed to see threats against America coming from Saudi Arabia can be ascribed to this largesse, and the War on Terror that came because of this willful blindness is nothing more or less than the most recent and bloodiest example of blowback we have to reckon with.

There is one other area of the world where Bush's love for his fellow energy business compatriots can clearly be seen. One need only look to the south.

News of the abortive coup in Venezuela against the government of President Hugo Chavez came fast and furious in April 2002. No mainstream reports managed to reveal the story in its entirety, but an amazing picture began to coalesce, thanks to the work of independent media organizations like Narco News. Venezuela's democracy was attacked by business interests that wished to wrest control of that nation from a legitimately elected leader. It is an old story in that part of the world, but this time around the ending was different. Democracy in Venezuela survived its attempted murder, essentially because the people took to the streets and saved it.

The details in brief: Hugo Chavez won two presidential elections in Venezuela, in 1998 and in 2000, by the largest margins in 40 years. Upon his rise, he instituted a number of socially progressive programs, based upon a concept called Bolivarianism, aimed at raising the standard of living for the common people. Chavez ratified a new Constitution guaranteeing new rights for women and indigenous peoples. He cleared out the plague of graft and corruption in the Venezuelan government by restructuring the legislative and judicial branches. He instituted a government-funded breakfast and lunch program for schoolchildren which has helped increase enrollment by over a million students. He provided free health care and public education up to university level.

How did he pay for all these programs? This is the $64,000 question ... or to be more accurate, the multi-billion dollar question. The answer lies in the small word that has so dominated American foreign policy: oil. Venezuela is a major source of petroleum, historically providing between 15% and 40% of America's imported supply. Canada and Iraq, by comparison, make up only 26% of our imported oil. Chavez's country is, without doubt, the most important nation to America on this side of the planet because of this.

Chavez redirected vast sums of money from Venezuela's petroleum production away from the multinationals, which had been profiting wildly, towards his progressive government programs. That alone was enough to draw the ire of the American petroleum industry and the International Monetary Fund. But Chavez also became deeply involved with OPEC when Venezuela took over the presidency of that entity, giving Chavez a burst of new influence. Not long after Bush took office, the decision was made: Chavez had to go.

It began with propaganda, as it always does. After Chavez won for the first time in 1998, he was labeled a demagogue and an authoritarian by members of the mainstream American media. The drumbeat of criticism from 'journalists,' whose fealty to the truth apparently came second to their support of business, continues to this day. A spokesman for Bush's administration chimed in at one point, making the claim that Chavez's earning of a majority of the vote in two separate elections did not necessarily confer legitimacy upon his administration.

Yes, they actually said that. Go figure.

All this reached a crescendo in April 2002. According to mainstream media reports, Chavez was forced out of office after several anti-government protesters were gunned down in the streets. He resigned, we were told, to preserve democracy in the region. Said democracy was delivered into the hands of the Venezuelan military and the leader of that nation's business (read: petroleum) community, a man named Pedro Carmona.

Carmona and his allies misjudged the level of public support Chavez enjoyed. When Carmona abolished the Venezuelan Congress and the Supreme Court, when he changed the country's name to the Republic of Venezuela, and when he instituted a house-to-house search for congress-men and former cabinet members, the hours-old coup flew apart at the seams.

A popular uprising against Carmona erupted almost immediately in every quarter of Venezuela. The people took to the streets in support of Chavez and in defiance of the coup. Simultaneously, rank-and-file soldiers and officers in the Venezuelan military refused to accept Carmona's regime and began what ultimately became a successful counter-coup. In short order, Carmona's rule in Venezuela was finished, and Hugo Chavez was reinstated as President.

It seems, despite media reports to the contrary, that Chavez never actually resigned. Reports proffered by the *New York Times*, CNN, and even Ari Fleischer, that Chavez ordered the shooting of anti-government protesters, were wildly inaccurate. In fact, it appears that those killed were uniformly supporters of Chavez. The puny anti-Chavez protests that received so much play in the American media were funded by the Venezuelan business community as a means to give a 'populist' veneer to their coup.

Narco News reported the existence in Venezuela of a CIA command bunker operating under the name MIL GROUP. This operation greatly increased its staff size in the weeks before the coup. Chavez himself has commented upon the appearance of a private jet with American markings that arrived on the island where he was briefly held before being reinstated. Individuals loyal to Carmona urged him to board the plane and fly into exile, but he refused. Chavez has vowed to get to the bottom of that strange aircraft and the curious timing of its appearance.

A potentially explosive story hit the wires on the afternoon of April 18: officials within Chavez's presidential office claim that the American military attaché to Caracas was present with the coup leaders at that city's main military base in the days leading up to the coup attempt.

A number of Venezuelan military officers reported some days after April 18 the name of this American military official – US Army Lieutenant-Colonel James Rodgers, aide to the US military attaché in Caracas – and reiterated that he was present with the coup leaders at Fort Tiuna in Caracas, where the operation was planned. Rodgers, it was reported, was with these leaders at Fort Tiuna when the coup leaders brought Chavez there to be held after he was deposed. These officers interpreted Rodgers' presence at Tiuna as a green light from the United States to overthrow Chavez.

Officials from the Organization of American States, the powerful political and economic alliance between North and South America, publicly accused a number of influential Bush administration members of actively assisting the coup. Otto Reich, an anti-Castro Cuban and former US ambassador to Venezuela in 1986 who serves as Bush's main policy advisor for Latin America, was accused by OAS of meeting several times with the coup leaders in the months before the coup attempt. John Negroponte, US ambassador to the United Nations who was ambassador to Honduras during Iran/Contra, was accused by OAS of having been informed of 'some movement in Venezuela on Chavez' as early as the New Year. OAS also named Eliot Abrams, a member of Bush's National Security Council and best known for his criminal involvement in the Iran/Contra affair, as having been deeply complicit.

The Senate Foreign Relations Committee made plans to begin an investigation into the Bush administration's involvement in the Venezuelan coup, and names of Rodgers, Reich, Negroponte, and Abrams will likely play a central role.

A number of shoes must still drop before the full story of what happened in Venezuela comes clear. This much, however, is evident: petroleum interests attempted to overthrow a democratically elected leader because he was interfering with oil profits and because he was engineering the rise of what some have called the purest democracy in the world. A number of major American news outlets, including the *New York Times* and the Associated Press, either completely misreported or flat-out lied about the happenings there.

The implications of this are grievous. If the US government is implicated in a plot to destroy a democratic government in its own neighborhood, its international stature in this dangerous time of war will suffer a mighty blow. More significantly, it appears the Bush administration assisted oil interests in the overthrow of a democratically elected leader so as to re-establish corporate hegemony over that nation's petroleum production.

Amid this blizzard of fraud, economic woe, looming indictments, shredded freedoms, and dead civilians, George W. Bush made an executive decision to spend the entire month of August 2002 on vacation down in Crawford, Texas.

There is an old story about a lady who found an injured snake while walking down a road. She picked it up, brought it home, and nursed it back to health. In the ensuing weeks, she and the snake became great friends. Then, one day, the snake bit her on the neck while she was working in her garden. As she lay dying, she gasped to the snake, 'Why did you bite me? I was your friend. I took care of you. Why did you do this?'

The snake replied, 'Lady, you knew I was a snake when you picked me up.'

A Bright September Morning

Turn on the television and find a news station, and you will be greeted within minutes by a graphic, and by suitably dramatic music, that tells us we are engaged in the War on Terror. You will be reminded that we were attacked out of nowhere by entities that hate our freedom. You will be counseled to understand that everything has changed. This is, you are told, a new war.

In a prime-time press conference not long after September 11, George W. Bush took the long walk, *à la* Reagan, down the red carpeted hallway to the East Room of the White House and answered about twelve questions. In one response, he professed amazement at the hatred our new enemies hold for us. We're so good, he claimed. How could they miss that?

The answer to that question embarrassed all the networks that tell us we are involved in a 'new' war, and should embarrass a president whose oft-repeated disdain for reading has left him with little historical understanding for our current circumstances.

This is not a new war at all, nor is it a new world, nor has everything changed. This is a very old war and has been raging for generations. There are nations, some of whom are apparently complicit in the September 11 attacks, who believe that they have been at war with the United States for two decades. The destruction of the Trade Towers and a section of the Pentagon was not a lightning strike from a blameless sky. It was a bold tactical stroke by an enemy that has managed to strike back within our borders.

This is not a new world and nothing has changed. America has been rudely and horrifyingly awakened to the circumstances of the world around them. The cushion provided by two oceans, countless nuclear missiles, and a media establishment that shrinks from reporting what is actually happening elsewhere because of our policies, has been ripped from under us.

Welcome to the world, America. This is what life is like for many, many nations.

Defense Secretary Rumsfeld has described this conflict as a 'new Cold War.' That war lasted from Truman to Bush Sr, and the circumstances we are currently enduring are a direct result. The old Cold War gave us nuclear weapons in all corners of the globe, Korea, Vietnam, Laos, Cambodia, Nicaragua, Iraq, the Gulf War, the Red Scare, the Black Lists, McCarthy, Hoover, anthrax weapons, smallpox weapons, Star Wars, massive ecological destruction, and yes, Osama bin Laden and the Taliban.

The ultimate fallacy behind the idea that this is a new war lies in the fact that we are fighting it in a very old-fashioned way. Bombing Afghanistan will not stop terrorism. It will not allay the fears of our populace. All the bombing of Afghanistan will do is create new jihad warriors who are ready to die so as to see you die. In their rage and despair, they will willingly sign up. Our so-called endless war will become a reality, as we manufacture droves of the very people we seek to destroy. It will never end.

If we cannot stop terror without becoming a barricaded, isolated, totalitarian state – a dark choice that is the only sure cure – then what is left? More bombs far away? More civilian deaths? More feeding of the cycle that will surely bring more of the same to our shores and theirs? There is no way to win this old war if we fight it the way we have been. The only way to guarantee victory is to transform the conflict into a genuine new war, one that looks inward as well as outward.

It has been almost two years since September 11. We have heard many debates, accusations, and arguments about the genesis of the attacks. Every major news agency, and every talking head with a whisper of breath in their lungs, has weighed in. We have been told how we should respond. We have been told how we should feel. We have been told how we can help. In all that time, however, something essential has been missing. We have yet to be told how such a thing was allowed to happen in the first place.

It is a curious phenomenon. Whenever anything occurs in this country, be it a shark attack or the disappearance of a Capitol Hill intern, the media drumbeat has always played the same tune: Why? Why? Why did this happen? This Greek Chorus has fallen silent since the Towers came down. Rather than question the genesis of our woe, we have been afforded endless observations about how we have and should react. There is no looking back. There are no answers.

Thousands of Americans died on September 11, and thousands of Afghan civilians have joined them in the days since. Millions, nay, billions worldwide have been affected. American soldiers stand in peril. Yet we are afforded no answers, no understanding, no succor. All we have are threads of data flapping in the winds of battle and response. We deserve better.

The time has come to take those threads and weave them together as best we can.

It cannot be denied that the attacks of September 11 represent the most spectacular intelligence failure in the history of the nation. The planning required to pull off such an audacious air strike likely was years in the making, formulated by people all across the planet. Somehow, these people managed to locate and exploit a security loophole left by the mighty FBI, CIA, and NSA (National Security Agency), and flew four deadly bombs laden with fuel and humanity right through it.

The beginnings of an explanation came from a totally unexpected source on May 30, 2002. Recent revelations have surfaced that the Bush administration had been specifically warned of September 11-style attacks by a host of foreign intelligence services, and failed to address them properly. Enter Larry Klayman, General Counsel for the conservative activist group Judicial Watch.

Klayman has been on the scene for years, coming to prominence as one of the foremost anti-Clinton bombardiers on the Right. Best known for his preponderance of the theory that Clinton Commerce Secretary Ron Brown was assassinated and that the plane crash that killed him was a cover-up, Klayman spent a great deal of time spreading the story of the 'Clinton Body Count' – those unfortunate souls whacked by Bill because they got too close to his drug-running out of Arkansas airports or because they asked too many questions about his sex life, etc. Klayman managed to sue the Clinton White House some 18 times before 1999.

On May 30, Klayman emerged from the mists of anti-Clintonism and fired a stupendous broadside across the bow of the Bush administration and the FBI. Appearing before members of the press in a news conference broadcast by C-SPAN, Klayman introduced an eleven-year veteran FBI agent named Robert Wright. Judicial Watch has claimed Wright as a client and intends to defend him against what Klayman describes as a serious campaign by the FBI and the Department of Justice to intimidate and destroy him.

Why?

According to Klayman, Wright had been sounding an alarm within the FBI for years about terrorist activities within the United States. Rather than heed Wright's warnings, the FBI deflected and obstructed his efforts to curtail dangerous movements by agents of Hamas and Hezbollah. Wright's activities within the FBI were geared towards thwarting money-laundering activities by these agents, and he is claiming that his efforts were stymied because important government officials such as Colin Powell have been coddling these pro-Palestinian groups to protect the reputation of Yasser Arafat.

Klayman leaned across the podium at the press and claimed that the FBI 'did not do its job' regarding September 11, that Wright had been trying since 1999 to get the FBI to clean its house before disaster struck, and that his reward for doing so was the threat of civil suits, loss of employment, and criminal charges. Klayman juxtaposed this against the recent praise heaped upon Colleen Rowley, the Minnesota FBI agent whose whistle-blowing memo to FBI Director Robert Mueller outlining all of the agency's failures to see September 11 coming was lionized by the Director as he announced the dawn of a new improved FBI. Wright was threatened while Rowley is praised, said Klayman.

The FBI bore the brunt of Klayman's lashing, but it was definitely not alone. The Bush administration was blasted as 'an administration which, despite being elected on the basis of restoring national security, slept for nine months, and did virtually nothing to shore up the inadequacies of the FBI.'

Klayman went on to describe the Bush administration as 'an administration which comes forward yesterday to cover their backside after it becomes apparent that they hid information from the American people for nine months – material information as to how, in the new admission of FBI Director Robert Mueller, the 9/11 attacks could have possibly been prevented.'

Klayman addressed Vice President Cheney specifically, lambasting his claim that America is defenseless against future terrorism. According to Klayman and Wright, our defenselessness is based on nothing more or less than rank incompetence on the part of the FBI. That incompetence reaches into the highest offices of government and into the responsibility of men like Cheney and Bush, who should be doing more to change the inadequate capabilities of intelligence branches like the FBI.

'What have you, the Bush administration, been doing for the last nine months,' railed Klayman, 'that just now you're advising the American people that we don't have the defenses even after having lost 3,000 lives?'

Klayman yielded the podium moments later to the speakerphoned voice of David Schippers, another infamous anti-Clinton warrior standing forth for Robert Wright. Schippers recapitulated the threats levied against Wright by the FBI regarding his intended disclosure of intelligence failures, calling Wright 'a great American.' Before his voice was cut off, Schippers warned Wright, 'Don't go into any specifics, any particulars about any case, even though you and I both know there is no case. But they claim there is, so we'll follow their guidelines – the same guidelines that put 3,000 people on the street, dead.'

Wright stepped up to the podium and presented himself as a vividly different breed of man from Klayman and Schippers. Somberly dressed and adorned with the severest of conservative hairstyles, Wright appeared to have come straight out of FBI central casting. He began by stating that he did not in any way stand as a representative of the Bureau; he was speaking freely here of his own views and opinions, and was not representing the FBI in any capacity.

Wright went on to describe his work with the FBI. For many years, he had worked in the Chicago office on counter-terrorism cases that focused on money-laundering efforts by terrorist cells operating within the United States. His work developed into an operation named 'Bulgar Betrayal,' which seemed on the verge of becoming officially designated as a major case because of its far reach and national security implications. Before he had finished, a Saudi businessman named Yasin Kadi became implicated in the terrorism funding. Wright was careful to note that, one month after the September 11 attacks, Kadi was named by the Federal government as a financial supporter of Osama bin Laden.

Yet Kadi's name was known to Wright well before September 11, when the Bulgar Betrayal investigations were taking place. Did his work take root within the FBI? Did his superiors note the dangers implicit in the activities of the terrorists Wright had pinpointed? 'FBI management,' said Wright on Thursday, 'intentionally and repeatedly thwarted my attempts to launch a more comprehensive investigation to identify and to neutralize terrorists.'

Wright had to purchase computer software and hardware necessary for his investigations because the FBI failed to allocate the necessary funds to help his work. A week after September 11, Wright attempted to deliver his concerns to several members of Congress so the glaring gaps in American national security could be addressed, but was threatened by the FBI and the Justice Department. In fact, he was told that he could not travel beyond Chicago without specific permission from the FBI.

Wright's frustration at the FBI's inaction regarding his warnings led him to write a 500-page manuscript detailing the Bureau's anti-terrorism failings entitled 'Fatal Betrayals of the Intelligence Mission.' Beyond describing the myriad ways the FBI and the government have failed to protect Americans from terrorism, the manuscript goes on to demand a thorough house-cleaning within the FBI. It seems clear after listening to Wright's press conference that the main reason why FBI Director Mueller has chosen to embrace whistleblowing agent Rowley while threatening agent Wright comes down to the existence of that manuscript.

Wright concluded his remarks in dramatic and emotional fashion. 'My efforts,' he said,

> have always been geared towards neutralizing the terrorist threats that focused on taking the lives of American citizens, in addition to harming the national and economic security of America. However, as a direct result of the incompetence, and at times intentional obstruction of justice by FBI management to prevent me from bringing terrorists to justice, Americans have unknowingly been exposed to potential terrorist attacks for years.

He went on to state, 'Knowing what I know, I can confidently say that until the investigative responsibilities for terrorism are removed from the FBI, I will not feel safe.'

At this point, Wright paused a long moment before continuing through choked voice, and wiping a tear from his eye, 'To the families and victims of September 11th, on behalf of John Vincent, Barry Carmody and myself ... we're sorry.' These last words were essentially sobbed into the microphone, and with that Wright fled the podium. The names he mentioned – Vincent and Carmody – were later described by Klayman as FBI agents preparing to come forward 'with the truth' as Wright had done.

What to make of all this? On one side stands Larry Klayman, clown-man *extraordinaire* who shattered his credibility years ago by spreading tales of Clinton death squads. On the other side stands FBI agent Robert Wright, shadowed by agents Vincent and Carmody. Anyone who watched the Wright press conference – available via link at JudicialWatch.org – could sense the man's earnestness. Perhaps he believed Klayman was the only vehicle he had to get his story out. Perhaps, after eight years of anti-Clinton jihad along the halls of the FBI, Klayman was the only lawyer he'd ever heard of.

Wright's claims of FBI malfeasance became only a part of the roar of accusation that include Rowley's assertions and dozens of terror warnings from foreign intelligence services such as the French Directorate of Territorial Security (DST). The DST was screaming at Rowley's Minnesota FBI office about Zacarias Moussaoui and terrorist plans to crash airplanes into important targets, but no one from Rowley's office could get FBI headquarters to pay attention to these warnings until it was too late.

What the FBI and the Justice Department will do with the information coming from these truth-telling agents, who squat above Ashcroft's door like the raven, remains to be seen. The immediate return upon this informational investment does not bode well. On the same day that Wright revealed his information, the FBI released a warning for everyone to be on the look-out for terrorists bearing shoulder-launched missile weapons.

More ominously, Ashcroft announced the same day that the Justice Department planned to extend its PATRIOT Act mandate to the surveillance of churches and political groups. Congressman John Conyers, Democrat of Michigan, blasted this move:

> The Administration's continued defiance of constitutional safeguards seems to have no end in sight. This decision decimates the Fourth Amendment. The Justice Department is intent on another power grab when it has become clear that a lack of competence – not law enforcement authorities – prevented the Administration from connecting the dots before September 11. I call on the Bush Administration to immediately halt any efforts to unilaterally expand surveillance authority and to consult Congress before implementing further intrusions on our civil liberties.

We have here the central problem regarding anyone trying to peer behind the curtain and find out what exactly happened on September 11 and why. Klayman is a kook, for years a political hatchet man, and yet there he was before the national press corps denouncing Bush and the FBI for allowing the attacks to happen through criminal malfeasance. Whatever goofball credibility Klayman had was augmented by orders of magnitude when FBI veteran Wright burst into tears. There are many threads to be pulled here.

Robert Frost once penned some compelling lines: 'We dance around a ring and suppose / but the Secret sits in the middle and knows.' This was never more true than after September 11. The Secret indeed knows, but we can parse some of its whispers if we ask the right questions and look in the right places. Klayman may be a charlatan, but by putting Wright and his accusations about the FBI before the press, he wrapped his hands around one of the ropes that make up this web.

The questions, then. The data I have compiled to answer them may prove to be wrong – and the soul within me that loves this country often prays that it is – but they are questions that demand answers.

- How did American intelligence services fail to see this attack coming? Was it simple negligence or is there more to the story?

- Was the Bush administration dealing with the Taliban in the months before September 11? What was the substance of this parley?
- In what ways does Saudi Arabia play a part in the whole scenario? If so, why has it been excluded from the War on Terror's target list?

The last question must come first, for there is no doubt that Saudi Arabia is the most important country on the face of the earth. The Saudi regime, put in place decades ago with America's direct help, provides more oil to our nation and the world than any other country. In short, this makes them Bush's boss – his administration blows whichever way the petroleum winds happen to be gusting, after all.

This stands as the main reason why Saudi Arabia has been conspicuously absent from Bush's list of nations accused of harboring terrorists, and yet 13 of the 19 terrorists who commandeered the aircraft on September 11 were from Saudi Arabia and some 80% of all Al Qaeda recruits come from that oil-rich nation. It stands to reason, therefore, that American intelligence agencies would have a vested interest in paying a great deal of attention to Saudi Arabia. Somehow, however, these terrorists managed to elude notice until they appeared in the blue New York sky.

American security concerns overseas fall primarily within the bailiwick of the Central Intelligence Agency. This agency was run in the 1970s by none other than George Herbert Walker Bush, father of the sitting Commander-in-Chief and a former president himself. Bush Sr ranks among the most venerated members of the Old Guard from the Nixon and Reagan days, and commands the loyalty of government officials past and present. Because of his long years in politics, Bush Sr also enjoys a vast array of business connections. This is common knowledge.

Since his departure from the political scene, however, the activities of Bush Sr have not been paid much attention by the national media. Supporters of the former president would be pleased to know that he has done quite well for himself. He has, in the days since his defeat at the hands of William Jefferson Clinton, secured a position on the advisory board of an organization called the Carlyle Group.

The Carlyle Group is a multinational, multi-billion-dollar private firm, managed by former members of the Reagan and Bush administrations, and is involved in everything from soda bottling to pharmaceuticals manufacturing. It is here that Bush Sr, whose contacts with Saudi Arabia were cemented in the forming of the Gulf War coalition, comes into play. As early as January 2000, Bush Sr was courting the favor of Saudi Crown Prince

Abdullah in the name of Carlyle, which was working with the telecommunications giant SBC to gain control of a large share of the Saudi phone system. He has, over the years, done similar outreach work for Carlyle's oil interests, because the petroleum/energy business is central to the Group's financial strength.

It has long been true that the business of America is business, to the detriment of many other important factors. Given the connections between the former president and head of CIA, a major energy business player, and a nation that contains oil and terrorists in equal measure, questions about conflict of interest must be raised.

The American petroleum industry relies upon the stability of Saudi Arabia to keep their oil flowing in the proper fashion. Because the business of America is business, it is not too far a leap to conclude that the business of the American intelligence community is also business, and deliberately so. Public questions about and investigations into Saudi Arabia's hosting of terrorists like Osama bin Laden, whose family calls that nation home and whose vast fortune is still banked there, would certainly make it difficult for the American petroleum industry to work comfortably with the Saudi regime. Add to this the fact that the CIA, whose job it would be to investigate terrorist connections in Saudi Arabia, claims as its former head Bush Sr, who has a vested financial interests in healthy and unobstructed US–Saudi relations.

The result of this line of inquiry is chilling. Could the CIA have been dissuaded from fully investigating the roots of terrorism in Saudi Arabia because such investigations would have conflicted with the interests of entities like the Carlyle Group? If this was not the case, the explanation must be chalked up to simple incompetence. Considering the complexity of what transpired on September 11, the simple answer is not reliable. Occam's Razor fails in the face of the facts.

The importance of Saudi Arabia to the formulation of American policy, and the manner in which the Bush administration directed its counter-intelligence work, is further highlighted by the words of a man named John O'Neill. A Deputy Director of the FBI, O'Neill was America's chief bin Laden hunter. He had been in charge of the investigations into the bin Laden-connected bombings of the World Trade Center in 1993, the destruction of an American troop barracks in Saudi Arabia in 1996, the African embassy bombings in 1998, and the attack upon the USS *Cole* in 2000. Simply put, no one person in America's counter-terrorism apparatus knew more about Osama bin Laden than John O'Neill.

Two weeks before September 11, O'Neill quit the FBI in anger and disgust. He believed his government was actively hindering his ability to pursue dangerous Islamic terrorists. O'Neill was quoted as saying, 'The main obstacles to investigating Islamic terrorism were U.S. oil corporate interests, and the role played by Saudi Arabia in it.' Upon leaving the FBI, O'Neill took a position as head of security for the World Trade Center and was killed doing his job on September 11.

Egypt, Germany, Russia, and Israel warned us. The German intelligence service BND told US and Israeli intelligence that Middle East terrorists were 'planning to hijack commercial aircraft to use as weapons to attack important symbols of American and Israeli culture.' Egypt relayed warnings that same month regarding aircraft attacks. Russian intelligence, no stranger to domestic terrorism, warned us, 'in the strongest possible terms' of 25 pilots trained for suicide missions. The Israeli intelligence service Mossad, another agency well versed in dealing with terrorism, delivered a warning to both the FBI and the CIA detailing 'a major assault on the United States' against 'a large-scale target' that was 'very vulnerable.'

The hole in the ground in midtown Manhattan and the crushed wing of the Pentagon are evidence enough that these warnings had no purchase within American intelligence agencies.

Lawyers call this a conflict of interest. The CIA, charged with defending the nation internationally against threats to the homeland, dealt with a de-emphasis of Saudi Arabia as a matter of energy policy that is excused as a matter of national security. At the same time, the backroom fact that the former head of the agency has been directly doing business with Saudi Arabia since leaving the White House must be considered.

The FBI, whose charter dictates the defense of the country on the domestic front, has been accused by one living agent and one dead one of failing egregiously in their task. The living agent, Wright, chalks it up to institutional incompetence on the part of the agency. The dead agent, O'Neill, believed there was something more fundamental in play.

Generally speaking, the Bush administration had a vested economic interest in not pestering such an important country with anti-terrorism investigations focused on individuals and groups residing within and ranging without their borders. Such questions might offend that all-important regime and disrupt the flow of oil that so many American petroleum companies depend upon. Until September 11, this was a relatively safe course to take. Certainly we had absorbed terrorist attacks from individuals connected with Saudi Arabia. The first bombing of the Trade Center, the bombing of the Khobar Towers, the destruction of our

African embassies, and the explosion that ripped through the USS *Cole* all came at the hands of terrorists connected with Osama bin Laden and Saudi Arabia. None of this affected the continental core of America until that bright September morning.

The Bush administration's willful dismissal of Saudi Arabia as a threat worth focusing on is based on decades of American policy. If you drive a car and do not want to spend $10 a gallon on gas for it, if you have done so for any length of time, then you have benefited from this policy. America's economic lifeblood is oil. The price of a barrel affects agriculture, industry, and pretty much everything else. An average American citizen forced to spend extra cash on gas every time they tank up does not have those spare dollars to spend on clothes, food, booze, cigarettes, video games, vacations, and a pile of other things that have become basic to our lifestyle. This adds up. When gas gets expensive, the American economy begins to slip.

Clearly, September 11 made this situation no longer acceptable. One would hope and expect that nobody in America would be willing to absorb such brutal death tolls to save money at the gas pump from now on, but this is hardly something to be laid at the feet of the Bush administration. They were playing by the rules as they found them – indeed, as some within their administration helped establish them.

The tooth-grinding aspect of all this comes when we consider the Bush administration's reaction to September 11. Of course, they knew that our addiction to oil played an indisputable role in what happened. Yet Bush did not charge out and begin advocating for a full-court press to establish alternate sources of energy that would free us from our deadly entanglements with Saudi Arabia and the Middle East. Instead, he obfuscated the whole issue by blaming the attacks on freedom-hating evildoers. He declared war on a sizeable chunk of the planet. He demanded that we drill for oil in the pristine Alaskan National Wildlife Preserve, an act that would yield exactly six months' worth of oil by the most optimistic estimates. He left Saudi Arabia off the list of nations whose terrorism affiliations are a clear and present threat to American security at home and abroad.

Is this more willful ignorance? Of course not. This is nothing more or less than the actions of an oilman unwilling to part with a substance that has been so lucrative to him personally and to the men who stand behind him financially. If America is addicted to oil, George W. Bush is a stone junkie far past the help of any rehab program. The words of John O'Neill take on a deadlier accent upon further consideration.

If Bush was playing by the rules, did those rules lead him to direct US policy towards activities that led directly to the attacks of September 11? Some months ago, a book was published in France entitled *Osama bin Laden: The Forbidden Truth*. The authors, intelligence analysts Jean-Charles Brisard and Guillaume Dasique, described a connection between the September 11 terrorist attacks and a stalled plan to build a pipeline to exploit the vast natural gas fields along the Caspian Sea in Turkmenistan. Their story pointed damning fingers at American petroleum companies and the Bush administration, citing instances where US anti-terrorism efforts were thwarted in order to smooth the way for the pipeline deal.

The story begins in 1998, with an American petroleum corporation called Unocal. Unocal had heavily invested in a planned pipeline that would run from Turkmenistan, through Afghanistan and Pakistan, and out to a warm water port. From there, natural gas piped down from the Caspian Sea would be made available for sale to American and Asian markets. The deal required approval from the governments of all three nations, including the Taliban. If terms could be met, Unocal and its investors stood to reap enormous profits. Saudi Arabia played a vital role in these plans.

The deal was destroyed, along with two American embassies in Africa, victims of terror attacks by Osama bin Laden. Because bin Laden was based in Afghanistan and supported by the Taliban, the Clinton administration forbade any American company from dealing with them. A blizzard of cruise missiles soon followed this order, and Unocal was forced to wait for calmer days before it could continue to pursue the pipeline deal. Without Afghanistan, the puzzle-piece at the center of the arrangement, everything ground to a halt.

On a rainy January day in 2001, Unocal was given reason to rejoice. Oilman George W. Bush had just taken the oath of office, and the power of the US government was immediately brought to bear in the situation. Enter Afghan-American Zalmay Khalilzad, who, in the early 1990s, served Unocal as an advisor on the nascent pipeline project. In 1997, Khalilzad was present with Unocal representatives when they hosted a delegation of Taliban officials in Houston.

Khalilzad was part of a full-court press by the Bush administration to see the pipeline deal through to completion. Their main objective was to bring the Taliban, who had become decidedly disinterested in the project, back on board. The project would never happen unless the Afghan government somehow became legitimized. In bargaining for the pipeline, the Bush administration put forth the requirement that the Taliban reinstate King

Mohammad Zahir Shah as ruler. They further demanded that the Taliban hand over Osama bin Laden to face Western justice. The Taliban had been playing host to bin Laden for years, paying off a debt they believed they owed him after he financed and led the effort to eject the Soviet Union after it invaded Afghanistan in 1979.

The American pitch to the Taliban became so intense that the Taliban hired an American public relations expert named Laila Helms to broker negotiations. High-level meetings between the Bush administration and the Taliban continued through August 2001, but with little gain. The Taliban simply was not interested in becoming part of the deal. To do so would have been suicide; besides losing power when the king returned, they faced brutal repudiation from far-flung corners of the extremist Islamic world for giving bin Laden to a Western nation for trial – a violation of Koranic law.

It was at this point, according to Brisard and Dasique, that the story takes a darker and more dangerous turn.

Pakistani news agencies reported in the weeks before September 11 that America had threatened war against the Taliban if they did not agree to the pipeline deal. 'Accept our carpet of gold,' the Bush administration is reported to have said, 'or be buried under a carpet of bombs.' If Brisard and Dasique are to be believed, the Bush administration was actively courting the Taliban, protectors of Osama bin Laden, on behalf of Unocal. That courtship gave way to dire threats of war, framed by demands that would have spelled the end of Taliban rule.

The September 11 attack could well be seen as a pre-emptive strike by bin Laden and the Taliban. The Taliban's doom had been unmistakably spelled out by the demands of the Bush administration, either by war or dissolution and disgrace. Rather than face this ignominy, they chose to attack and let the chips fall where they may. Bin Laden's ability to attack the United States was made far easier by the Bush administration's standing-down of American anti-terrorism agents like John O'Neill, so as to avoid discomforting the very regimes they were seeking to bring into the pipeline deal.

In the aftermath of September 11, we were told the terror was brought upon us by people who hate our freedom and resent our way of life. In point of fact, however, it appears possible that the attacks came as part of a broader game. The Bush administration willingly entered parley with the Taliban, despite their care and feeding of wanted killer Osama bin Laden in order to further the goals on an American petroleum interest. In the process, they watered down American anti-terrorism measures to such a degree that a deputy director was compelled to quit in protest, and another has since filed suit against the agency.

Did threats levied against the Taliban on behalf of Unocal spur Osama bin Laden into murderous action on behalf of his host nation? Was his attack made easier because the Bush administration willfully weakened our intelligence apparatus so as to avoid offending potential client states? Is it possible that the dust and ruin in New York and Washington are byproducts of a pipeline deal?

Stanley Hilton, a San Francisco attorney and former aide to Senator Bob Dole, filed a $7 billion lawsuit in US District Court on June 3, 2002. The class-action suit names ten defendants, among whom are George W. Bush, Dick Cheney, Condoleezza Rice, Donald Rumsfeld, and Norman Mineta.

Hilton's suit charges Bush and his administration with allowing the September 11 attacks to take place so as to reap political benefits from the catastrophe. Hilton alleges that Osama bin Laden is being used as a scapegoat by an administration that ignored pressing warnings of the attack and refused to round up suspected terrorists beforehand. Hilton alleges the ultimate motivation behind these acts was achieved when the Taliban were replaced by US military forces with a regime friendly to America and its oil interests in the region.

Hilton's plaintiffs in this case are the families of 14 victims of September 11, numbering 400 people nationwide. These are the same families that rallied in Washington to advocate for an independent investigation into the attacks. The September 11 hearings were being conducted by Congress behind closed doors, a situation these families found unacceptable.

Mr Hilton, by filing his lawsuit, has joined the ranks of an ever-increasing body of Americans who subscribe to what they call the LIHOP Theory. LIHOP stands for Let It Happen On Purpose. The LIHOP Theory puts forward the accusation that Bush and his people allowed the September 11 attacks to take place, despite the fact that they had been repeatedly warned of an impending strike.

The LIHOP Theory is straightforward. In the months before September 11, American intelligence agencies received ominous warnings from the intelligence services of nations like Israel, Russia, Egypt, and Germany. These warnings were pointed – an attack involving hijacked aircraft and prominent American landmarks was imminent, our security forces were told. Bush himself was briefed of these warnings weeks before they happened. Instead of responding vigorously, the Bush administration and its security apparatus did nothing.

LIHOP is, of course, the purest breed of conspiracy theory, involving high-ranking members of government from both parties, as well as the CIA, FBI, and NSA. Like all good conspiracy theories, LIHOP is surrounded by disturbing facts and bits of evidence that are difficult to ignore.

For LIHOP Theorists, the evidence is clear. The Bush administration got the legitimized Afghanistan government it wanted. Along the way, they used the horrors of September 11 to place themselves beyond reproach. In the patriotic fervor that resulted from the attacks, both the press and the Democratic opposition were bracketed by the administration-espoused idea that any questions or criticism were tantamount to treason.

The passage of the PATRIOT Anti-Terror Act has given the US government sweeping abilities to snuff dissent by defining it as terrorism, thanks to the loosely defined wording of the bill. Bush enjoyed stratospheric approval ratings and American citizens were given new enemies to hate. The Defense Department, and the weapons contractors who cater to them, received billions from the Federal budget to do with as they pleased in order to address the objects of that hate.

Even the most naive political observer must admit the dismal truth – September 11 was the greatest thing ever to happen to Bush and his administration. Attorney Stanley Hilton has brought LIHOP Theory into the Federal court system with his class-action suit, and with the families of September 11 victims he represents. It will be interesting to see what transpires when these two facts collide in an American courtroom.

With all this in mind, we must face the final and most difficult issue: Are such questions even conscionable? Is it within the realm of decency even to inquire about such things? If proven true, Bush and his administration have much to answer for. They took a standing economic policy and bent it around the coddling of the Taliban in the interest of furthering the financial aspirations of the petroleum industry. They did so with threats and tactics that led directly to the deaths of thousands of Americans, and to a state of war that, in all aspects, feeds the avarice of those interests as well as the desires of prominent American weapons manufacturers. Along the way they accumulated political capital worth its weight in pure gold.

Could an American president and an American government ever be called to task for such a thing? Is this not totally indecent, and worse, viciously unpatriotic?

Answering these last questions requires a look into America's recent past. In the early months of 1962, General Lyman Lemnitzer, Chairman of the Joint Chiefs under Kennedy, wanted a war. Part of a cabal of extreme right-wing anti-communist Cold Warriors within the Pentagon, Lemnitzer believed Kennedy had gone soft on communism and Castro. Kennedy had put any and all provocative action against Cuba on hold, and ordered only the gathering of intelligence data.

For Lemnitzer, this was totally unacceptable. Further frustrated by the fact that Castro himself had failed to do anything that would demand an invasion of Cuba, Lemnitzer and his cabal planned an operation called Northwoods. Bluntly, this operation called for acts of terrorism within the United States perpetrated by agents of the United States loyal to Lemnitzer.

A plan, crafted in exquisite detail, was drafted describing the scope of Operation Northwoods, and was later signed in approval by all of the Joint Chiefs of Staff. Citizens would be shot in the streets. Boats of Cuban refugees would be sunk on the high seas. Bombings would be perpetrated within Washington, D.C. and Miami. There were even plans to fake the hijacking, and later the destruction, of a civilian aircraft.

Phony evidence would then be provided pointing a finger at Castro. The American people, in their outrage, would demand a full invasion of Cuba. General Lemnitzer would have his war.

Needless to say, Operation Northwoods was never put into effect. When directly asked by Congress whether plans were afoot for the invasion of Cuba, Lemnitzer swore an oath and said no. Eventually, he was removed from his position. Northwoods was buried under subsequent events, a forgotten idea for more than forty years.

It is an appalling thing to know that such an idea could even be spoken aloud in the Pentagon. It is comforting to believe Lemnitzer was on the lunatic fringe, a man obsessed with Cuba to such a degree that he would be willing to attack his fellow citizens to create the pretext for war. Yet Operation Northwoods was signed by all the Joint Chiefs of Staff, leading to the inevitable conclusion that this cavalier and bloodthirsty attitude towards the lives and safety of American citizens and military personnel was not the exception, but the rule.

Such vicious motivations all too often come into play in the formulation of American policy. Operation Northwoods is but one example, and a deadly one at that. The current War on Terror may well be another. All of this – the pipeline, the stand-down of our anti-terror capabilities, and the intimate interest of George W. Bush in all things oil – appears to have played a far more central role in the events of September 11 than anyone who hates our freedom.

Ask the questions. Pay attention to the men behind the curtain. Nothing could be more important. Doing so, no matter what anyone may say, does not make you a traitor. The LIHOPers may be completely wrong, and the connections between the pipeline, Saudi Arabia, American intelligence services, and the petroleum desires of the Bush administration and its backers may all prove to be balderdash. The questions, however, must be asked. The dead remember.

The Light of the World

Imagine being placed under arrest. Your clothes are stripped off and divided among your captors. You are whipped until blood flows from your back, you are beaten, you are spat upon. You are taken to a hillside where many people have gathered. You are laid upon two large pieces of wood. A man comes with a large metal spike and hammers it through your right wrist, into the wood. Tendons tear, bones crack, arteries rip and spray. The same is done to your left wrist. Your ankles are crossed together, and a third spike is smashed through them.

The pain is unimaginable.

The wood that now holds you is hoisted up and planted in the ground, so that every inch of your body weight is suspended by the spikes that have been smashed into your flesh. You immediately begin to suffocate as your lungs become paralyzed. A spear is thrust into your side.

Finally, a sign is hung above your bleeding form that insults you and your people. Those who have done this stand before you and mock you as you drown within your own body.

What would your last words be? Would you rage at them with your dying breath? Would you rally your friends and allies to kill and maim among those who have tormented you? Would you cry out for vengeance?

I can tell you what the fellow who actually endured this torture said. He raised his eyes to the sky and spoke these words:

'Forgive them, Father. They know not what they do.'

Whether you believe or not, the human moral of the story speaks to all of us. Vengeance is the wrong answer, even amid terrible suffering and pain. We must learn this lesson as we pursue justice. If we do not, we doom ourselves and our children to a cycle of violence and horror that has stalked the earth for far too long. These attacks have raised the ante. The final cards could destroy us if not played just right.

America considers itself to be the light of the world. Our freedoms and democracy are a beacon to all those nations and peoples who suffer injustice, who have no voice, who yearn for the liberties we so casually took for granted before the attacks. If we are to continue to be the light of the world, we must forgive them even as we seek our justice. We must rise above the hatred that brought them into war with us.

If we do not, we become them. If we do not, they win, even if we kill them all.

September 11 was a national trauma on the level of the assassination of John F. Kennedy. Along the way, we saw bravery on a scale unmatched perhaps since a June day in 1944, when average Americans ran through a hail of steel and fire on a beach in France. What the police and firefighters ran through on September 11 was no less deadly. What our soldiers face in Afghanistan and Iraq is likewise proving to be deadly.

Yet we must be cautious as we appraise the time that has passed since that wretched day. For all the good that has come from a nation united, there has been a surge of dangerous misdirection, folly, and polished ugliness passing itself off as patriotism.

We must remember that no explanation for the events of September 11 has been forthcoming. September 11 was many things, but above all it was an intelligence failure of spectacular dimensions. The CIA, FBI, and NSA were all caught flat-footed, and not one official has come forward with an explanation. We have been told the attack came because certain individuals in the world hate our freedom, and that is all we know. Demands by the families of September 11 victims that an open and independent investigation be immediately undertaken were rebuffed by the Bush administration. Instead, a secret committee of congress people met behind closed doors.

Bush and Cheney pressured Senator Daschle on the eve of Bush's first State of the Union speech to avoid too many pertinent questions about why September 11 happened. These are the two men whose chief responsibility it is to ensure that such an attack never comes again. Ostensibly, the War on Terror serves that purpose. The war, however, cannot correct institutional flaws within our security apparatus.

If we do not dig deep and hard into the reasons behind why September 11 was allowed to happen, we leave ourselves open and vulnerable to another attack. This is unacceptable. We must put pressure on the White House to avoid blocking any investigations that seek answers to this most vital of questions. If they do not, we must demand from them an explanation of their motives.

We must also look hard at the War on Terror itself. It remains an undeclared war, and yet more and more resources are being poured into it. Bush announced some new steps to be taken in this fight. Chief among them was his intention to push the battle into fully one third of the nations on earth. This is unilateralism on an unprecedented scale and pushes his 'With us or against us' rhetoric onto truly hazardous ground.

The *Los Angeles Times* broke a story about a secret Pentagon report detailing their intention to broaden the definition of circumstances in which nuclear weapons might be used. The report also outlined the need for a whole new galaxy of weapons that could be brought into Bush's terror war.

All of this takes place within the context of a fight in Afghanistan that is far from finished.

Not long ago, an army of surpassing might swept into the high, remote regions of Afghanistan, bent upon domination. They carried with them all the superior firepower and training that any advanced, modern army could wish for: powerful aircraft, rolling armor, and special units of trained men who were considered the best their military could offer.

Arrayed against this force was a rag-tag army of warriors armed with outdated weapons, whose loyalty adhered more to their ancestral tribes than to the centralized government. Though they had repelled every invading army that had set foot in Afghanistan for well over a hundred years, it seemed farfetched to believe they stood a chance against the juggernaut facing them. They fought barefoot in the highlands, using guerrilla tactics for the most part. Against an army that could erase them with great gusts of artillery, napalm, and bombs from the sky, it appeared that only Allah Himself could rescue them from rout and defeat.

This was Christmas Eve, 1979, when the Spetznaz Special Forces of the Soviet Union roared into Afghanistan. They seized roads, communications installations, killed President Hafizullah Amin, and swept the seemingly pitiful Afghan resistance from the field. Soviet forces rapidly occupied several key cities in Afghanistan, installing a puppet regime in place of the government that had been left in smoking ruins by the invasion.

The world, caught flat-footed by this bold stroke, assumed *en masse* that Afghanistan had been defeated and was now to be considered an incorporated fiefdom of the Soviet Empire. Soon after their arrival, the Soviets believed they had secured absolute victory.

No one, however, thought to tell the Afghan warriors that they had been defeated. Weeks after the invasion, the Soviets believed all resistance had ended. In truth, it had only just begun. On the night of February 23, 1980, almost the entire Afghan population of Kabul took to the roofs of their homes and bellowed their defiance into the sky. 'God is Great!' they chanted into the faces of an army that could have obliterated their city from the air in one day's work.

The boldness of this night quickly spread to the hills and villages, where Afghan warriors armed themselves with everything from US-made Stinger missiles to flintlock muskets. Arranging themselves into small bands, these warriors began attacking Soviet forces and sabotaging their infrastructure at every opportunity. Suddenly, the smug Soviet Spetznaz began taking casualties, and their helicopters were blasted from the sky.

The history of this conflict is not kind to the Soviets. Before their time in Afghanistan came to a close, they had committed 642,000 troops to the conflict. The dead and missing from this number amounted to nearly 15,000; and 469,685 fell as wounded casualties in combat or to the ravages of indigenous diseases, amounting to 73% of their overall forces. Along the way, the Soviets killed 1.3 million Afghans and forced another 5.5 million to flee the country as refugees. Another two million were displaced within the country. The truth of this did not come fully to light for years.

The war lasted ten years, and when all was said and done, the mighty Soviets were forced to return home humiliated and defeated. Their dreams of annexing Afghanistan so as to gain a competitive edge with the West in the exploitation of the energy reserves in that region lay in ashes. The money poured into the conflict helped to shatter an already teetering Soviet economy, and not long after their defeat, the fearsome Soviet Empire ceased to exist.

This disaster came about for several reasons. The Soviets failed to appreciate the extreme environment in which they were forced to fight. They had scant capability to defend themselves against the slow bloodletting caused by tactically efficient guerrilla fighters, who seldom cooperated by waiting for artillery or air strikes to fall. Finally, they totally underestimated the fighting spirit of the Afghan warriors, whose religious belief combined with an ability to fight under conditions of extreme deprivation made them formidable opponents. One of the men they faced was named Osama bin Laden. His financing of the war against the Soviets, and his leadership under fire, elevated him to hero status among the Afghan rank and file.

Not long ago, another powerful army swept into Afghanistan, filled with the zeal of the righteous and armed to the teeth with the most advanced weapons known to human history. Immediately, they seized roads, communications, wiped out the sitting government, and invested the main cities. Along the way they churned the dusty earth with fire and bombs from above, killing scores of civilians and scattering whatever organized resistance that lay before them.

Before the smoke had cleared, the leader of this army began speaking of wars with other far-flung nations such as Iraq, Iran, Somalia, Yemen, and North Korea. The battle for Afghanistan was winding down, it seemed. The world believed the Afghan army shattered, and the nation pacified.

Again, no one bothered to tell the Afghan warriors that they had been defeated. On March 3, 2002, two missiles reached into the sky and struck down helicopters carrying US troops. Nine were killed in the attack. This came on the heels of media reports that a massive battle in the region surrounding Gardez demanded a larger investment of American troops. After the reports of American dead reached home, the American president announced in somber tones that his country would 'pay any price' to achieve victory in that nation.

After a series of events no one could have believed possible on September 10, America finds itself occupying Afghanistan. A victory that seemed well in hand for a time slipped a bit when the first true casualties from our War on Terror came home. Many said this was to be expected, but few seemed to fully understand what is to come. If history is any guide whatsoever, those brave American soldiers we have lost will be followed by many more.

The author Rudyard Kipling, after encompassing the ravaging defeat handed to the British empire after their army attempted to play a hand in Afghan domination, penned the following lines:

> When you're wounded and left on Afghanistan's plains,
> And the women come out to cut up what remains,
> Jest roll to your rifle an' blow out your brains
> An' go to your Gawd like a soldier.

The frustration and humiliation living within these words fairly burns the page. Kipling knew, as the Soviets now know, that Afghanistan is little more than an army-eating land mass, which has never known conquest. All the soldiers that have been sent there, all the blood and treasure spent in search of conquest, have evaporated into the air above the Khyber Pass. The last two armies, ours and the Soviets, went filled with confidence in their ability to tame the region, fully expecting to reap profit from the resources to be found there.

No one told the Afghan warriors how easy it was all supposed to be. No one, apparently, ever does.

Americans demanded action after September 11, and they have had it. Yet we must examine the dangers inherent in an open-ended and ill-defined global engagement. As we polish our nuclear weapons and claim the right to invade whatever nation we wish, all the while sinking deeper into a murky quagmire in Afghanistan, it appears we have gotten far more than we bargained for. An explanation of what defines victory in this fight, and a setting of clear parameters, is required.

We must look to define patriotism. Senators Daschle and Kerry chose to question, in the mildest of terms, the direction of this war. Daschle stated that if bin Laden, the purported author of this horror, fails to be captured and convicted for his crimes, the entire war itself will have failed to achieve its goal. They were pilloried on all sides for this and their commitment to America was called into question. It seems the White House would like nothing more than to marginalize congressional oversight, in defiance of the Constitution, and will resort to whatever hyperbole is available to do so.

Senator John Kerry won the Silver Star, the Bronze Star and three Purple Hearts during his service in the Vietnam War. Upon his return home, he became active in the Vietnam Veterans Against the War. Of all those active in politics today, it is Kerry's wise voice we must listen to. He knows the needs of war personally, and also knows when a war has crossed the boundaries of common sense and control.

Many of his detractors – Dick Armey, Tom Delay, Trent Lott, Dick Cheney, and George W. Bush among them – used family influence to avoid combat in Vietnam. Rather than attack the messenger, these people should take note of Kerry's concerns, as he is far more versed in the truths of war than they. If we are to be truly united, these men should avoid attacking the patriotism of a man who gave so much to his country while they stayed home when the call to serve came.

On every car and every porch flutters an American flag, symbol of pride and strength for the people of this nation. Bumper stickers make declarations of unity and lapel pins speak wordlessly for citizens who still weep at the thought of the dead and the lost. Those symbols, so proudly displayed, represent a nation racing towards ignominious defeat. We are losing this war, not because of the actions of a clever enemy, but because of dangerously poor leadership in Washington. As William Shakespeare said, 'When valour preys on reason, it eats the sword it fights with.' In the end, we may all be forced to eat the sword being wielded in so cumbersome a fashion.

In one notable barrage of attacks upon Afghanistan, errant US munitions struck yet another civilian village. Eight members of a family were wiped off the face of the earth while gathered at the breakfast table. The mother, the lone survivor of the attack, was quoted by BBC reporters: 'What shall

I do now? Look at their savageness. They killed all of my children and husband.' More recently, Canadian soldiers were killed by an American attack. Some weeks later, a wedding party was strafed with cannon fire from American combat aircraft, killing dozens of women and children.

United Nations relief workers anticipated that between 300,000 and one million refugees would find themselves in dire straits as the winter began to wind a shroud around the country during the onset of war. These relief workers were helpless, trapped by the knowledge that they would be unable to do much of anything to prevent massive death and misery.

Rumsfeld and his warriors took great pains to inform the Afghan populace that this war was not being waged against them. This message was blunted by an effective Taliban propaganda campaign that used deaths like those described above to good effect. Many fighters in Pakistan do not even need to hear well-crafted messages within the media. They could look across the border to Afghanistan and see the thousands of civilians living in filth after fleeing the bombs.

Ten thousand Pakistani warriors left their homes to join the Taliban forces. Armed with Kalashnikov rifles, rocket launchers, missiles, grenades, anti-aircraft guns, and even swords, members of the Tehrik Nifaz-i-Shariat Muhammadi militant group surged across the border towards Kabul. Joining their ranks were thousands of ordinary villagers who volunteered for duty.

This is the nightmare scenario, one whose rise was all too apparent. Every time we kill a civilian, every time we level a house, every time we strike terror into the innocents and cause them to flee into misery and death, we give birth to new warriors for the jihad. Every one of these new volunteers must be killed, according to the Bush battle plan, and their deaths will give rise to more and more warriors seeking revenge for a lost loved one.

The Greeks feared the Hydra for a reason. Every time one head was cut off, two rose snarling in its place. We are creating, every day, more enemies who will die in the fight against us. It is clear that the order of battle, comprised in haste and fear by the Bush administration, is not only failing to defeat the chosen foe, but is in fact making the task more difficult by orders of magnitude.

The failures of leadership in Washington are even more evident on the home front. The administration, in concert with the CDC (Centers for Disease Control), decided to publicly play down the threat of anthrax contamination when it appeared in our midst, despite the fact that a virulent strain made its way through the postal service to Senator Daschle's office. Two dead mailmen later, we saw the result of this.

The envelope addressed to Daschle passed through the mail system, apparently spraying spores in all directions. Rather than rush to determine the scope of contamination possible when anthrax passes through a major mail processing system, we were told to hush, relax, be at ease, shop. Mail carriers were specifically told there was no danger. Two dead mailmen later, we knew better.

In the rush to determine who is responsible for the anthrax attacks, administration officials were quick to suggest Iraq as a likely suspect. Certainly, a possible biological weapons program in that nation is of great concern. Focusing on that one possibility alone, however, caused Federal investigators to miss what appears to be the most likely set of suspects: home-grown American extremists on the Far Right.

The letters mailed to Daschle and to broadcaster Tom Brokaw were dated September 11 but mailed many days later, an apparently craven attempt to link their attack to the airplane bombers. The date itself was written in the American style, 9–11–01, rather than the European/Arabic fashion, 11–9–01. The handwriting on the letters sloped from left to right; an individual schooled in the Arabic style would have handwriting that sloped from right to left.

The extreme American Right, represented by groups like the National Alliance, the Army of God, and the Aryan Nation, have long coveted biological weapons of mass destruction. Survivalist militiaman and micro-biologist Larry Wayne Harris successfully placed an order for *Yersinia pestis*, the organism that causes bubonic plague, in 1995. Members of a group called the Minnesota Patriots Council were arrested in 1994 for making the toxin ricin. There are many examples of these groups making, or trying to make, weapons like anthrax.

These groups greeted the attacks of September 11 with what can only be described as savage glee. Fearful of a Zionist world conspiracy, as hateful towards American multiculturalism as the narrowest fundamentalist Muslim cleric, many of these groups decided that the enemy of their enemy was their friend. It is not so far out of bounds to believe that one group may have gone beyond angry rhetoric to action.

One hundred and thirty family planning clinics across the country, including Planned Parenthood and the National Abortion Federation, received threatening letters that contained an unidentified powder during the week of October 15. Several of the letters mentioned the Army of God, a rabid anti-abortion group that actively espouses the killing of doctors who offer an abortion service.

According to Attorney-General Ashcroft, any act that threatens the use of anthrax shall be considered terrorism and shall be prosecuted to the fullest extent of the law. Clinics where women go for prenatal care and gynecological exams, as well as for abortions, received 130 such threats. This was by far the largest terrorist act to take place in this country since September 11.

If Ashcroft's political predilections distracted him from instigating an investigation into groups that could well be responsible for the anthrax threats leveled at Washington and these clinics, a deadly enemy within has been allowed to range abroad unpunished and unrestrained. It is difficult to imagine a worse failure.

Yet imagination is a terrible thing, especially when its darkest forebodings burst into reality. Calls for unity from the Republican leadership, in concert with an effort to quash any questions about their handling of this crisis, may shatter under the weight of their own hypocrisy. Partisanship must be laid aside, we were told, and the Democratic Party surged *en masse* to salute this ideal. They bare throats begging to be slashed by GOP profiteers who are only too happy to wield the knife.

To understand how completely these calls for unity have been betrayed by the actions of many within the GOP and the Bush administration, we must begin by reaching all the way back to the heady days of the Reagan administration. There were two hot wars blazing then, and both were used by Reagan to further Cold War goals.

The first was the protracted fight between Iran and Iraq which lasted ten years. Saddam Hussein, now known as a bloodthirsty demon, was in those days a boon compatriot of American interests. We armed him and his military to the teeth in their fight with Iran, because that nation was receiving weapons and funding from the Soviet Union. American SEAL teams fought alongside Iraqi troops, blowing up bridges and fighting the kind of covert guerrilla war for which they are famous. In the end, Iraq fought Iran to a stalemate and found itself at the end of the war among the most well-armed and well-trained nations in the region.

We all know how this ended. Barely two years later, Hussein's army was charging into Kuwait and threatening to disrupt the flow of oil from the Middle East. America, under the leadership of the first George Bush, mustered a coalition of nations and drove him in flames back to Baghdad. In the process, however, we established military bases in Saudi Arabia, the original home of Osama bin Laden. Bin Laden, appalled that the

'Crusaders' were again assembled under arms in his homeland, swore eternal holy war against the United States.

The other hot war being waged at the time was much more vividly a Cold War conflict. When the Soviet Union invaded Afghanistan, the newly minted Reagan administration poured untold millions of dollars' worth of weapons and arms into that nation, to be used by the Afghani Mujeheddin. The Mujeheddin freedom fighters, compared by Reagan to our Founding Fathers, were pledged to drive the Soviets from their land and were more than happy to accept the help of the United States.

In the end, the Soviet military smashed themselves into oblivion against the unyielding Afghani landscape and were bled nearly to death by the stings of the American-armed Mujeheddin fighters. When they left, the once-united freedom fighters splintered into various factions for control of the nation.

Not long after, the group now known as the Taliban assumed near-total control of the country and instituted a regime based upon a harshly inter-preted version of fundamentalist Islam. Bin Laden, deeply involved in the fight against the Soviets, made a home with the Taliban and was given their protection. In 1998 agents of bin Laden used an American plastic explosive called Semtex to destroy two American embassies in Africa.

This tangled web of Cold War loyalties and conflict has as much to do with our present state as any other factor. Arguments regarding the right-eousness and validity of our involvement in these wars can, and have, raged for years. Both sides can boast persuasive arguments to bolster their opinions. Facts, however, have a way of interfering with American political goals.

You guessed it. The whole mess is Bill Clinton's fault. Forget the Cold War. Ignore the Gulf War. Leave aside the Mujeheddin warriors who became the Taliban by using American weapons to gain power and influence. In our darkest days, Republican political opportunists attacked, once again, a former president whose political viewpoint they disagree with.

The facts of the matter betray the political goals of these vultures. In 1999, the Clinton administration initiated a plan to capture or kill bin Laden by training approximately 60 members of Pakistani intelligence for the task. This was done in response to the attacks upon the US African embassies, and may well have succeeded. The plot collapsed when Pakistani Prime Minister Nawaz Sharif was overthrown in a coup by General Pervez Musharraf, who remains today the leader of Pakistan. Musharraf refused to support the plot and it withered on the vine.

Earlier, the Clinton administration, acting upon information provided with an imprimatur of certitude by the Pentagon, launched some 66 cruise missiles into Afghanistan. These missiles were aimed at a training camp the Pentagon believed was sheltering bin Laden. The information proved to be erroneous, and bin Laden was unharmed. Again, the Clinton administration acted boldly, but was foiled by circumstances beyond its control.

The Clinton administration spoke often about the need to augment America's defenses against terrorist attack. Clinton, having presided over the first bombing of the World Trade Center, the destruction of the Murrah Federal Building in Oklahoma City, and the destruction of American embassies in Africa, knew in an acutely personal way what needed to be done.

His attempts to address the threat were not only foiled by circumstance, and by an American mood that neither knew nor could even conceive of an attack like that which transpired on September 11, 2001; Clinton's attempts to address the threat of terrorism against the United States were disrupted and diverted by the same Republicans who seek today to blame him for the tragedy.

The most potent weapon Osama bin Laden has to wield against America is his financial resources and the means to move that money secretly from cell to cell. Bluntly, it takes a man of means to fight a nation of means. During his administration, Clinton offered legislation that would give the Treasury Secretary broad powers to ban foreign nations and banks from accessing American financial markets unless they cooperated with money-laundering investigations that would expose and terminate terrorist cash flows.

The legislation was killed by Texas Republican Senator Phil Gramm, who was working on behalf of his friends at Enron, the company that used those same shelters to hide their ill-gotten profits. It is certain that his wife Wendy, who was an Enron board member and knew how badly that company needed those shelters, had a hand in his work. Asked in September 2001 to defend his actions, Gramm responded, 'I was right then and I am right now. The way to deal with terrorists is to hunt them down and kill them.'

The idea of choking off their financial resources, now so popular as to be almost axiomatic, apparently does not resonate with Senator Gramm. In the guise of this failed presidential candidate lives yet another wall thrown up by opportunistic and narrow-minded Republicans, whose desire to stick it to Clinton aided and abetted the murderers who visited New York.

The hypocrisy behind current Republican attempts to blame Clinton for the World Trade Center attacks finds its roots far beyond the opportunistic posturing of Phil Gramm. It reaches back to the viciously partisan, Republican-controlled Congress of 1996, which thwarted legislation offered by Clinton that would have substantially augmented America's ability to defend against terrorist threats.

In 1996 Senator Orrin Hatch referred to several threats which Clinton warned us of, threats that now are as commonplace as stores that have sold out of gas masks, as 'phony threats.' He used these words to attack Clinton's legislation, helping to create a legislative environment that gave birth to a watered-down, Congress-driven version of an anti-terrorism bill that has been proven to be utterly worthless.

Senator Trent Lott, with his powers as Republican Majority Leader, did everything he could to hamstring Clinton's attempt to enact real protections against American threats in 1996. Yet he found within himself the unmitigated gall to stand in the well of the Senate during a debate about the current iteration of Clinton's anti-terrorism measures on October 2, 2001 and say, 'If anything happens, if there is a terror attack, the Democrats will have to explain to the American people why they didn't pass this bill.'

On February 12, 1997, Vice President Al Gore delivered to President Clinton a report entitled 'White House Commission on Aviation Safety and Security.' In this report, Gore outlined numerous ways in which the airline industry could protect its aircraft and passengers from the threat of terrorism. Many, if not all, of these recommendations would have gone a long way towards thwarting the September 11 attacks. Like Hart–Rudman, the warnings voiced by Gore's report were ignored by the Bush administration.

What is most reprehensible about the treatment the Gore report has received can be explained through the simple geometry of the airline industry marketplace, which has one of the most powerful lobbying voices to be found on the floor of the Republican-controlled Congress.

It has been no secret within the airline industry that security at American airports had been a bad joke. These checkpoints were mostly manned by poorly trained workers who made minimum wage. Between 1991 and 2000, Federal Aviation Administration agents managed to smuggle grenades, guns, and other weapons aboard aircraft at Logan airport in Boston with a 90% success rate. Logan, it must be noted, was the point of origin for the aircraft that struck the Towers. The terrorists had done their research.

The FAA, during the Clinton administration, proposed sweeping changes to the way security was enforced at airport checkpoints. These measures were fought every step of the way in the Republican-controlled Congress by the aforementioned airline industry lobby, and to good effect. None of the changes desired by the FAA was legislated, because the airline industry did not want to pay for them.

On January 31, 2001, the Hart–Rudman report was published. This report voiced dire warnings about threats to American security posed by terrorist attacks. Further, the report recommended the creation of an Office of Homeland Defense which would be responsible for the implementation of defensive measures to combat this threat. The Hart–Rudman report was summarily dismissed by the Bush administration.

No credence was given to the Hart–Rudman report or the Gore Commission report by the Republican-controlled Congress, on whom falls the responsibility for enacting legislation based upon such warnings. This was done for purely partisan reasons, and nothing more.

The New Republic, in an article published in 1997, commented prophetically about the demise of the Gore Commission report:

> The truth is, there is not a whole lot that can be done to stop a trained professional terrorist. Terrorism will continue, and, in calmer moments, people will recognize that any attempt to stamp it out completely would impose such extraordinary costs and time delays as to destroy the airline industry altogether. The Gore Commission ... inaugurated with such fanfare, will likely see their recommendations disappear into archival history. And everything will settle down until the next explosion.

In the aftermath of September 11, the Republican-controlled Congress gave a multi-billion-dollar bailout to the airline industry, whose culpability in the events of September 11 is beyond question. This industry was given approximately four times the amount they had lost while grounded, money that was once earmarked for Social Security and Medicare. Immediately after receiving this bailout, United Airlines ordered almost a dozen planes from a French airline manufacturer.

Since the attacks of September 11, anyone who dares criticize Republican President George W. Bush has been labeled a traitor. Reporters have been fired for doing so, talk show hosts have been repudiated for doing so, and the White House Press Secretary himself has warned all of America to 'watch what we say.'

The reasons for this intellectual lockdown are articulated as being necessary to combat the threat of terrorism and to present a united front against our enemies. Most of those demanding this united front are Republicans who have wrapped themselves in the flag. They do so not out of patriotism, but to hide their faces from a public that deserves to know the truth.

The politically motivated blame game directed at Bill Clinton cannot deflect the fact that the Bush administration appears dangerously in above its head. Recent events in the Middle East have proven beyond a shadow of doubt that the Bush administration's complete lack of engagement with Israel and Palestine will stand as an historic example of deadly poor judgment. What we see is an administration that is groping for a solution far past the time when one could be reached, and all the while hedging its bets to keep a conflict with Iraq on the table.

Consider the timetable of events. The Bush people came to Washington filled with scorn for the peacemaking efforts of the departing Clinton administration. On the eve of the election of hardliner Sharon as Israeli Prime Minister, the Bush administration refused to send a peace envoy to the last-gasp talks between Israel and Palestine in Egypt. Weeks later, Bush pulled out the highly visible CIA brokers who had been stagemanaging a cessation of the conflict. All the while, Bush and his people parroted the same asinine rhetoric: we'll help make peace once y'all stop shooting at each other ... or, to put it another way, we'll help make peace once you make peace.

As scenes of horror flash across CNN, Israeli and Palestinian representatives speak out. Salting their comments are heartfelt laments at the absence of Bill Clinton and American engagement in any peace talks. The current administration's opinion of the efforts made by Clinton were summed up by White House Press Secretary Ari Fleischer, who stated, 'You can make the case that in an attempt to shoot the moon and get nothing, more violence resulted.' Though he was later forced to apologize for the claim, there is no mistaking the truth that Fleischer was stating the opinion of the Bush White House.

Attempting to explain the Bush administration's appalling negligence in dealing with this conflict requires an examination of several factors. Foremost among them is what appears to be an astounding lack of ability among Bush's foreign policy people. The one true 'policy wonk' on the staff, Condoleezza Rice, is a world-renowned expert on a nation that no longer exists – the Soviet Union. No one else seems capable of dealing with the complexities of the issue. Beyond that lies a deep fear of failure: no one in the White House wants to make an effort at peace in that region and risk the appearance of falling short. This combination of ignorance and cowardice has borne bloody fruit.

There is one man in the administration with the clout and deft touch to have an impact in this conflict. Secretary of State Colin Powell is well known and much respected on the world stage, yet he was noticeably absent. He visited the region rarely after taking his position. When the administration needed to gather support for a war with Iraq, it was not Powell but Vice President Cheney who made the whirlwind tour of the Middle East. Cheney's efforts came to naught, at least publicly; after his trip, the Arab League released statements warning America against a war.

Powell's silence on the Israel/Palestine conflict lies at the crux of the matter. He is ensconced in an administration that wants nothing to do with the conflict. Because Powell holds deep reservations about a war with Iraq, he does not want to undermine his standing in the administration by taking an unpopular position on the current situation. Powell is keeping his powder dry because he will need all the clout he can muster to direct Bush and the administration's chief Iraq war-hawk, Paul Wolfowitz, away from a conflict with Saddam Hussein that could set the entire Middle East aflame. The one man who could pull Israel and Palestine away from each other's throats has his hands tied because this administration wants war elsewhere in the region.

The whole ball of wax can be summed up in two words: political cowardice. The administration has its priorities seated elsewhere and must sling blame in any direction it can to distract people from their goals. Bush and his allies in the House passed a $100 billion 'stimulus package' that was wrapped securely in the flag and soaked with patriotic rhetoric. The package is needed, we were told, to bolster a weak economy further damaged by the September 11 attack. The fine print of this bill revealed it to be nothing more than the second half of a financial windfall promised to Bush's corporate campaign backers.

Only 30% of the money earmarked for this bill will go to individuals. The rest of the money was delivered to General Motors, IBM, and scores of other corporations which were faring well in the new economic climate. The effect of this stimulus plan will be felt most acutely by individual states, who will lose billions of dollars in tax revenue because of it. How this will generate an economic revival is a mystery and a betrayal of all the states-rights arguments we have heard from the GOP for generations.

In fact, this package was nothing more than compensation to corporations and their lobbyists who supported Bush's enormous and irresponsible $2.1 trillion tax-cut bill. That bill did not do for these corporations what they wanted and they were rewarded for their patience with this one. This has nothing to do with patriotism, national defense, or the revival of the economy. This is old-school patronage passed under the veil of national mourning, and it is a travesty.

This from the people who held up the defense appropriations bill in the Senate in an attempt to force the Democrats to accept right-wing judicial nominations. The very idea that such attempts were made is nauseating and dangerous. If our political unity in the face of this terrorist threat is shattered by the greed of the GOP, the nation's safety will be imperiled even further.

Speaking of imperiled safety, Bush and friends didn't want airline security jobs to become Federally controlled, because doing so would swell the ranks of the unions. This was, like the stimulus package, a partisan decision that affected the safety and well-being of millions of Americans. In Bush's mind, however, more people carrying union cards are a greater threat to America than airborne bombs made of jet fuel and people. Better to keep them free of union entanglements. Better to have people at the airport security booths guarding our lives who would, in the words of Democrat Max Cleland, see a job at a fast-food restaurant as a promotion. Better to have politics rule the day.

The politics of September 11 became an earthquake on Thursday, May 16: The Bush administration had been warned by the CIA months before September 11 of Al Qaeda terrorists and plans to hijack airplanes. Nothing of substance was done to address the threat – 'The proper agencies were warned,' we were told, but no representative of any pertinent agency has since stepped forward to acknowledge receipt of any warnings.

In fact, the spokesman for Massport, the Massachusetts state agency responsible for security at Logan airport, stated bluntly in the pages of the *Boston Globe* that his agency never heard from the Federal government regarding any hijacking threat. The two aircraft that destroyed the World Trade Center towers and killed thousands of Americans went wheels-up at Logan.

By Friday, the news was sprayed across the headlines of virtually every newspaper on the planet: Bush knew. So much for blaming Clinton.

The implications were deadly for the Bush White House. Information had been given that indicated terrorist attacks were imminent, but little if anything was done to prevent them. Concern for the profit margins of the airline industry, which would have been crippled had a serious terrorist warning been disbursed in high summer, were first offered as a good reason why no true measures were taken to prevent the hijackings.

Later, spokesmen such as Ari Fleischer and Dick Cheney came forward to claim that the warnings were 'vague' and 'non-specific' and therefore not worthy of notice. We were told that the hijack warnings pertained to 'traditional hijacking' scenarios, as if that forgave the lapse in security. The weekend political talk shows became a showcase for spin, and the word went out for all to hear – the Bush administration is blameless, and anyone who says otherwise is a traitor.

The truly interesting part came the following Monday. All of a sudden, the world was coming to an end. FBI Director Mueller claimed there was no chance that another terrorist attack could be stopped. Dick Cheney thrust out his jaw and stated bluntly that another terrorist attack was inevitable. Don Rumsfeld said terrorists would definitely get their hands on nuclear or biological weapons and then use them to terrible effect. The news wires vibrated with images of suicide bombers on New York subways, and a warning went out to apartment building landlords – watch for suspicious characters, because the next WTC-type catastrophe could be yours. The Statue of Liberty and the Brooklyn Bridge were draped with bullseyes by the administration, though no one spoke of means to prevent these horrors.

The effect of these warnings was dynamic. People from coast to coast felt the grip of fear in their guts as images of smallpox and mushroom clouds flickered behind their eyelids. New York City, battered and bruised, clenched its collective fist in a spasm of dread. It must be real, these threats, because the president and his people say so. Let there be terror and meekness in equal measure on the streets of the greatest city on earth.

And yet came the next Wednesday and an extraordinary series of revelations. An article in the May 21 edition of the *Toronto Globe and Mail* reported that 'the White House quietly acknowledged that the threats are not urgent and that they are partly motivated by political objectives' and that 'the blunt warnings issued yesterday and Sunday do not reflect a dramatic increase in threatening information but rather a desire to fend off criticism from the Democrats.'

It seemed that everyone could calm down. Horrific terrorist attacks were not, in fact, imminent. Everything was well in hand. The Bush administration was merely using the fear and horror that another September 11-type attack may happen again as a means to deflect legitimate criticism from the Democratic Party. Nothing to see here. Go about your business. This is, after all, just politics.

It was bad enough that Bush had made his crass 'trifecta' joke 15 times. You know this one: someone reported that Bush promised not to raid Social Security or dive into deficit spending unless the nation was faced with war, recession, or national emergency. After September 11, Bush was heard to crack, 'Lucky me, I hit the trifecta.' Let it be noted that the country was running a $66.5 billion deficit seven months into the budget year, and the September 11 death toll between America and Afghanistan stands above 5,000 souls. That is one hell of a trifecta and no laughing matter.

It was bad enough that Bush and his people were selling photographs of his phone calls during the September 11 attacks to raise political funds. Al Gore called the practice 'disgraceful;' the word is not strong enough. The English language is deficient in words required to describe those who seek to profit from a day of such blood and horror.

We had well-known members of the Bush administration going on national television to terrify the American people so as to avoid any questions. It wasn't enough for Condoleezza Rice to go on CNN's *Late Edition* to state that the administration was against a public investigation into September 11, as she did on May 19. The American people needed to feel the wrath of pure terror from this administration, to ensure that it would get what it wanted – a continued veil of secrecy and the surety that prickly questions would go unasked.

Why the veil of secrecy? Perhaps it is as simple as the story told by respected British journalist Gordon Thomas, who has reported that Israel warned the US government on five separate occasions of terrorist plots to attack prominent targets. As late as August 24, 2001, the Israeli security agency Mossad informed the CIA that 'terrorists plan to hijack commercial aircraft to use as weapons to attack important symbols of American and Israeli culture.'

There are those who believe the absolute worst – that Bush and his cronies knew of the September 11 attacks in advance and allowed them to happen so they could advance nefarious personal and political goals. The truth in hand, however, is worse than the darkest conspiracy theory. The Bush administration had specific information in hand from the CIA pointing to an airplane-based attack on American targets. They did not warn agencies responsible for security at American airports, nor did they beef up airline security by fiat. The FBI had specific warnings of terrorist attacks in hand earlier in the summer of 2001, but these warnings went unheeded.

The same administration that had the September 11 attacks happen on its watch has fought tooth and nail to keep any investigation into the security failures that led to the attack from happening. Basically, those security failures are still there, intact, deadly to us all. The warnings of impending catastrophe from the likes of Cheney, Rumsfeld, and Mueller may prove to be a self-fulfilling prophesy because this administration refuses to take responsible action to address them.

In fact, the Bush administration has proven itself more than willing to go to wretched extremes to keep any investigation from gaining steam, by frightening the public with warnings of doom that they themselves admit have far more to do with politics than reality.

We were wide open to attack on September 11 because of these security failures. We are wide open to attack today, because the same irresponsible leaders in charge on September 11 are calling the shots today. Rather than work to protect Americans, they seek to terrify Americans as a means to cow any Democratic move towards an investigation into the causes behind the attacks.

If we are attacked again, they will have no one but themselves to blame. The Democrats asking for an investigation are doing so because they want to protect Americans. Bush and his people are fighting this because they want to protect themselves. They are purposefully making people afraid to further this agenda. They play politics on a field littered with the bones of American dead, and they peddle fear to a nation already saturated with woe.

Our bombs in Afghanistan are not bringing to justice those who perpetrated the acts of September 11, and are creating more enemies who will fight to see us die. The Justice Department has stumbled about like fools trying to ascertain the source of the anthrax threat with no notable success. Our tax dollars, vitally needed to defend the economy and the country, are being spent to reward corporations for their support of the GOP agenda. Our airports remain sieves through which more deadly threats may pour unchecked. Our homes and private communications are made of glass.

The world paused as we passed the first anniversary of September 11. From this stillness must come action. We must look around and determine whether this nation is forging the proper course. The world is a dangerous place, as the crater in Manhattan clearly shows. If we are to make it less so, then a hard appraisal of our actions to date is required. The greatest defeat of all would be if our course, begun with such fanfare and support, brings us into a world where September 11 seems mild by comparison. We are a fair piece down that road already.

None of this matters to the dead. They trusted the president and his people to take care of the business of security and knew nothing of the conflicts of interest inherent in a mob of energy company CEOs running the store. If America is to move intact through the minefield of the twenty-first century, we must redefine the threat that faces us. It is not the shadow men with the deadly eyes that cause us to lie awake at night, but the treason of divided loyalty along the halls of power in Washington.

That infection has led us to global war. The cure is not to kill, to invade, to make war and excuses. The cure is the understanding of consequences and the cleansing of our sacred governmental institutions. When entities like Enron control our foreign policy, blood runs in rivers down our streets. The best interests of the people are not represented, but are in fact completely disregarded in pursuit of new markets and profit.

Victory will be found by exposing, in public and for all the world to see, the roots of our common catastrophe. In the aftermath of September 11, it was the expectation and the demand of all that we stand to defend the nation, in the name of the common good. Victory will come when our government and foreign policy meet this goal.

One Crazy Summer: The Media Before and After September 11

In the early morning hours of Thursday, June 22, 2001, a man named Jared T. Bozydaj took to the streets of New Paltz, New York with a semi-automatic assault rifle. He fired pointedly at police officers, wounding one officer named Jeffery Quiepo in the arm. The shooting went on for several hours before Bozydaj was disarmed and arrested.

Bozydaj was described as being highly upset by the execution of Timothy McVeigh. He apparently had decided to take revenge in McVeigh's name on the police, whom Bozydaj referred to as 'control mechanisms for the government.' Weapons and literature in his apartment indicated that Bozydaj had been planning this attack for some time.

New Paltz is a small community near the Hudson River about an hour north of New York City. The downtown district is filled with small stores, as well as a number of bars that cater to the students of SUNY New Paltz, the campus of which is only a few blocks away from where this shooting occurred. The best word to describe the place is 'quaint.'

My fiancée was born and raised near this town. I have spent many drunken hours with her in the bars that bore the bullet holes from Bozydaj's rampage. Her parents reported that much of downtown New Paltz was roped off with yellow police tape the day after the shooting. One could see quite clearly the damage done by Bozydaj's assault rifle, and the police believed it was a miracle that no one was killed. One SUNY student reported that eight bullets passed through her bedroom wall, and said that she would have been shot in the head if her radiator had not deflected the rounds.

I discovered this story on the forums of DemocraticUnderground.com, where someone had posted it as a topic for discussion about McVeigh-oriented violence. I forwarded the link to my fiancée, for obvious reasons. She called her parents and got the story from the ground. The local New Paltz paper, the *Times-Herald Record*, covered the shooting in detail, and she sent me the link to the story that was carried on their website.

The next day, she called me.

'I haven't seen this story in any of the newspapers,' she said. 'It wasn't on CNN or MSNBC last night. Why do you think they aren't reporting this? Some guy shot up my town, and shot a cop.

I am a news junkie, and had myself noticed that this interesting and disturbing story had not appeared anywhere in the national news media. Using the words 'New Paltz' and 'Bozydaj,' I searched the *New York Times*, an obvious place for this story to appear, and came up empty. I did the same at CNN.com, the *Washington Post*, ABCNews.com, and several other news outlets, and found nothing.

A man, motivated by the execution of Timothy McVeigh, had gone on an hours-long shooting rampage directed exclusively at cops in a small New York town with a sophisticated assault rifle. He blew a hole in a cop and shot hell out of every storefront in the vicinity. He nearly put a bullet through the head of a sleeping college student. Somehow, this was not deemed newsworthy by every major news outlet in America, including the *New York Times*, the paper of record for the state where this shooting took place.

Why?

An immediate explanation is that the editors of these news sources were acting out of a sense of responsibility. For most Americans, the name Timothy McVeigh is synonymous with pure evil. It is likely that a decision was reached among the purveyors of our information that nothing should be published or broadcast that will give ear to those who consider McVeigh a martyred hero. The fear, I suppose, is that if enough of these kinds of stories get out, some of our militia-oriented citizenry will think the Revolution is finally at hand, and will take to the streets of their own small burgs with rifle at the ready.

This kind of quiet censorship, however, raises some disturbing questions. If unreported McVeigh-motivated shootings like this are happening in New Paltz, where I am lucky enough to have eyes on the ground, where else are they happening and going unreported? I have no friends in Akron, Butte, Silver Springs, Kissimmee, El Paso, or Needles. Where else in America is violence like this breaking loose?

Why are we not being told of it? What else is being withheld?

Noted linguist Noam Chomsky has observed many times that the national media are not the information-disbursing entity created by our love for the First Amendment of the Constitution. Rather, the national media are the propaganda wing of the status quo. The national media tell us things in a certain way to keep our eyes on our shoes and to keep us from questioning power too closely. When no other avenue is available to control the masses, the national media simply refuse to inform us at all.

We have seen this phenomenon many times in many places. How many of us truly know the level of poverty that exists in America? How many of us know the toll our sanctions in Iraq have taken on the civilian populace of that country? How many of us know the number of dead left at the hands of CIA-trained and armed murderers in Nicaragua during the Reagan administration? How many of us truly know the extent to which corporations run the government of this country? Who can say for sure what happened on September 11, beyond the obvious calamity that we saw on television? Why did that happen?

Were we told all the facts in unpolished newspaper prose, a howl of outrage the likes of which has never before been heard would rise from the throat of the American populace. This, more than anything, is the reason we are left in our uninformed state of bliss. Were we to be truly informed by the media outlets, so much would change so fast, and so many of those who hold the power and the purse strings would be run out of town on a rail, that the very nature of power in this country would be shattered forever. Those who sup on the teat of the status quo want nothing to do with this. We are left in the dark.

Such a condition is beyond concepts of Left or Right. Political affiliation is mere window-dressing in the high apartments of true power in America. One need only look at the corporate connections of Gore and Bush, our last two presidential challengers, to know that party politics doesn't matter a damn at the end of the day. Everything boils down to the central question: Who rules?

Not us, friends. Not when we are kept safe and uninformed. It is better this way, when the tree-shakers are kept out of the loop.

The fact that Mr Bozydaj's shooting rampage went completely unreported by the national news media, an entity entrusted with informing this vast nation about the truths that happen within its borders, should shake your confidence in what we are told to its foundations. I don't care for Mr Bozydaj's views and I despise anyone who would attack police officers with an assault rifle. But, simply put, he happened. We deserve to know.

If the news media can report on a consensual relationship between adults for two years, they can report on Mr Bozydaj. If the news media can report on every school shooting, despite the real danger of inciting copycat outrages, they can report on Mr Bozydaj. And if they can report the actions of Mr Bozydaj, they can certainly report other stories, as well.

We deserve to know many things we are never told of or are lied to about. When we are not told, we are deprived of the right and ability to determine the course of this country, as is our purpose as citizens. We all know the dangers of making uninformed decisions, having done so to our woe many times in our daily lives.

How many decisions have we made in the name of this nation without all the relevant facts in hand? How many more such decisions will we make?

Too often, others do our thinking for us. The story of Mr Bozydaj is just one example of this phenomenon. If you love this country, fear in your soul what other areas in the life of our country you are not allowed to participate in, simply because someone else decided you didn't need to know.

The attack by Mr Bozydaj, and the subsequent media silence surrounding it, happened before September 11. Cast your mind back to that innocent summer. If you were not a shark on the attack, or Gary Condit on the run, you did not make the news. I am a journalism teacher and I know the damage this myopia has done to our politics and our place in the world. This country was meant to function with the informed hand of the populace guiding the way. When that hand is removed, when the people are stoned on televised stupidity, the machinery of the state is overtaken by entities that do not have the best interests of the people in mind.

If you think the sorry state of journalism has nothing to do with September 11, think again. Below is a running diary of a day in the life of the Fox News Channel from the first week of August, 2001. Can you think of anything we should have been hearing about besides this?

10:56 am – I turn on Fox to see a pearl-festooned announcer named Patty Ann Brown with a remarkable beehive hairdo talking about Steve Fosse's balloon trip. I haven't seen a do like this since looking at the pictures of Jackie at the JFK library.

10:58 am – The Condit coverage begins ...

11:00 am – They have a female reporter standing on the Levy lawn getting sprayed by the sprinklers. I wonder if this is where she saw her career heading.

11:08 am – Graphic claims Levy neighbors are parking their cars around the Levy house to block reporters. I needed to know that.

11:11 am – Many grinding seconds with a totally useless press conference from D.C. police chief Ramsey. No evidence, no crime, no suspects, no nothing, and yet the media tracks Condit like he's a fugitive Nazi.

11:16 am – It continues back at the studio ... will the Levys sue Condit in civil court? Will Condit be booted from Congress? Sixteen minutes in and I want to gouge out my eyes.

11:18 am – At last, they move on to lightning strikes and the new *Star Wars* movie. That was 20 minutes of nothing. The graphic spun up before the commercial with the voice-over: 'A fair and balanced report is coming up.' Well, praise Jesus.

11:20 am – Shark attacks in Florida and the Bahamas. The businessman who was attacked in the Bahamas was named Krishna and his wife is named Ave Maria. I'm eating my own face.

11:27 am – A segment on the dangers of having a heart attack while working out at a gym. Bear in mind that these Fox broadcasters are getting paid for this. The graphic reads 'Killer Workout.'

11:30 am – Today's headlines: clones, Libby Dole might run for Jesse Helms' seat, Shug Knight is free.

11:32 am – A new face: David Aspen talking about the dangers of being struck by lightning.

11:35 am – First mention of Clinton! They're rebroadcasting a portion of last night's Hannity & Colmes, and the subject of Bill's book is broached. The segment is called 'Condit & Clinton.' Is Bill an honest man? No! His book will be a self-serving grasp at a legacy that intends to rewrite history! Who would buy this book?!? Jack Kingston (R-GA) is calling Bill's memoir a 'How-To Manual' for deceiving your wife and selling state secrets to foreign intelligence services.

11:37 am – Back to Condit and the rally his supporters had for him in California. They're all stunned that such a thing could exist.

11:38 am – The microburst of Clinton/Condit bashing has concluded. That was amazing.

11:44 am – A Market report called 'Fox Stox.'

11:46 am – They've got a weatherman dancing around the studio to the tune of 'Hot Fun in the Summertime.' He just said, 'Yeah baby, sing it to poppa!'

11:47 am – A commercial for Bill O'Reilly's show: 'Who's looking out for us, the working people of America?' When was the last time you actually met a working person, Bill? How's that trust fund treating you?

11:52 am – The new *Star Wars* movie!

11:53 am – They're running a phone poll: 'Would you read Clinton's memoir?'

11:56 am – I've made it through the first hour. I counted seven mentions of Bill Clinton, and 24 minutes of Condit coverage that offered absolutely nothing in the way of news.

11:58 am – The 'Fair and Balanced' graphic is back … we report, you decide. I might decide to walk into traffic before too long.

12:00 pm – A rehash of previous headlines, and the Condit show begins anew. That reporter is still standing in the sprinklers on the Levy lawn. The pro-Condit rally is getting lots of play, as are the wingnuts who arrive to bust it up. According to Fox, 65% believe Condit was involved in a murder that hasn't been proven yet because no body has been found.

12:06 pm – First Bush sighting. He's on his working vacation down there in Hell. 110 degrees in the shade in Crawford.

12:07 pm – A discussion on how police locate decomposing bodies. Yes, they're talking about Chandra.

12:11 pm – Rehashing the old news, heavily spiced with commercials.

12:26 pm – Is Gary Condit's political career over? Is there such a thing as 'Doggy Profiling' that gives some pooches a bad name?

12:28 pm – Cloning again. Breezy overview of the Academy of Science roundtable on the subject.

12:29 pm – According to Fox, 75% of Americans think Bush's month-long vacation is not too large a time to be off the job. Another random mention of Clinton's name wedged in there.

12:36 pm – 'As the search for Chandra gets cold, will the Levy family turn up the heat?' We're back on Condit again, and a writer for *The Nation* named David Corn is debasing himself and his magazine by participating in this conversation.

They're running captions at the bottom of the screen titled 'Fox Facts.' Among these facts: 70% of people say Condit isn't telling all he knows; 51% say Condit is acting guilty; 47% think he should resign. It's a drumbeat across the screen.

12:38 pm – A talking head named Cliff May, former RNC Communications Director, claims that no one is using this story for political gain.

Fox Flash! The bombing of Iraq 'according to national policy.' We bombed Iraq? Whahuh?

Cliff May: 'Condit is not shameless enough to survive this.' More Fox Facts: 50% say the cops are giving Condit special treatment.

12:41 pm – Condit was just compared to Marion Barry. They are leaving no stone unturned here on Fox.

12:42 pm – Condit microburst is concluded. Commercial break. My eyes are beginning to feel dry and scratchy. A tremor shakes my hand.

12:44 pm – Was Tom Selleck drunk and disorderly on the streets of Manhattan? They called him 'Magnum Pie-Eyed.' I wish for death.

12:48 pm – After an agonizing wait, filled with anticipation, they're finally doing the story on 'Doggy Profiling' giving some loveable mutts a bad name. The music in the background is 'Bow wow wow, yippie-yo, yippie-yay.'

Oh my God. They stuffed some Fox reporter into a puffy padded suit and sicced this massive bulldog/mastiff hybrid on him.

12:55 pm – Here comes a phone poll – What would you name Clinton's memoir? I see this generating scads of intelligent dialogue.

12:56 pm – Two hours down. A truly disturbing blizzard of Clinton, Condit, and cloning just paralyzed my higher brain functions.

12:59 pm – They've been lobbing teasers about the cloning debate all day. Here comes the first real substance on it, given in the appearance of straight reporting. The Fox Facts scroll on the bottom describes, in chopped sentences, how one might go about creating a human clone. I hope everyone at home is taking notes.

1:01 pm – Cloning conversation concludes, on to a 'tax revolt' happening in Nashville, TN. The Governor of Tennessee is daring to institute an income tax. I guess these folks didn't get their check from Bush yet.

1:03 pm – First mention of the missile defense plan. The Russians are in Washington, D.C. to talk turkey. I hope they don't mind if Bush peers into their souls.

1:04 pm – Back to Chandra and Condit. They're rehashing the last two hours. That reporter is still in the Levy yard.

1:09 pm – A 'Breaking News' graphic interrupts the Condit coverage. An Italian scientist is defending his desire to clone humans. His English is completely incomprehensible. You haven't lived until you've heard someone say 'spermatozoa' with a heavy Italian accent. Still, this man deserves my thanks. He may be getting ready to breed monsters, but at least he got Fox off the Condit story.

1:11 pm – An amazing wall of commercials. It won't end.

1:16 pm – We're back to Condit. Two more talking heads have appeared to regurgitate all the non-news that I've been listening to.

1:18 pm – Condit rant over. They're back to 'What would you name Bill Clinton's memoir?'

1:22 pm – I am logging on to the Internet to check if any non-Condit-related events have transpired. Lo and behold! CNN.com says we bombed Iraq, and the story here was posted at 11:51. Fox was talking about the new *Star Wars* flick. It seems we blew up a rocket launcher. With the exception of that quick blurb at 12:38 pm, Fox has made no mention of it at all.

1:23 pm – I've fled the Internet because Fox has callers on the air offering potential Clinton memoir book titles. The suggestions:

'How to Tell a Lie and Get Away With It.'
'Bill and Hillary's Greatest Blunders.'
'Memoirs of an Unrepentant President.'

The last caller gets on and froths all over the phone about Clinton. His final remark: 'Harlem is a good spot for him.'

Wow. I hope a CNN executive saw that. These are the people they wish to attract for the sake of ratings. Where is Willie Horton when you need him?

One caller squeezes in an impressive list of Clinton accomplishments and dismisses the other titles that have been offered as partisan nonsense. While he speaks, the Fox broadcasters smile and shake their heads.

1:26 pm – Back to the heat wave, the shark attack, a tad on cloning.

1:29 pm – Condit. A car accident in California. Ave Maria, Krishna, and the shark. The heat wave. Condit. Scary lightning.

1:36 pm – I need a context check, so I'm switching quickly to CNN. They are focusing on the cloning debate.

1:39 pm – Back to Fox, and 'The Chandra mystery continues.' They have a graphic up which reads, 'What went wrong?' The fact that Condit hasn't taken a second lie detector is damning proof of culpability as far as Fox is concerned.

1:43 pm – 'It's amazing with the 24-hour news coverage that they haven't started a grand jury investigation yet,' says Fox person. Perhaps that is because evidence is needed to present before a grand jury?

1:44 pm – Saith Fox: 'It definitely wasn't a suicide because women who kill themselves always make sure their bodies can be found.' OK, lock the bastard up.

1:45 pm – Condit screed over, back to the report about scary lightning. Didn't we blow something up in Iraq today?

1:51 pm – More lightning, and a teaser for a show coming on at 6:00 pm: 'The Levys turn up the heat.'

1:53 pm – Condit again.

1:54 pm – Kool and the Gang are reuniting.

1:59 pm – Back to Condit again. That reporter is still in the Levy driveway. Her parents must be very proud.

2:02 pm – Condit rant over, back to the headlines. Bush playing golf, the TN anti-tax protest.

2:04 pm – Back to Condit. 'Bill Clinton did it. Gary Condit did it. They all get away with it.' A talking head from Fox in Dallas claims Chief Ramsey is protecting Gary Condit.
    I need a break.

2:21 pm – Back from the store, they're talking about the heat wave.

2:24 pm – Sharks.

2:27 pm – A teaser about a segment where they will check out Wilt Chamberlain's fabulous bachelor pad.

2:30 pm – Heat wave.

2:32 pm – More non-news about the cloning debate.

2:38 pm – They're walking through Wilt's house. I wonder if they'll find Chandra in there. Background music: 'Love Shack' by the B-52s.

2:41 pm – An exposé about women who wear shirts that expose their belly buttons. Background music: 'Stuck in the Middle with You.'

2:44 pm – Fox lets me know that a fair and balanced report is coming up next. I wait with baited breath.

2:48 pm – The comeback of Kool and the Gang. Two Gang members are in the studio. Homogenization Breach! There are two African American males on the set of Fox! These are the first non-Caucasians I have seen all day, commercials included.

2:50 pm – Blurb at the bottom: Bush says US will not intervene in Middle East until fighting stops.

2:53 pm – Condit. It's the same stuff warmed over again.

3:03 pm – Top stories again. Hey! We bombed Iraq! Sharks. The heat. And, of course, a story about a race in the UK involving riding mowers.

3:04 pm – Back to Condit. That reporter is still out on the Levy lawn. Ramsey says the only reason the press is pursuing the case is because they want to play up the sex angle. No, say the Foxies. It's about lies and deception and obstruction of justice. So there.

Fox Fact: Chandra's mom, Susan Levy, is a community volunteer. She has a son named Adam. A picture of Condit being pursued by cameras flashes on the screen. The caption reads, 'Obstruction of Justice.'

3:11 pm – Sharks.

3:14 pm – Sean Hannity in the radio booth, ranting about how Condit is using his father, Reverent Condit, to defend himself. Hannity wants to know if the Reverend has read that commandment – Thou shalt not commit adultery.

3:17 pm – Clinton again, and the poll question about naming his memoirs. A mention of the cloning debate, which the Fox broadcaster refers to as 'The whole sheep thing.'

3:21 pm – Sharks.

3:30 pm – Back to the 'tax revolt' in Tennessee. They've shown this several times now, and I count maybe 50 protesters. I've been to a number of Bush protests that have drawn at least as many people. I assume that is not newsworthy, however. Not one little bit.

Two car accidents, one involving a plane that crashed on a highway. Roger Clinton has plead guilty to a misdemeanor reckless driving charge. The republic is saved.

3:32 pm – The latest from Wall Street; everyone's waiting for Cisco's earnings report.

3:34 pm – The Clinton book deal rises again. Caption at the bottom reads 'Scandal Storie$.'

3:37 pm – Back to Condit. What are the PR moves he can make to salvage his career?

3:42 pm – They've got a publisher named Judith Regan on to talk about the Clinton book. Regan has her own show on Fox, on Saturdays and Sundays.
   Fox Fact: Clinton plans to write the book himself. I'm stunned.

3:46 pm – O'Reilly asks once again who is watching out for the working folks.

3:50 pm – They're airing callers again who have suggestions for a title to Clinton's memoir:

'I Beg Your Pardon.'
'Feeling Your Pain.'
'How to Lie, Cheat, Steal, and Get Away With It.'
'A Leader's Contribution to America's Decay'

3:52 pm – Moment of high comedy: they're actually having a conversation about why Clinton won't use these titles.

3:53 pm – Bill from Texas offers his suggestion: 'Born to be President.' He then shouts at the top of his lungs, 'We love you in Texas, Bill Clinton!' How that got past the screeners is a mystery.
   I am reminded that this news is fair and balanced before they break for commercials.

4:00 pm – Top stories: bacterial meningitis in college dorms; a bit on the cloning debate with the caption, 'Cloning Humans?!?'

4:12 pm – This has been a straight Wall Street report thus far. Microsoft seeks redress from the Supreme Court. Everyone is waiting for Cisco's earnings report.

4:29 pm – Another blurb about the Tennessee 'tax revolt' before a return to Wall Street. It has been a full half an hour since anyone has mentioned Condit or Clinton. I feel like I've been paroled.

5:00 pm – The vacation is over. John Gibson and the Big Story dive right back into the Condit story, with a teaser about the Clinton memoir.

John Gibson has the most remarkable hair I have ever seen: an ivory pompadour helmet that rises impossibly above his brow. As he reminds us that it is Day 99 of the Chandra search, I am mesmerized by the studio lights glittering in his blond locks.

5:02 pm – They are rehashing the last six hours' worth of coverage again. Parrots do not get this redundant.

Did Chandra want Condit's baby? Did Chandra confront Condit's wife? Wendy Murphy, a criminal defense attorney, stokes the soap opera fires to a glowing blaze.

5:11 pm – The first commercial break from the Big Show. It has been wall-to-wall Condit.

5:13 pm – Gibson is back and the Condit crucifixion continues. A detective from the New York Police Department adds to the talk about how there is nothing to talk about. That reporter has been on the Levy lawn all day.

5:16 pm – Another commercial break, but first: 'The police say Condit is not a suspect. Is he guilty in the court of public opinion?'

The fair and balanced graphic sails by.

5:20 pm – We're back, and it's Condit again.

Fox Fact: Obstruction of justice is a Federal offense.

5:24 pm – Gibson raises the specter of a House ethics investigation. Nothing is happening there, because the ethics board only investigates Congress people who break the rules while acting in their official capacity. Gibson finds this absurd.

5:27 pm – They have said nothing new about Condit all day. As we fade to commercial, I realize that Gibson has just spent 27 minutes talking about nothing at all.

5:30 pm – An ad for the Brit Hume show coming up at 6:00 p.m.: 'Is Condit's career over? A fair and balanced report.'

5:31 pm – Top of the hour recap: Sharks; car crashes; the Roger Clinton misdemeanor pleading; the actress Rebecca Gayheart is being sued for running down a 9-year-old boy with her car while talking on a cell phone.

5:32 pm – Cloning. Fairly straight report.

5:42 pm – The Clinton book deal again. What will he have to do to sell it? People won't want to read about his brokering of the Middle East peace accords. They want to know about Monica, they want all the dirt. Gibson refers to Clinton supporters as 'fawning droolers' who will accept everything he says.

6:00 pm – That was 18 full minutes of sarcastic venom from Gibson aimed at Clinton's book, which isn't due out until 2003. Good news for Fox. They'll never run out of material with that kind of a timeline.

6:01 pm – Brit Hume, and the first story is not about Condit. I am jonesing already. Instead, a recap of the cloning debate.

6:04 pm – Look out. Here's some real news. Ashcroft spoke at a meeting of the American Bar Association to defend his dumping of their traditional review of court nominations. He points to a column from the *Wall Street Journal*, which carried an analysis by the conservative Federalist Society that claimed the ABA leans wildly to the Left. The ABA president, Martha Bennet, calls the report balderdash.

6:10 pm – A rebroadcast of Bush's comments regarding the Iraq bombing and the state of the Middle East peace process. Some tasty Bush quotes:

'Sanity must prevail there before we get involved.'
'It's important for people to get outside, and work.'

6:12 pm – Unlike Clinton, Bush never takes a mulligan while playing golf. He can't remember what the Patients Bill of Rights legislation is called. He refers to it as 'The Gansky Something Something Bill.' Then he told the press guys to 'get lost' and walked away. All the Fox broadcasters are chuckling at the president's delicious wit.

6:13 pm – Back to Condit and a total rehash of everything. Thirteen minutes of other news was all they could give.

According to my calculations, There were 42 distinct occasions where the name 'Clinton' was raised, not including an 18-minute rant by Gibson. Bush was mentioned 14 times. They showed the same picture each time – George on his golf cart. Monica Lewinsky was mentioned twice and her picture was shown once. The missile defense program was mentioned once. The tax cut was mentioned once. The Iraq bombing was mentioned twice. The chaos in Israel was mentioned twice.

Perhaps the most astounding aspect of my quest into the land of Fox News is this: I watched for exactly 437 minutes. Of that, by my calculations, 133 of those minutes were directed solely at rehashing the fact that Condit did it, he did it, he did it.

That accounts for nearly a full third of the time I watched. Another third of the time was dedicated to the commercials that were shown approximately every five minutes. The rest of the broadcast dealt with shark attacks, heat waves, car crashes, the new *Star Wars* movie, and the upcoming Clinton memoir.

God, what a summer. Gary Condit was driving me insane.

I wanted to see him punished, driven through the streets like the mangy cur he is. I wanted to see posters emblazoned with his face on every wall in the city. I wanted to see children spitting at that image. I wanted him to go down bleeding from the ears and cursing his mother with his dying breath for birthing him in the first place.

Didn't I?

After all, he was all that I saw on television for two months. His name was on every lip and his picture was perpetually broadcasted into millions of homes at the speed of light. Mothers were frightening their children to bed with the mere mention of him. Off to bed now, children, or Gary Condit will get you.

For weeks I tried to ignore the sordid tale of Gary Condit. I assiduously avoided any and all TV news broadcasts dealing with him, which pretty much means that I didn't watched Fox (except for the purposes of the diary). I turned the page on any newspaper article that bore mention of him. I refused to talk about it with friends at the bar.

For a time, I thought I was in the clear. After an orgy of coverage about a parking lot in Virginia where Chandra Levy's bones purportedly lay, it seemed the media had finally manufactured enough shame to be embarrassed with themselves. The botched election coverage didn't do it, but 22 straight hours about an asphalt blacktop brought about a subdued silence from those who were trying to build careers on the Levys' front lawn.

Then the man had to go and prostrate himself before one Connie Chung for an interview. It was as if a bomb went off inside my television. Anchor people ran amok like startled chickens, dramatic graphics flashed all over the place, and stridently martial music blared from the speakers. Onward Condit soldiers …

There was the preview of The Interview, but before that was the preview of the preview. Preceding that was the recap of the last three previews, plus a forecast of what was to come. Woven through it all was this breathless anticipation: he's gonna talk.

I pledged to ignore The Interview and started a small boycott of the broadcast. I surfed my way past every news station that was hyping it, which meant all of them. It was wall-to-wall Gary, and things were not looking bright for the man with the fantail hairdo.

After The Interview, of course, came from the media what my female students call 'the dish.' How did he do? What did he do? What do we do now? The answers to these three questions, predictably, were 'Badly,' 'Nothing,' and 'Let's keep kicking the tar out of him.'

That night, I left the state to attend a wedding over the weekend. I had neither television nor Internet access until two days later. I came home and flipped on CNN, wondering what I might have missed. 'Coming up next on CNN,' crooned the authoritative voice. 'Gary Condit has spoken up, and no one is satisfied. We'll discuss the total annihilation of the California Congressman next on ...'

How could this be? What happened to the brilliantly democratic institution we once called the free press? We shall cease to exist as a free nation if the fair and open exchange of information is stopped or further distorted. The point cannot be made more clearly.

In all but the poorest homes there is a television and electricity to make it work. Across the dial are stations that broadcast a signal virtually every second of the day. In Utopia, such a marvelous means of mass communication could be used to ensure that every flavor of opinion representative of diverse peoples is shared with all, with the obligatory sitcoms and soap operas spiced throughout.

This isn't Utopia. This America, Jack. Nobody knows what's happening here, but you can bet your bottom dollar we've got our breads and circuses. Gary Condit was the sacrificial goat that season. There will be another next season. You can count on it.

Part of me wants to rage against the media. They are responsible for this. They are the ones showing it every hour of every day. It is a plot, a smoke-screen, designed to keep us distracted from what is happening in this country. They have trained us, over many years, to prefer swill over content.

I sat at a table over that wedding weekend and spoke with a woman who did not know that the surplus was gone, that Social Security and Medicare were screwed, that there will be no money for education reform. She knew all about Gary Condit, though. This was no rube I sat with. She was a very smart lady, but she depended almost entirely on television news for information. In this, she is like a vast majority of Americans.

I want to denounce the media for blinding and deceiving us, because I believe it to be true. But another part of me whispers about the geometry of the marketplace. It tells me that the media lives and dies at the altar of capitalism. If nobody is buying what they are selling, they are doomed. They broadcast what sells.

For many weeks, Fox was the only network devoting a majority of their broadcast time to the Condit story. CNN began to notice that they were losing swaths of their market share to Fox. People were watching Murdoch's stations because they liked what they saw. The folks at CNN made the fiscally intelligent move and became the Condit News Network virtually overnight. Soon, the other news networks followed suit.

This happened for one reason: the networks took the temperature of the marketplace, and served up what it wanted. The marketplace obviously preferred Condit's bloody head on a platter over foreign affairs reporting or dire news of looming financial catastrophe.

In the words of Pogo, we have seen the enemy, and he is us. We are the marketplace.

Some will read this and believe I am defending Gary Condit. I am neither defending nor defaming him. I am dismissing him. Whatever crimes the man committed, at the end of the day he was answerable only to his constituents, his family, the police and the Levys. The millions who followed his destruction have no say in his fate. Their lives will be the same after he is gone.

It is said that Nero fiddled while Rome burned. That summer, the American empire was burning and it is the people who fiddled in the face of the flames. As much as the media are to blame for it, at the end of the day it is our responsibility.

If we cannot change this bastardized sham that comes in the guise of news and information, there will some day be words engraved upon our tombstone: 'Here lies America. They didn't pay attention.'

While Social Security was pillaged, the media reported breathlessly of shark attacks. While Medicare was imperiled, they went around and around the Condit mulberry bush. While election reform lay fallow, they squealed over the newest Powerball zillionares. Any political press conference played second fiddle to airplanes without landing gear or mangled trucks spread across a highway.

There are many possible explanations for the conspicuous lack of meaningful coverage of the issues that lie at the heart of our national interest. Perhaps corporate sponsors fear a decline in ratings if the nightly news speaks of budget shortfalls instead of missing interns. Perhaps journalists, seeing this trend, seek to make careers out of covering sensational stories to ensure their names become known.

Whatever the case may be, the trend towards news-as-entertainment instead of news-as-information has been happening for years. It took off with a bang via Pentagon-purified coverage of the Gulf War, and became pure art during the trial of O.J. Simpson. By the time the Clinton impeachment came along, infotainment became standard fare for the masses.

In a nation so vast, with a government so large and with such power, it is impossible for our citizens to govern as we are tasked to if we are not given the information necessary to make informed decisions in the voting booth and elsewhere. Thomas Jefferson and the Framers were great admirers of the concept of a free press. They believed no democracy could endure without one. John F. Kennedy, speaking for all politicians, was in agreement, saying once, 'Even though we never like it, and even though we wish they didn't write it, and even though we disapprove, there isn't any doubt that we could not do the job at all in a free society without a very, very active press.'

This is a great burden and responsibility the modern media have, and they have not been doing the job. The summer of 2001 was but one glaring example of this. The situation begs the question: If the American media are not constituted to represent the people, to help them with the free and open exchange of information so as to further or ability to rule as we are tasked to, whom or what do they represent?

Let's take a look.

The major television news sources familiar to Americans are NBC, ABC, and CBS, along with the cable news channels CNN and Fox.

CNN is owned by AOL/TimeWarner. This massive company also owns HBO, Cinemax, and Comedy Central, not to mention an Internet empire that includes America Online, Netscape, and Amazon.com. They own the magazines *Time*, *Life*, *Fortune*, *Money*, *Sports Illustrated*, *People*, and *Entertainment Weekly*. They are involved in a variety of joint ventures with Hughes Electronics Corp., General Motors, and CitiGroup. They own the Atlanta Braves and the Atlanta Hawks. This is a mightily abridged list.

ABC is owned by Disney. Disney also owns television stations in Chicago, Fresno, Houston, Los Angeles, New York City, Philadelphia, Toledo, and San Francisco. They own radio stations in ten cities, with multiple stations in each city. Disney also owns ESPN. Disney holds a partial interest in the Sid R. Bass company, which is involved in crude oil and natural gas production. Again, this is a partial list that does not reflect their entire holdings.

CBS is owned by Viacom. Viacom owns television stations in 36 American cities, along with MTV, BET, UPN, Nickelodeon, VH1, Showtime, and TNN. Viacom owns well over 100 radio stations in 40 cities. They also own Simon and Schuster, which publishes books. This is, once more, a partial list.

Fox is owned by Rupert Murdoch's News Corporation. Murdoch owns 33 television stations across the country. He also owns television stations in Germany, England, Australia, China, Japan, Canada, India, Italy, Indonesia, and across Latin America. Murdoch owns the *New York Post*, as well as 36 other newspapers across Australia and New Zealand. Murdoch owns the amazingly conservative *Weekly Standard*. This is a partial list.

NBC is owned by the General Electric Corporation. GE owns television stations in Dallas, Chicago, Houston, New York City, and ten other cities. GE also owns the stock market channel CNBC, and holds partial ownership of MSNBC along with Microsoft. GE has several wholly owned subsidiaries in the insurance realm, including Harcourt General, Union Fidelity Life Insurance, and The Pallas Group, along with 19 other entities in America, Europe, and Japan. GE's industrial interests run the gamut from aircraft engines to power systems based on gas, electricity, and nuclear fuel services. GE is quite involved in the satellite communications business. They have for years been part of America's military industrial system. In the 2000 election cycle, GE's industrial wing contributed $1,264,159 to political campaigns; 64% of that money went to Republicans. Once again, this is a partial list.

History tells us that the rise of militant fascism in Germany during the 1930s did not draw worried notice from European news outlets – radio and newspapers – because those media entities were owned by chemical and steel interests that were reaping the profits from Germany's explosive military buildup. Only when it was too late did the alarm bell begin to sound. This we call a conflict of interest, and a damned deadly one.

Today in America, we face a similar crisis. These five broadcasters listed above reach into every American home on a daily, nay, hourly basis. Sometimes the conflict of interest is blatant, as in the example of General Electric. Sometimes it is slightly more subtle, as in the conservative shilling performed by Murdoch's Fox. All of them, however, are greatly invested in the status quo, and all have given vast swaths of campaign money to our politicians to maintain that status in their favor. In nearly every example above, the profits made by delivering journalistically sound news to

Americans is a tiny fraction of their overall haul. At bottom, because they are so widely divested, it does not pay to inform.

What would be the result if a democratic nation was suddenly deprived of a free press dedicated to true journalism? Leave that door unlocked and tyranny must soon follow. Some will tell you it is already here.

The indolent summer of 2001 ended on September 11. On that day, the news media became more important to the health and welfare of the nation than all the flags and patriotic songs we could muster. Not only were they required to inform a stunned populace what was happening on the ground minute by minute. Sooner or later, they were going to have to roll up their sleeves and help us all figure out why this wretched thing happened.

But then George W. Bush got on television and told us we were attacked because the terrorists hated our freedom. That was that. The American news media said, 'Yes, sir' and proceeded to avoid questions of causality regarding September 11.

Since September 11, I have often fantasized about having one hour alone with George W. Bush, armchair to armchair as it were, so I might put five questions to him. The questions change from week to week; this busy administration hardly passes a day without saying or doing something that, 20 years ago, would have obsessed the national media for weeks. It would be nice to hear him speak on these things, to listen to the insider's view.

After all, Bush is privy to virtually every decision made by Dick Cheney. It stands to reason, therefore, that George would know better than most what motivating factors move the White House. Cheney would never deign to sit with me; power like that has no time for the truth. Bush, on the other hand, could easily spare me an hour down in Crawford. He's there all the time, inspecting the patch of desert he calls a 'ranch.'

Below are the questions I'd ask if he called me down there tonight. They'll probably change twice before Monday, but only if we're lucky.

1. What is the true nature of the Saudi Arabian connection to September 11, and why has this connection not been a priority for Bush's State Department?

American Undersecretary of State John Bolton gave a speech to the conservative think tankers at the Heritage Foundation not long ago entitled, 'Beyond the Axis of Evil.' In it, he leveled a military finger at Lybia, Syria, and Cuba, accusing them of pursuing development programs for the creation of weapons of mass destruction.

In essence, Lybia, Syria, and Cuba have joined the long line of potential targets along with Iran, North Korea, Iraq, Yemen, the Republic of Georgia, the Philippines, and Colombia. For some of these nations, it is the suspicion of the presence of the aforementioned weapons program that draws the ire of the State Department. For others, it is the shadowy accusation of fealty to the Al Qaeda cause that brings forth our attention. Afghanistan has already been invested.

In all of this, there is scant mention of Saudi Arabia. The vast majority of the September 11 hijackers called Saudi Arabia home. Many Saudi Arabians fought with the Taliban in Afghanistan against the Soviet Union. One of those was named Osama bin Laden. The Bin Laden Group, a massive construction firm with deep business ties to America which was created by bin Laden's father, is based in Saudi Arabia. The extreme fundamentalist Wahabbi sect of Islam is rooted in Saudi Arabia, and it is from this movement that scores of terrorists have grown.

The silence surrounding Saudi Arabia has been huge. How can we fail to pursue Saudi Arabia with the Bush Doctrine guiding our way? Nations that sponsor terrorism, or have terrorists operating freely within their borders, are in grave danger of invasion and destruction. This Doctrine was established in Afghanistan, and it appears many other countries face a similar fate. Yet Saudi Arabia, a veritable birthing bed for international terrorism, escapes taint.

Is this silence due entirely to Saudi Arabia's supply of oil? If so, please explain the details behind this necessity. Thousands of Americans have died, and the world has been plunged into war. If the prime suspect behind the September 11 crime has been given a free pass, it is essential that we understand exactly why. Names and numbers, please.

2. Why has the Bush administration not been the loudest, most strident advocate for a far-reaching investigation into September 11?

On the eve of Bush's State of the Union address, it was reported that he and Cheney issued a request to Senator Daschle that many interpreted as a veiled threat. Soft-pedal the investigation, Bush said. Don't interfere.

In the time between, the Bush administration has changed its tack somewhat, claiming to welcome an investigation. Yet there is silence, and silence, and silence on this front. Relatives of September 11 victims rallied on the steps of Congress to demand an independent investigation. This evoked even more silence on Pennsylvania Avenue.

How can this administration fail to be the most ardent, vociferous advocate for an investigation into September 11? How is it possible that the glaring security loopholes that allowed the attack to take place are not publicly dunned in the vigorous fashion that is required? These missed signals must be investigated and deconstructed, so that the security gaps they slipped through can be closed.

What role did a planned natural gas pipeline through the subcontinent play on September 11? What role does it play in the post-September 11 international relations situation?

The American people deserve to know exactly what happened on that day, and why. 'The attackers hated our freedom and our way of life' is unconscionably insufficient. As this happened on this administration's watch, how is it you have failed to push relentlessly for answers that will undoubtedly enhance our security?

3. What, precisely, is the legal basis for a war with Iraq?

The resolution agreed to by Congress and the White House on September 14, 2001, gave Bush wide latitude to 'use all and necessary and appropriate force against those nations, organizations or persons he determines planned, authorized, committed or aided the terrorist attacks.'

The resolution further allowed Bush to use military action 'to prevent any future acts of international terrorism against the United States' by those who perpetrated the September 11 attacks.

Iraq falls under neither heading. No proof whatsoever has linked Saddam Hussein or his government to the September 11 terrorists. No proof exists that he intends to help any entity or nation to perpetrate future attacks. The state of his weapons program exists in a state of innuendo, as there were no inspectors there for some time. In the seven years of UNSCOM inspections, Hussein's ability to manufacture weapons of mass destruction – every tool, every piece of equipment, every factory and laboratory – was leveled and burned and destroyed. To have these weapons now, he'd have been required to start completely from scratch, buying tools and equipment on the international market. Such activities are eminently detectable, and no such activity has been detected.

Why do we threaten Iraq with war while leaving Saudi Arabia unmolested and unthreatened? Which aspect of the Bush Doctrine applies to this apparent double-standard?

Speaking tactically, how do military threats levied against Syria, Jordan, Iran, Lybia, and Yemen strengthen our fighting capabilities in the region surrounding Iraq? We'll need those countries to keep their powder dry, as they did during the Gulf War, to avoid a region-wide conflagration. Moreover, we'll need neighboring allies (Saudi Arabia again) unmiffed enough to allow us to base troops and fighters for jump-offs towards Baghdad.

It looks as though we are cruising towards a conflict with Iraq that has little to do with the September 14 resolution, and in the process we seem to be alienating and infuriating other nations in that region in a manner that will make a war with Iraq far more dangerous and destabilizing. Please explain the wisdom of these policies.

4. Where is the anthrax killer?

There is not much to add after the initial query. There's a killer with deadly poison in hand wandering free in this country. The evidence points directly to home-grown terrorism and to someone on the government payroll. What is the status of this investigation, and how is it that such a dangerous killer has escaped detention?

5. What role did America play in the failed coup in Venezuela?

When Venezuelan President Hugo Chavez was ousted from office in a coup perpetrated by Venezuelan military officers and businessmen early in April, the Bush administration fell over itself in a rush to welcome the new government into the family of nations. Never mind that Chavez won two popular elections in that democratic nation. As administration officials admitted, winning an election does not necessarily convey legitimacy.

The collapse of the coup and the reinstatement of Chavez left a lot of egg on the face of the Bush White House. As the story behind the failed coup has begun to coalesce, several prominent American officials have been named by the foreign media, and by Chavez himself, as having had a hand in the overthrow. Among them are:

Eliot Abrams, member of the White House National Security Council, once convicted for lying to Congress about the Reagan administration's role in the Iran/Contra scandal, is reported to have given US approval for the coup.
Otto Reich, senior White House policy advisor on Latin America, once the American ambassador to Venezuela under Reagan, met several times with Pedro Carmona, the erstwhile coup leader ousted after 24 hours of rule. Reich, after the coup began, gathered the Latin American ambassadors to him and stated bluntly that democracy had not been violated in Venezuela, and that America would support Carmona.

John Negroponte, American ambassador to the United Nations, former ambassador to Honduras under Reagan who held that post during the worst atrocities of the Iran/Contra affair, was reportedly warned of the coup as early as last January.

Lieutenant-Colonel James Rodgers, assistant military attaché to Venezuela, who was spotted with the coup plotters right up to the moment the plot unfolded.

What is the truth behind all of this? Where are America's hands, and are they as dirty as they seem? As Venezuela leads OPEC and is a major petroleum source for the United States, are we dealing with yet another foreign policy fiasco based upon oil? How can the Bush administration condone the overthrow of a democratically elected government?

So ... those are the questions for today. I will have more tomorrow. Hopefully, someone in the mainstream press with access to Bush will read these and choose to ask them, tape recorder in hand. I'm still waiting for my call from Crawford.

As I write this, my friends are in the other room watching some amazingly vapid reality show called *Dog Eat Dog*. Did the summer of 2001 ever really end?

American Elections: 2000 and Beyond

In all the history of American democracy, there has never been anything like the 2000 election. There has never been a president elevated to his position by a majority of the Supreme Court. It goes without saying, then, that there has never been such an elevation performed by a majority that is ideologically identical with the man to whom they're giving the job.

If there has ever before been vote fraud on the scale seen in Florida during that November, it has never been reported on to any great degree. The fraud that existed in 2000 still remains almost completely uninvestigated by American journalism. Only Greg Palast of the BBC has taken a swipe at it and what he found should disturb anyone with a care for the manner in which we choose our leaders.

The intentional removal of thousands of names from the voter rolls before the presidential election was performed by a company hired by Clayton Roberts, head of the Florida Elections Board. That company was called ChoicePoint. The vast majority of names removed from the rolls were African American, who went for Gore nationally by a 9–1 margin. People make a lot of Nader's role and even more of the Supreme Court's action, but I believe ChoicePoint's nefarious work was the single most important factor in the outcome of that election. Bush 'won' by 537 votes, a margin that would have been wiped out had ChoicePoint not scrubbed tens of thousands of black people from the rolls for no legitimate reason.

Without ChoicePoint, Nader would have been an asterisk. Without ChoicePoint, the Supreme Court would never have been able to get involved. Without ChoicePoint, the 37-day disaster of lies and propaganda that followed the vote would never have taken place. Without ChoicePoint, Al Gore would be president today. Taken to the furthest extreme, it can be argued that, without ChoicePoint, the soaring towers of the World Trade Center might still be standing.

Read Palast's book *The Best Democracy Money Can Buy* for an in-depth report on ChoicePoint and the Florida fiasco. Those who say we should all 'get over it' are either not in possession of the facts, too jaded to defend the essence of democracy, or have something to hide.

Even before the disaster in Florida, I sensed a lethargic strangeness to the whole process. The country was being offered a choice between a sitting vice president, who had been in politics for 24 years, and a Governor from Texas, who appeared at times utterly flummoxed by the English language. It was a race of establishment candidates, with Nader agitating from the Left and Buchanan frothing from the Right.

Worse, the level of journalism committed to the coverage of the race seemed sorely lacking. We heard about Gore's choice of suit color and Bush's nebulous descriptions of 'compassionate conservatism.' We heard little else. I decided one day to reach out to the one man who could shake things up a bit. If there was ever a man who could breathe some bombastic life back into campaign reporting, it was The Doctor.

Date: July 12, 2000

To: Dr Hunter S. Thompson, Woody Creek CO

From: William Rivers Pitt, Boston MA

How can you stand it? We have been chest-deep since the fall in one of the most abominable political races ever run. The dubious cast of characters we have endured since November is only part of the story. Beyond the milkfed sons of privilege carrying the banner for the Main Parties is a swirling morass of corporate overminds and a deteriorating environment. One of these boobs will be charged with handling it all, and there is a large fog of doubt as to whose interests they plan to represent.

I waited for you during the primaries. Those days after the New Hampshire primary surely quickened your blood. At the very least the players were far more engaging. There came former jock Bill Bradley, dragging his marsupial chin north after Iowa to absorb another beating from a shark-toothed Al Gore. However entertaining that may have been, it's fair to say that all the action was on the Republican side. When John McCain wiped that vapid grin off the face of heir-presumptive George W. Bush in New Hampshire, my feet tapped and my fingers snapped. There was no joy in Mudville, because the voters around Manchester could not be bought.

There was Orrin Hatch, who, I learned today, has a website where you can download MP3s of him singing religiously patriotic songs. Stop laughing, it's true. Dan Quayle clawed his way onto the stage for a time, but the snickering drove him back to Indiana. Gary Bauer shrieked of God's vengeance and the evils of China until, like Bob Dole, he tumbled off a platform and out of the race. And there was Alan Keyes. At full bellow he was the grandest speaker out there, on any night. But when the voters stared into his crazy, swirling, sweat-lined eyeballs they saw more than they were prepared to deal with.

Did you heave a sigh of relief when McCain finally was brought low? I surely did. I watch baseball, and coming from Boston I am privileged to be able to observe two naturals at work: Pedro Martinez and Nomar Garciaparra. They are the best at what they do. John McCain was a natural, a gifted politician with a resumé of service and pain so vast that to question him on issues was tantamount to treason.

I close my eyes and see boardrooms with fuming moneymen chewing cigars, cracking their knuckles in rage because they'd given all the money to George. They didn't count on John, and he made their investment seem foolish, and worse, beatable. When the GOP establishment rousted the diehards and finally beat McCain down South, I felt as much joy as Bush did. John McCain would gobble up Al Gore in a general election, even though he carries Barry Goldwater in his genetic code. And Al Gore is one of the Good Guys ... isn't he?

Behind them all was Bill with his fly unzipped and a sheepish look on his face. Nixon was the raven over the GOP convention in 1976. The shadow of William Clinton will cast long and deep across the Democratic Convention of 2000.

I don't have to tell you all this. You know. Where are you?

It's another Hobson's Choice, Hunter, perhaps the worst one we've ever faced. Back when you were writing politics all the time it wasn't just a game you were watching. There were high stakes involved – a war, rights movements, a broader definition of freedom, and over it all the face of Richard Millhouse Nixon, whose ascendancy bode grave ill for the very soul of the nation.

The candidates you had to choose from back then were also a motley crew; some days simply throwing up your hands and abandoning it all as a bunch of bad noise seemed the only human option. I remind you of that because today, I believe, the stakes are even higher and the abyss darker than those bloody days when Altamont and Chicago were on everyone's lips. 'We were right, and we were winning.' Isn't that what you said in 1971 after all was lost? We're still right, Hunter, but we stand to lose even more.

Back then you knew the enemy, and there was no one better at pulling back the curtain to reveal what was really happening than you. Today the enemy is harder to find. It is the sneakers you wear, whose proud corporate logo was sewn on by a slave laborer in Micronesia. It is the shirt on your back. It is the coffee you drink, the megastores you shop in, the gas you put in your car. The First Amendment protects us from government intrusion, but nothing in those old documents provides us with protection from the corporations that hold the puppet strings. Al Gore and George W. Bush are their greatest creation. No matter who wins, corporate America comes out ahead.

This year we have some surprise entries who appear poised to stick the entire race out until November. Pat Buchanan, the old speechwriter/populist, is still crashing around, biting off heads and slobbering on babies. Raise high the pitchforks, my pallid tribe! We burn the temple of NAFTA tonight! Who would have thought Buchanan, the last echo of Watergate, would become a sympathetic character? He's mean and he's dirty, but he was right about those trade bills. When the WTO protesters rail against that shadow corporate government, Pat Buchanan can lean back and say, 'I told you so.'

Did you know Ralph Nader is running? Actually, seriously running? You might have missed it, because a lot of the mainstream news outlets on cable and the Internet pay him little mind. That's no accident. I think, in a tiny corner of their minds, a lot of very powerful people are rabbit-scared of Ralph Nader. He's been nipping at the heels of corporate America for thirty years, and he knows all their weak spots. He won't win this year, but if he pulls 5% of the vote his party will be eligible for Federal matching funds the next time around.

I watched the Thrilla in Manila tonight on ESPN. Ali was magnificent then. He's all used up now. We're running out of champions, Hunter. Bush and Gore, Buchanan, and Nader ... and Thompson? It's so crazy that it just might work. America A.B. (After Bill) is a strange and dangerous place. But the hope is still there, as fresh as ever. Hope is the best drug of all, as it was thirty years ago. Write for us again, Doc. Once more unto the breach, dear friend ...?

Yours in Jesus,

William Rivers Pitt

Needless to say, I never heard from him. I do take a certain level of pride in noting that, some weeks after I posted this to Woody Creek, HST started writing a column for ESPN.com's Page Two.

To understand how demented and deranged the 2000 campaign was, even before Florida, requires a delving into the minute-to-minute realities that defined it. I spent the evening of October 3, 2002 hunched over my television with one of those hand-held tape recorders. My purpose was to capture a detailed picture of the entire presidential debate that was taking place that night in Boston. What came was the running diary below. I reread it some months later, and was chilled by the line about independent voters in Florida. Sometimes we find the truth by accident.

Time to put on your memory caps, folks. This is how it was:

8:17 pm: The moment is almost upon us. Gore the Shark *v.* Bush the Shrub, an encounter that could well decide this whole race. They're tied in the polls, with gender balances tipping everywhere. Gore leads mightily among women, while Bush holds a huge lead among men (Bush is from Mars, Gore is from Venus?). The other polls are all over the map, and not one of them offers clarity beyond one razor-edged truth: this is the closest race in 20 years.

(From October 3, 2000, *Washington Post*: 'The inability of either candidate to gain an obvious advantage has helped to heighten the stakes for the debates, which will provide Bush and Gore with their best and perhaps last opportunity to influence wavering or undecided voters.')

This is my Christmas. I love this crap. I live for it. All day long I've been hearing prizefight shills ringing in my head:

> *Innnn the far corner, wearing the environmentally sound patchouli-scented wraparound sarong made of recycled Truman leaflets – he's a Vulcan automaton from Planet Q, the man with antifreeze in his veins, the man who invented invention, faster than a speeding policy seminar, more powerful than Bill Clinton's libido – ALBERT ... GORE ... JUNIORRRRRRR!!!!!!*
>
> *Aaaaaand in the near corner, wearing the feetie pajamas with his thumb in his mouth, the man who'll give your tax money to rich people, the man who makes Gerald Ford look like Mr Wizard – he couldn't say 'Yugoslavia' if you put a gun to his head, but he's ready to throw down tonight. He stole Reagan's brain and he's out to steal your heart, from the great nation of Texas, give it up for GEORGE ... DUBYA ... BUUUSH!!!!!*

Well, I doubt it'll start like that, but I can dream. I have been waiting for this shindig for weeks, ever since George took off his chicken suit and decided to come to Big Bad Boston after all. The funny part is that nobody in Boston is watching this thing. Everyone is stuck in traffic out by Morrissey Boulevard. Thank you, Secret Service. As if we don't have enough trouble with the roads already.

8:21 pm: Gotta decide which network to watch. Peter Jennings on ABC might be the choice. He always develops a certain gravity for events like this. I HAVE to stay away from CNN and Bernie Shaw. The man is an assassin, a total fiend. For those who are playing along at home, it was Shaw who asked Dukakis that question about Kitty getting raped and murdered. Might as well have gone Capone on him with a baseball bat. The Duke was dead on the floor before the curtain came down, and he knew it. Bush ought to be grateful Shaw didn't get tapped as moderator. *Mr Bush, how have you been running for President when it is painfully clear you cannot speak the English language?*

The horror ... the horror ...

(From October 3 Reuters story: 'The vice president got a boost from a Reuters/MSNBC daily tracking poll on Tuesday that gave him a six-point lead over Bush, the governor of Texas, 46 percent to 40 percent.')

8:23 pm: ABC it is – but I'm sticking around to watch the glitterati of the national political punditry salivate on themselves. This is their Big Night – the Super Bowl and the World Series combined. These guys have hyped this encounter to such an obscene degree that anything short of full decapitation with sprays of arterial blood will be considered a letdown. I'll bet none of them slept last night.

8:25 pm: I wonder if CNN's Bernard Shaw is named for George Bernard Shaw? G.B. Shaw had a great quote that fits well with tonight's festivities: 'A government that robs Peter to pay Paul is assured the support of Paul.' Who is Peter? Who is Paul? Does Bernie know? Does he care?

(From October 3 New York Times: 'A New York Times/CBS News Poll shows that most Americans regard Gov. George W. Bush and Vice President Al Gore as strong leaders, but they consider Mr. Gore far more prepared for the White House.')

8:30 pm: Sometimes CNN does it just right. They've got Wolf Blitzer sitting with a panel of undecided voters in Florida. That's pretty much the election right there.

8:50 pm: God, this is killing me. I'm bouncing off the walls. Will we see the Bush smirk? Will Gore turn to petrified wood? Will one of them stumble? Will one of them fall? Will Ralph Nader, who was barred at the door, sneak past security and charge the stage?

8:53 pm: Jim Lehrer, the moderator, is saying hello to the crowd, and the CNN talking heads are talking right over him. Snarl. Lehrer is the wild card in this thing. How will he phrase his questions? What will he ask? Any curveballs? I found it interesting this week when it was revealed that Lehrer hasn't voted in 40 years, the better to maintain his objectivity. A serious man.

8:59 pm: It begins ...

9:00 pm: Lehrer covers the ground rules and opens the floor. The candidates are wearing almost identical suits – somber blue with red ties. Looking at them, you'd think they belonged to the same Kiwanis Club.

9:04 pm: The first question is about experience – who has more, and does it matter? Gore is specifically asked if Bush has enough moxie to do the job. Gore says he doesn't question Bush's experience, he questions the programs. The two candidates play nice, ply the audience with their stump speeches. If people were looking for a barn-burner, they ain't getting it yet. It took all of six seconds for Bush to mention 'the great state of Texas.'

9:10 pm: Suddenly some life. Gore begins beating what I imagine will be a common theme of the evening: Bush plans to give the wealthiest 1% of Americans more of the surplus in his tax-break than he plans to spend on any other program. There's some back and forth on this. Gore looks for all the world like Reagan, and Bush has gone Quayle – sputtering, getting shrill. Calls Gore's figures 'phony numbers,' but Gore seems to win the exchange.

9:12 pm: Interesting bit here: Bush says Gore has promises to fix Social Security, Medicare, etc., but Clinton/Gore promised this in 1992 and didn't deliver. Bush says Gore is campaigning on past failures. This is effective for Bush, until you remember Clinton and Gore's Earned Income Tax Credit, perhaps the most successful tax-break for the middle class ever created. And of course, there is the pesky fact that a good deal of Clinton's 'failures' were in fact destroyed by the GOP-controlled Congress.

9:16 pm: Gore says 'lockbox' regarding Social Security for the first time – isn't that a GOP phrase from last year? The wealthiest 1% take it in the chops again. Bush is really getting flustered, fires out a pitiful line: 'Not only did my opponent invent the Internet, he invented the calculator.' God. Memo to George: fire your joke writer. Gore goes into berserk wonk mode regarding Medicare, butchers Bush's plan seven ways from Sunday, challenges the audience to check Bush's website to prove that his 'fuzzy math' is right on point.

9:21 pm: Lehrer's next question is about the skyrocketing oil prices: what will the candidates do to control the situation? Gore charges the ramparts of alternative fuel sources, cleaner cars and buses, tax breaks for non-polluting factories, etc. Pretty green stuff here, and good to hear. He concludes by saying he won't shred the Alaskan wildlife refuge to plumb more oil, but instead is 'betting on the future.'

Bush jumps on his 'this administration had no energy plan' bandwagon. 'You bet I'll open Alaska,' he says, and give the proceeds to the poor. (*belly laugh*) He doesn't even touch the concept of alternative sources of fuel. He talks about coal miners – I get the feeling that as far as Bush's fuel plans go, if it ain't dirty, it ain't worth it.

9:28 pm: Lehrer asks Bush if he'd overturn the FDA's approval of the abortion pill, RU-486. Pat Robertson has just leaned forward in his easy chair somewhere out there. Bush goes Yellow Alert – must pander to conservative base without alienating women voters. Bush doesn't think a president can overturn the FDA – but Gore reminds him that *just yesterday* he promised to have that very idea reviewed if he wins. Bush retreats into a stump speech: we must cultivate a culture of life. Bashes partial birth abortions, doesn't mention how they are usually performed to save the mother's life.

Gore picks up the banner of *Roe* v. *Wade* and waves it to and fro. Sudden ominous turn – we're talking about the Supreme Court now. Bush will appoint strict constructionists to the bench, and won't have an abortion litmus test. Gore counters that 'strict constructionist' is a code word for the overturning of *Roe*, reminds us that Bush loves Scalia and Thomas, says the Constitution is a living document and the Justices he'd appoint would treat it as such. Bush blusters again, whines – and an audible sigh from Gore? Easy, big fella. You're ahead on points. Don't rude yourself out of the contest.

9:36 pm: Foreign policy question!!! What to do with Milosevic? Gore says he'd take measured steps – huh? – believes the Yugoslav people will see the problem through. Bush says he'd ask the Russians to lead the way and assert themselves again on the world stage. A great answer, until Gore reminds him that Putin has yet to recognize that Slobo lost, and maybe he should do that before we invite him to the table. Bush should have stayed in Austin – Gore is visibly drooling before every question.

9:42 pm: A bunch of happy talk about rebuilding the military – but that foreign policy discussion was pretty light, and it begs the question: rebuild the military for what purpose?

9:45 pm: Lehrer: Which of you is better suited to make the Big Decisions? Gore reels off an impressive list of responsibilities he's had: Vietnam, Congress, the NSC. This is Gore country. Bush comes off with a 'What, me worry?' reply. Says he'd decide on principles and not polls, tries to draw a parallel between Gore's resumé and his own from his time as a constitutionally weak Governor of Texas.

9:49 pm: Lehrer: Is this election major choice in political philosophy? Gore says Big Yes, back to using the surplus to help people and not to stuff the wallets of the rich. Bush goes to the 'fuzzy math' complaint, warns us that under Gore the government will swell beyond the boundaries envisioned by LBJ. Paints a picture of three zillion IRS agents prowling the countryside doling out Gore's targeted tax cuts. The Michigan Militia just reached for their shotguns. That line will resonate in a lot of places.

9:52 pm: Lehrer: Change and/or reform public education? Bush says he'd demand responsibility from schools and teachers, goes into warm fuzz story about at-risk kids in charter schools, accountability in grading. This works, says Bush, as he dives into education policy. This is his one area of policy strength, at least rhetorically. 'Don't subsidize failure.' Gore: Accountability and local control are good, he's agreeing with Bush. Smart. Adds more policy re: teacher testing, 100,000 more teachers, shrink class size. Tax deductible college tuition.

Bush won that exchange hands down. He knows the stuff cold. Gore was playing catch-up the whole time, agreeing left and right because challenging Bush here would be folly.

(*Note*: Noam Chomsky has a book out: *The Miseducation of America*. Read it and compare his brutal wisdom to the candidates' ideas.)

10:05 pm: Lehrer: Can you point to a decision that illustrates how you'd handle an unexpected crisis? Gore: Kosovo solution, I had Russian PM get involved, was risky but paid off in the end. Other examples are there if he had time, touts public service – some rah rah about him being a Middle Class Warrior fighting HMOs and Big Oil.

Things suddenly get riotously ugly for Bush: respond to crises? He talks about handling wildfires in Texas, that he's got a big heart, and would cry with the victims of catastrophe.

10:09 pm: Lehrer: What would you do in the event of a financial crisis? Bush would talk to Greenspan, get facts, get Congress involved, and somewhere in there they'd all come up with game plan. Perhaps the most glaring non-answer of the night. Gore reminds us he's worked on this stuff, recalls the peso crash and the Southeast Asia market meltdown – and then lets us know that our prosperity is due to the deciding vote he cast in Congress that rammed through the current economic plan.

Bush says entrepreneurs made this economy, not Big Al. Zing! Gore says they were working hard eight years ago and struggled. Papa Bush gets blasted.

10:14 pm: Bush backhoes, knocks the middle-class tax cut of 1992 promised by Clinton/Gore that never came, rips Gore economic plan. Gore sighs audibly yet again, perhaps remembering the EITC (Earned Income Tax Credit). Gore: His quotes are from partisan report from GOP Congress, not worth tax-funded paper it's printed on. We shrunk government. Gore is scolding Bush, Bush about to blow, more whining about fuzzy math.

10:16 pm: Some back and forth about Social Security and lockboxes, mostly a repeat of earlier barbs. Bush looks like he needs a nap, Gore looks pompous.

10:24 pm: Lehrer: The Inevitable Character Question. Bush says Gore loves his family, and that's good. Hits 'no controlling legal authority,' Lincoln bedroom, the Buddhist fundraiser. I'll keep the public trust and won't let you down.

Gore: We should attack the problems of the nation, not each other. You focus on scandals, I focus on troubles of our country. I am my own man, family man, not exciting but will fight for you, won't let you down.

I question Bush's tactics here. He's beating on Clinton, not Gore. Big Al invokes McCain – big whiff for Bush, who could have used that name – and promises to sign McCain/Feingold. Reminds us that everyone is dirty when it comes to campaign financing. A deft defusing of a thorny issue, in my opinion. Yet Gore here had the chance to dismantle the raft of allegations that have been floated about him, and he fails to do so.

10:29 pm: Lehrer invokes McCain, and asks if the candidates will support his campaign finance reform push. Bush says yes (*belly laugh*), if we can kill labor donations and soft money. Gore casts a baleful eye at Bush and says, 'You've attacked my character, but I won't respond.' Says the system undermined by special interests, he knows how bad it is and will fix it.

A glaring example of the jaundiced state of journalism during the 2000 campaign came when virtually every pundit on television handed the debate victory to Bush. Somehow, they missed what I was watching that night. Gore sighed and looked pompous, yes, but he also manhandled every barb Bush sent his way. The media handed the debate to Bush basically because their expectations regarding his performance were preposterously low. Bush didn't fart audibly, drool, or babble about being 'misunderestimated,' and therefore 'won' the exchange.

The fallout from this sad example of reporting was clear in the next debate – Gore was tentative, polite to the extreme, and lost. By the third debate, the opportunity was gone. Gore has always been known for his awesome mastery of the details of policy and historically had an eye for the jugular in any debate. These strengths were negated by the skewed reporting that surrounded the first debate, and Gore never seemed to regain his equilibrium.

As the weeks passed, I began to develop a sick sensation in the pit of my stomach. Nothing Gore said or did seemed to gain him any traction with the TV people tasked to report on the campaign. For the first time, I began to truly fear that Bush would win the thing. His policies were poison, the people he would bring with him were poison, and the very real possibility that this man would be afforded the opportunity to reform the Supreme Court in his image kept me up nights.

And then came the election. Then came Florida.

They say the apple never falls far from the tree. Sons will be as their fathers are. I am like my father in many things, but in the madness of politics we share a special bond. A talking head on CNN will spew some ideologically demented grunt into their lapel microphone and my phone will be ringing six seconds later. My father's breath, redolent with indignation, will surge out of the headset saying, 'That guy is dumber than a bag of hammers.'

As he knows more about politics than any living human I have ever encountered, with the notable exception of my grandfather, an assessment like that has some teeth. I almost always agree with my father's observations, because we share a similar view of the world. Some fathers talk baseball with their sons. The sport my father and I share is politics and has had a season 18 months long, with many close contests and restaurant-quality plays. As the Florida battle roiled its way into its fourth week, we knew our seventh game of the World Series was in extra innings. I was always waiting for the phone to ring.

I was forced to wonder if the phone lines between Kennebunkport and Austin were burning up during the last days of the Florida recount. It stands to reason that they would have been. After all, there was politics aborning and the stakes could not have been higher. George Herbert Walker Bush knew just about every player that was active for the GOP down in Florida. Most of them worked for him. Dick Cheney was his Secretary of Defense. James Baker was his Secretary of State. Colin Powell was his Lancelot. These men were the team that pulled together a coalition of nations and bombed Iraq back into the Stone Age, so they knew something of war.

George Herbert Walker Bush had a son who was deeply involved in the election contest in Florida. He is named Jeb, Governor of the State. Jeb Bush swore to deliver Florida to the GOP on November 7. Had he failed, he would have been humiliated and his political career may well have been ruined. Jeb Bush knew everyone involved down there, from the counters to the commissioners to the judges to the folks in the media horde, on a first-name basis. His Secretary of State, Katherine Harris, had dramatically ended the race prematurely with the stroke of a pen. The job description for Secretary of State contains the words 'representative of the Executive'; when Harris spoke, her words carried the authority of the Governor's office.

Did George Herbert Walker have any reason whatsoever to speak with his son George W.? The Governor of Texas had been literally out of sight during the final days in Florida. He was last spotted on a Sunday night seizing the throne on national television while being victimized by the daunting task of having to read simple words off a TelePrompTer. After that he went underground, leaving the talking and the explaining and the attacking to his father's graying gods of war. Two months before the election, George W. had a similar altercation with the English language that left him bloodied and embarrassed. His handlers threw a bag over him and forbade him from saying anything beyond their carefully crafted stump speeches, lest he wander into a linguistic thicket again and blow himself out of the race. The same thing seems to have happened in those last few days.

Why would George Herbert Walker Bush want to speak to someone so thoroughly removed from the game, someone whose public presence had actually become toxic? George Herbert Walker Bush was the chairman of the Republican National Committee during the Nixon administration, and weathered the storm of Watergate. He ran the CIA for a time. He was a formidable presidential candidate in 1980, and that year became vice president under Ronald Reagan, whose administration was among the most popular and powerful and corrupt we have ever seen.

In the fullness of time he became president himself, and though limited to one term, he redefined the definition of war as we knew it. After Clinton beat him, Bush Sr became a powerful backroom dealer for the monolithic Carlyle Company, whose various dealings with the regime in Saudi Arabia have made it one of the most potent players on the corporate scene. George Herbert Walker Bush is accustomed to speaking to powerful men. In those final days, his son George W. was not yet numbered among that breed.

The phone was certainly ringing down in Austin, but George W. was not called to the line. Dick Cheney was being given advice from Bush Sr on how to present the GOP's public case in a quiet, firm manner. James Baker was being advised about keeping the strong front as bristly and shrill as ever, so as to elevate passion and public exhaustion in equal measures. Colin Powell was being advised to simply let his armor shine, so as to dazzle the minds of otherwise reasonable people. Jeb Bush was being advised to get the legislature ready, in the event the mess required more drastic congressional measures.

None of these men was being told to speak slowly, remember your lines, don't get off the subject. Former President Bush has probably only had to say such things to three people in all his life: his old boss, his old running mate, and his Texan son. His son needed no such guidance in that time. George W. Bush was not involved in this contest, and so there was no strategic theorizing or even moral support required. A man with as active a resumé as former President Bush cannot give good advice on how to do nothing. If I had to make a bet on it, I'd wager that George W. Bush was playing with his dog while the phones rang around him and taller men carried the water for his candidacy.

It was commonly accepted a long while back that George W. Bush is a puppet dangling from many strings. His father's people were financing his campaign. His campaign managers were writing his scripts. There was little effort to disguise this fact, and the issue managed to hide in plain sight for the entire race. The degree to which George W. Bush had gotten used to being managed was truly exposed in those final Florida days. He was AWOL from what any rational assessment would have concluded was the political fight of his life. The defeated shade of his father's administration had possessed the contest. We were not witnessing the creation of a new administration in those days, but the return of an old one, with George W. Bush serving as little more than a mute, two-dimensional poster-boy.

The apple never falls far from the tree. In the final days of the Florida recount, George W. Bush dangled from one of his father's branches, green and unripened and unplucked. He was in his backyard, resplendent in cowboy hat and boots under the light above the door. He cast a tennis ball into the darkness and a shadow raced to retrieve it. George W. Bush was waiting for his dog to bring him the ball. He was waiting for his father's men to bring him the presidency. He had nothing to do besides play fetch. He might have been smart enough to be bored. Inside his house, the phones kept ringing. Nobody called his name.

A drenching rain was falling in Boston the night the Supreme Court decided the thing in favor of Bush. I heard thunder out my window. My lonely little plant was lashed by the wind coming through the screen, but it was a warm wind, carried on a storm from the south. Somehow, that seemed fitting. The pathetic fallacy was discredited as a literary contrivance long ago, but a part of me could not avoid sensing ill omens in the sounds of the night.

George W. Bush was coming to Washington, D.C. He, too, had been carried north on a southern storm. He brought with him a man named Andrew Card. Card has been for years the best friend of corporations like General Motors, which makes him the very personification of what the green-blooded folks who voted for Nader fear and dread.

George W. Bush was coming to Washington, D.C. with Colin Powell in his entourage. Powell was named Secretary of State, representative of the executive, the man who will be the face America shows to the diplomatic world. I was gladdened that an African American assumed that sacrosanct post, but I wondered if such a gesture could heal the wounds torn open by the systematic disenfranchisement of African American voters in Florida.

George W. Bush arrived in Washington, D.C. with many others in tow. His strongest allies, however, were already there. Trent Lott and Tom DeLay were there, as were Orrin Hatch and Strom Thurmond. These stalwart Republicans controlled both Houses of Congress, and the task of ramming through the new president's agenda fell to them. It was widely assumed that responsible budgetary planning or any manner of environmental protection were nowhere to be found on their wish list.

William Renquist, Clarence Thomas, and Antonin Scalia were there. Hopefully, George brought flowers, because he owed them his success. When these men asserted that the counting of votes in Florida would be 'injurious' to Bush, they all but assured his ascension. When they went further to claim that the December 12 Electoral College deadline was inviolate, a 'safe harbor' that could not be abrogated, they broke faith with the nation they swore to serve in order to cement the election for Bush.

Twenty-one states did not get their Electoral College votes in to the proper authorities by December 12. Those late states had their votes counted on December 18 when the College met to choose our leader. The most important votes, the ones from Florida, were chosen by that state's legislature because nobody in Florida actually had the right to vote in the election, according to those robed Justices mentioned above. See:

The individual citizen has no federal constitutional right to vote for electors for the President of the United States unless and until the state legislature chooses a statewide election as the means to implement its power to appoint members of the Electoral College ... the State legislature's power to select the manner for appointing electors is plenary; it may, if it so chooses, select the electors itself. (U.S. Supreme Court Decision, *George W. Bush et al.* v. *Albert Gore, Jr. et al.* December 12, 2000)

Basically, the decision in *Bush* v. *Gore* applied only to the state that determined the race in favor of the candidate whose politics agree with the majority on the Supreme Court. As my friend Will Shakespeare might say, something was out of joint.

Much of the media tried to sweep this unpleasantness under the carpet, to lull us into complacency, to turn our eyes towards the new administration and away from the mob action and judicial malfeasance that put them in office. We were lulled by the oft-repeated refrain, 'This is an orderly transfer of power ...' It was the safer course, to be sure. Let us watch the unfolding drama together and revel in the coming warfare between the parties, as if the inauguration actually has some legitimacy to it.

I refused to be a part of that national amnesia. I will not forget what happened and I have never accepted George W. Bush as my president. I will pay my taxes and if I am called upon to protect my country in a military capacity, I will serve, because thankfully George W. Bush is not America. But he is not my leader. He represents me not at all.

We have learned much about our country, and little of the lesson serves to warm the heart. We have learned to be patriotic, to pin flags to our car antennae. We have also learned to fear blue skies and airplanes. Somewhere along the way we learned not to care when the election process becomes despoiled. Do not forget what we have lost, what the country has had taken from it.

I hope those of you who were capable of doing so, yet did not vote in 2000, are properly chastened. If, after all that has passed and all that is to come, you people still refuse to take responsibility for the state of your own country and add your voice to the body politic, if you do not understand by now that every vote counts, you should be shunned as fools, cowards, and dead weight. There are 100 million of you right now. Do not dare complain about anything. You had your chance to have a voice. You may yet, in 2004.

It is the age of compassionate conservatism, and I intend to be the raven over the great seal of George W. Bush's ill-gotten office, bending a knee to his empty mandate nevermore. When he says the words, 'The people have elected me to ...', I remind all who would listen that the people did not elect him. George W. Bush stopped being the dull-witted fool we love to mock on December 12, 2000. He became the most dangerous man in the world, and he must be watched very carefully.

There is a long road ahead of us. Those of us who love our country and dread what their country has become must remain vigilant and angry for a long time yet to pass. It has been said that America works best when we have a common enemy. For years we had the Soviet Union. For a time, we had China. Now, we have the threat of terrorists and the prospect of eternal war.

My enemy is George W. Bush, and I am not alone. Never forget that Bush did not carry a majority of the vote in 2000. When you combine the votes earned by Gore and Nader it becomes clear that Bush is a minority leader. The most dangerous aspects of his plans for America can be thwarted if the Democratic Party and the army of activist progressives that people this country combine their strength and act. That, however, is the rub.

Water will get you wet. The sun rises in the East. There is no unity on the Left. Some things are so true as to be axiomatic. Under the wide-roofed definition of 'liberal' exists ideology after ideology, platform upon platform, all moving in a thousand directions at once. Liberalism by definition stands upon the elemental principle that change is necessary for survival, and that new ideas are not inherently dangerous. Ideas and idealism are the lifeblood of liberalism, yet it is in this bedrock core that division grows.

People as a rule tend to develop a vigorous fondness for the idea that resonates within them; liberals do this reflexively and energetically. That energy springs from the other basic principle of liberalism: ideas espoused by the Left stand for the little guy, the planet, and humanity as a whole. The words of Edward Kennedy, spoken at the funeral of his slain brother Robert, speak with simplicity and eloquence for all on the Left: We see wrong, and try to right it. We see suffering, and try to heal it. We see war, and try to stop it.

Yet in this plurality of hope, wisdom, and idealism rumbles a restless and fractious divide. Stop any ten liberals on the street and ask them what they believe in, and 95% of the time there will be unanimity of opinion. Put some of these like-minded individuals together in a room, however, and the likely result will be rage-faced natural allies who have screamed themselves hoarse in disagreement.

There is something to be said for this. After all, stubborn adherence to an ideology breeds a lock-step mentality which can become as narrow-minded and exclusionary as the worst form of conservative extremism. The Left thrives on ideas, and it is healthy for this nation to have a plurality of individuals and groups giving voice to them. It is healthy for the Left to have this, as well. Without it, liberalism is an empty well yielding only dust. In order to hear new ideas, one must accept without qualification the existence of those who will advocate for them with energy and passion.

The strife which inevitably follows cannot be avoided and should be welcomed. After all, the Framers conceived this nation to be a hotbed of debate and disagreement.

Unfortunately, that strife does not exist in a vacuum, safe in academia and coffee shops around Boston and San Francisco. The fractious nature of liberal ideology echoes with profound effect across the political landscape of America and the world. It changes voting patterns, dissuades many from participation, and worst of all opens a wide wedge for opportunists on the Right to exploit to profound and catastrophic effect.

It is a strange and disquieting phenomenon to behold the cognitive dissonance that arises from those who exacerbate the divide within the Left with infighting. One of the platforms upon which all liberals stand is the idea that an America which thinks only of itself is a dangerous country. Human rights are a global issue, as is economic equality, as is political enfranchisement, as is a well-seated fear of the rise of extremism in any form and in any nation.

The divided partisans within the Left in America, stubbornly adhering to their ideological isolationism, somehow believe they can have these arguments and continue the rift in an ivory tower above the fray. They miss the planetary consequences of their disunion, thus betraying the essence of that globalist world-view. American Democrats, Greens, Socialists, Communists, Progressives, and Anarchists are all guilty of this crime. It is an equal-opportunity error, one that must be addressed with all due haste. At bottom, the failure to consider tactics and pragmatism will be catastrophic for all involved.

Consider the recent elections in France as an example of the glaring con-sequences of disunion. On April 21, 2002, French voters went to the polls to begin the process of electing a president. In France, such elections operate on a run-off basis: the two candidates who receive the most votes in a pre-liminary and wide-open race win the ability to face off for the high office.

Jacques Chirac, France's Gaullist sitting president, faced off against a wide variety of challengers. Essentially a pseudo-conservative centrist, Chirac stood against Socialist Party Prime Minister Lionel Jospin and a number of lesser lights. The French media all but wrote off the initial April 21 vote as predetermined, anointing Jospin and Chirac as the obvious victors.

The importance of this cannot be overstated. France looked to be facing a presidential election where the ideology and opinions of an avowed Leftist would enjoy massive mainstream exposure. The nation would be faced with a decision between Centrist and Left, and whatever the result, an important European government would have the debate between these ideologies on the public record.

The prominence of a Leftist candidate would also likely ensure that some form of liberal ideology would make a home in France's government, especially if Jospin made a close race of it. Strong challengers tend to haul incumbents in their direction; France appeared destined to go Left no matter who won. In the context of Europe as a whole, this was of enormous significance.

Then the results came in.

An extreme Rightist politician named Jean-Marie Le Pen, representing the National Front Party, scored a stunning victory on April 21. Le Pen, age 73, managed to secure 17% of the run-off vote, edging Jospin's 16% by a statistical eyelash. Chirac, by comparison, secured 19.6% of the vote. Suddenly, the race for the presidency of France was between Gaullist Chirac and a man who came to prominence through virulently racist demagoguery, a man who proclaimed extreme French nationalism to the embarrassment of a vast majority of French citizens, a man who once dismissed the Nazi gas chambers as 'a detail in history.'

This disaster came about for a variety of complicated reasons that can be summed up in one phrase: disunity on the French Left. Three Trotskyite candidates ran, gathering 11% of the vote. The Green Party candidate earned 5%, while the Communist Party candidate earned 3%. Simple math delivers a plurality of 54.6% to Centrist/Leftist candidates, a sure sign that the voting majority in France wanted nothing to do with the ideology represented by Le Pen's extremist 17%. In this, the French Left mirrored the American voting electorate in 2000. A number of liberal candidates who earned between 1 and 2% of the vote serve to pad this total, and yet it will be Le Pen and his extreme Rightist ideology who stands center stage for the final showdown.

French fears of rising crime and immigration served Le Pen's fearful platform, as did a rising anti-Semitism based upon French sentiment for Palestinians in the Middle East. More than anything, however, it was the market rules of the burgeoning European Union, and by proxy globalization, that created rifts on the Left in France. Those rules, espoused by Chirac and Jospin, made it impossible for either candidate to entirely please their traditional voting bases.

These voting bases were aware of Le Pen's presence in the race and knew full well the danger he represented. Yet they chose to fragment, retreating to their various ideological islands in an expression of doomed defiance in order to make a statement. They did not support Jospin *en masse*, who was the logical target for votes based upon tactical political reality, and he went down to defeat.

Because of this, a historic opportunity for France and all of Europe was lost. That prime-time debate between a Centrist and a Socialist was gone forever, and the Continent was forced to endure the rantings of man labeled a Nazi in many quarters of Europe. Given the history of that land, such a charge carries incredible weight. France seemed destined for a leftward shift, but that opportunity was in ashes.

The silver lining in all this was found in France's electoral organization. In short, they have provided an opportunity for the correction of mistakes. Chirac defeated Le Pen with a plurality of some 80%. After Le Pen's victory, hundreds of thousands of Left-leaning French took to the streets in protest. In Lyons, Grenoble, Bordeaux, Strasbourg, and Paris they took to the streets in shame and outrage, and pledged in almost iron-clad unanimity to cast their votes for Chirac.

In the end, this averted the catastrophe of extremist Le Pen's assumption of France's presidency, and proved that Leftists can come together when push comes to shove. Nothing, however, can change the fact that the mainstreaming of a Chirac–Jospin policy debate never happened. It cannot alter the fact that similar Leftist fragmentations have opened powerful opportunities for the Hard Right in Italy, Austria, Denmark, Portugal, The Netherlands, and Germany.

Finally, it cannot obscure the shameful fact that some 28% of the French electorate, the highest number in 40 years, chose not to vote at all. While this dwarfs America's 100 million-strong voter abstention rate, a number that eclipses Gore and Bush's 2000 election vote totals combined, it is a baleful reminder that political disengagement is not purely an American phenomenon.

America recently endured an election where divisions on the Left were prominently featured. Ralph Nader's Green insurgency sapped strength from the Gore campaign, to be sure. Nader's strong pre-election focus on the traditionally Democratic states of Oregon, Wisconsin, Minnesota, and Washington required Gore to peel his time, money, and energy away from the pivotal contests in Tennessee, West Virginia, Florida, and New Hampshire. The loss of those latter states helped decide the election for Bush.

Yet a scattered Gore campaign that failed to capitalize fully on the boon years of the Clinton administration could not surmount the albatross of the Clinton scandals and fell victim to the machinations of Katherine Harris, ChoicePoint, and other conservative state officials in Florida. The dubious handling of the overseas ballots, the relentlessly partisan media campaign waged by Bush operatives, culminating with the onerous decision by the Supreme Court, all played their prominent role. Gore won the 2000 election; of that, there is no doubt. However, these complications fogged the issue to enough of a degree that a space was opened for that victory to be taken, and it was.

The history of this Bush administration serves to prove Nader's claims of identical similarity between Bush and Gore were less than accurate. In American politics, however, politicians go for votes. They do so by the most available means. Ralph Nader can be counted now as a politician; his activist days are over. For Nader, who sought only 5% of the liberal vote, painting Gore and Bush as twins was the surest way to success. Lambasting him for playing by the accepted rules of the game is intellectually dishonest. Beyond which, laying Gore's loss at the feet of Ralph Nader and the Greens ignores the multifaceted circumstances of the 2000 election and wrongfully scapegoats Green voters who were acting in good conscience.

In the final analysis, arguments surrounding the 2000 election should be laid aside by the American Left for one simple reason: looking backwards is the purview of the conservative. Liberals face today and tomorrow, taking lessons from yesterday to heart while free from the belief that the past has a vote on the future.

Le Pen's ascendancy in France and Bush's dominance in America must serve as a final, unavoidable warning to the American Left. Liberal fragmentation allows those whose views do not meet the will of the people to have an unnaturally powerful voice in politics. It is all well and good to believe what you believe, but if you are unable to translate those beliefs into policy that helps those for whom you speak, you may as well stay in bed.

Politics is nothing more than an expression of social will – the ability to translate moral certitude into effective governmental actions on behalf of the people. When the Left is fragmented, scattered, and unable to come to some form of consensus, that social will is useless. France had the social will to move definitively leftwards, and yet that energy was shattered into ineffective splinters because no one was willing to surrender specific ideologies for the common good. That nation had a second chance on May 5, when the presidential election was held. The French Left came together and fixed their mistakes. America will have to live with the consequences of a single vote in November of 2004, and there are no second chances allowed.

It comes down to this: unless the American Left can lay aside its decades-old infighting and unite behind the commonly held belief that the policies of George W. Bush are poison to the nation and the planet, he will win a second term and secure the ascendancy of a conservative ideology that has little to do with the well-being of the people. Democrats, Greens, and all American liberals must come together in the fundamental understanding that virtually any candidate within the spectrum of the Left is preferable to Bush, even one so Centrist as to be tickling the Right.

The planet suffers today under the yoke of what is shaping up under Bush to be an eternal state of war. In war, people are convinced that xenophobia is acceptable, and that problems are best solved at the point of a sword. If the Left weakens itself by refusing to stand for a candidate that can unseat Bush and bring forth policies that even vaguely resemble progressive ideology, then the Left will find nothing but ashes.

After all that has happened in the world, from the Cold War to September 11 and all the propaganda in between, no pure Leftist has a prayer in an American presidential election. The only candidates capable of victory are tainted by corporate funding and all the trappings of modern political life. A candidate with at least a nodding association with liberalism, however, is vastly preferable to the alternative – eight years of Bush and war and the erosion of constitutional liberties and deficit spending and environmental degradation and God knows what else.

Herein lies the secret: if the broad American Leftist community can find within itself the strength of will to support a pseudo-liberal candidate whom they might otherwise reject out of hand, and that candidate manages to win in 2004 behind such unprecedented support, a new dawn will have broken for the Left in America. It will take time and patience, because nothing so monolithic as American politics changes with anything resembling speed. It will require this coalition to hold together, in all likelihood, for another election or two.

If such a goal can be reached, the result will be incredible. The Left will have achieved a strong and resonating voice in the mainstream of American politics once again. The nation, which wanted to move to the Left by a majority of 52% in 2000, will find itself more perfectly free from the lies and obfuscations of the Right. The changes and progressive policies so ardently sought by the factions on the Left will begin to be realized. There will simply be no stopping it.

The alternatives to this is a further entrenchment of right-wing politics and policy in America and around the world. Make no mistake: this is a world-wide battle. The War on Terror is being used as a political tool bent on marginalizing anything even vaguely progressive on all points of the global compass, and it is a tool being wielded by America. 2004 stands as perhaps the last, best chance for Americans to take away control of the political agenda in this country from an extreme conservative minority whose views have little to do with the mainstream. Ideology is great fodder for debate, but is dust before this wind. Carve it on your tombstone for all the good it will do.

The time has come for tactics, pragmatism, and unity on the Left. Just ask the French – they had to face a Nazi on center stage because the Left could not unite against him. Imagine what the world may face by 2004 if that disunity continues, and shudder at the implications.

We cannot afford another debacle like 2000. We cannot afford another divided effort in 2004. We absolutely cannot afford, as a nation and a planet, a second term for George W. Bush. There will be more ChoicePoints, more media silence and skullduggery, and there will be the unavoidable juxtaposition between patriotism and the Republican Party. To overcome this, we must stand together. There is simply no alternative.

'We The People' Means You

A 14-year-old boy brings a pistol to school one day. The school is filled with the hustling bedlam between first and second period. Children move like cattle through the halls, carrying bags and books, passing through the dull repetition of routine that defines their daily scholastic existence. The routine is suddenly shattered as the boy stands in the doorway of a bathroom and begins to fire into the mass of people moving towards Biology or English or History class.

The sound of the pistol is deafening as it slaps off the institutional cement walls. Bodies spin and fall, blood sprays and flows, the air is spiced with the odor of gunpowder. Children scream and bolt for safety as the boy continues to fire with a cherubic smile splitting his face. Eventually he is subdued and arrested. Ambulances arrive on the heels of frantic parents. The television cameras devour it all from the parking lot and from helicopters hovering above the scene. Media representatives and politicians shake their heads and offer prayers. They say they are shocked.

This was Santee, California. I am certain that you watched this scene on your nightly news broadcast, on CNN, or read of it in the newspaper. Were you shocked? How long did you linger on the channel? Did you grab the remote and flip to MTV, a stock market report, ESPN, or a soap opera? How long did you wait before you changed the channel to something more palatable? Were you sickened? Did you think of your children or your friends? How long did the images of yet another school shooting stay in your mind? Did you write to your NRA-supporting congress person and president to voice your outrage? Did you wonder how Charlton Heston sleeps at night?

I can hardly blame you if you were not shocked by what happened in Santee. After all, a boy who decides to massacre other children in school with a gun has become routine in America. We have seen it in Arkansas, in Oklahoma, in too many other places. We saw it in Columbine High School, didn't we? It took 15 dead kids and teachers that time to create something that could even simulate shock among the populace. The president spoke of gun control. A million mothers marched on Washington, D.C. All the politicians and the media personalities said all the right things. Vigils were held and dirt was thrown over the caskets holding the dead. In the end, however, the status quo prevailed.

No effective gun laws were enacted. In their place, laws like California's Proposition 21 sailed through the vote to ensure that kids who kill kids will be treated like adults by the justice system after the shooting stops. The guns were safe, as were the politicians and the interest groups who support their pervasive presence in our society. The nation as a whole was compelled for a time, but eventually decided to see what was on the other TV station.

We are a nation of channel-changers. We no longer take an active interest in anything that causes discomfort or might require us to heave off the couch and do something. When the images of dead children flick across our screens, we turn to TBS to see if *Rocky IV* is playing again, because we love to associate with the blue-collar boxer who floors the Commie behemoth, thus proving America's righteous might. When we cheer him on as he batters the forces of evil into bleeding unconsciousness, we feel as if we are somehow participating. We have done our part. We are supporting good. The real blood, that sticky stuff staining the news, isn't worthy of attention. After all, we can't do anything about that.

One hundred channels of soothing television are the ultimate expression of choice. Our market-driven economy has given us unprecedented opportunity to decide what we will fill our eyes with. We can do the same with our video game machines and with the infinite pages on the Internet. These activities all involve one thing – sitting still somewhere, staring at a screen at realities contrived by others. We have become a nation of voyeurs, peering through keyholes at life lived by people that don't really exist. We live through these shadows, taking their emotions as our own, and become paralyzed by the very choice we equate with freedom.

Watching has come to mean taking action. We sit frozen in our chairs as we live through the deeds of others. We call ourselves righteous because we believe in what these imaginary people are doing, all the while doing nothing ourselves. And when it all gets too heavy, or if it requires thought beyond simple plot lines, we are free to change the channel. In the end, the vast majority of us decide to do exactly that. Shock doesn't even enter the equation.

We truly care about Dr Green's tumor on *ER*, but can't be bothered to listen to a debate about health care in America. We are worried about poor Matthew Perry's drug problems and whether it will affect the regular scheduling of *Friends*, but a conversation about the disastrous Drug War and the groundwork it laid for the constitutional perversions of the

PATRIOT Act will elicit a glazed look and a click over to Comedy Central. We love the president on *West Wing* and wish he could be our leader, but we don't make the connection that inferior men become president in real life when 100 million people refuse to vote. We laugh like hyenas at the political caricatures on *Saturday Night Live*, dimly unaware that the joke is on us.

Don't worry about this, though. You can't do anything about it. Besides, you have the American choice to ignore these problems, as you have ignored all the others. Pay it some lip-service, shake your head, and pretend to be shocked. There's always something better on another channel.

If these words leave you angry and disgusted, consider the story of Betty Ann Waters and her brother, Kenneth. In 1983, Kenneth was tried and convicted of murder despite his claims of innocence. He went to prison for a very long time. His sister, Betty Ann, did not accept the verdict. She was a high school dropout, a single mother of two children, one of the struggling faces we see every day who so often descend into despair.

Betty Ann Waters went out and got her high school equivalency degree. She worked nights and weekends and put herself through college. She worked nights and weekends to put herself through law school. She passed the bar exam and became her brother's lawyer. She started an investigation into his case, armed with the legal wisdom that she had lacked during his 1983 trial.

In the basement of the Massachusetts courthouse where her brother was convicted and sentenced, Betty Ann Waters found a long-forgotten box containing blood samples belonging to her brother. She had a DNA comparison done and it was revealed that her brother's DNA did not match the blood belonging to the murderer which was found at the scene.

Because of her work and dedication, because of her love, Kenneth walked out of prison and into the waiting arms of his mother and sister, a free man after over 18 years. This did not happen because of a miracle. It happened because Betty Ann Waters did not accept the injustice done to her brother and put her shoulder to the wheel. It took 18 years, but that wheel moved and true justice prevailed.

For those of us facing the daunting task of repairing the glaring ills of this nation and this world, it will serve us well to remember Kenneth and Betty Ann Waters. When your stomach sinks, when your shoulders sag, when your heart quails, when your mind tells you that there is no way in hell that you, one person, can do anything at all about the terrible noise coming from Washington, D.C., I task you to remember Kenneth and Betty Ann Waters. A man once said that if you gave him the right lever, he could move the whole world. For the Waters family, the lever was love, patience, and determination. It is not easy to shoulder the grindstone. But if you could have seen the look on Betty Ann's and Kenneth's faces, you'd know the effort was worth the price.

One of the hardest truths to face as a member of this American society is that change requires an enormous amount of time and effort. One cannot simply wish something into existence, even if that wish is for an idea or a reform that appears patently necessary. The seas are rising, the polar caps are retreating, the earth is warming, the coral reefs are dying, the air is filling with CO_2, the cities are choking on smog, the economy is falling apart, and 3,000 are dead from a terrorist attack. One must come to face the truth that, even when presented with such glaring catastrophes, it will likely require a lifetime of sweat to even scratch the surface of a solution.

We all know why. Who am I when compared to Enron and its influential millions? What are my resources? What is my capacity to do combat with such a monolithically wealthy foe? How can I possibly defeat those who profit wildly without care for the consequences? Where do I even begin?

The end result of this line of questioning is inevitable and disheartening. We lose interest, for who among us can climb Mt Everest? We cease to care, for caring becomes too painful when, despite our passion and our work, we know at the beginning that we are assured of failure. We become convinced of our inadequacy, of our powerlessness. We are tamed by the belief that one person truly cannot make a difference. We live and work and die and are buried burdened with the failure to act, despite the hard belief that any actions would have come to naught. We are broken very early, and we seldom heal.

The shattering of idealism happens during our youth, somewhere in the gulf between seeing the need for change and understanding what bringing that change requires. No one is better equipped to expose an injustice than a teenager. They are pure of mind and spirit and have yet to face the bruising compromises that mark the path to adulthood. From this plateau of purity they can see far and are not yet poisoned by the leaching of confidence in the very idea of change.

Teenagers are, however, even more powerless than the rest of us. They stew in the cauldron of adolescence, outraged by the world but unable to do much of anything about it. Even the strongest youth eventually pulls the plug sooner or later. It is simply too painful to care so much while being capable of so little. Thus, when they finally reach a place where they can actually accomplish something, they are finished with the thought of even trying.

This is a generalization, to be sure. There are legions of people in America who did not disconnect, who rise every day and wage the fight for change, who have not suffered the final crisis. But these people are vastly out-numbered by those who have died on the road to Damascus.

The world is as it is today because so many have lost the belief that they are in fact the heart and soul of this country, that in their combined strength they can rout utterly the forces that cage us, and steal our rights and our natural legacy. So much evil happens in broad daylight and is ignored with a shrug. This is the way it is. Who am I to think I can change it?

If I have painted here a portrait in colors of utter bleakness and despair, it is because we must recognize our common plight. Before change can happen on a national scale, or on a global scale, it must happen in the hearts and minds of individuals. We must never, ever surrender to the belief that we are powerless. If we do so, we are already defeated.

We must wake with the knowledge that we will certainly fail in our quest, yet we must square our shoulders and meet the day and our duty, for to do less is to admit that what is happening now in our country and our world is acceptable. Silence equals consent. Freedom begins when we say, 'No.'

There are too many days that have passed when I succumbed to the siren song of that silent complicity. I look out at a world that has been trained to never look beyond personal need. I see a lion named The American People that has been brought to heel because it believes it has no claws, no fangs, no strength of heart and soul. I have passed days when the very thought of awakening that great beast to its potential stills me, for I know the strength and guile of its trainer.

I have a memory that always stays with me. That memory is of exploring a cave out in South Dakota. In the center of that dark cavern was a rock with a deep depression dug into its core. The cave guide told me that the depression was created by drops of water falling from the ceiling high above. The drops fell about once a day, and had been doing so for thousands of years. Over time, the unyielding stone had been worn away.

I think of the weakness of water against the strength of rock, and I consider which had prevailed.

I am a teacher. I tend the flame of youth. I am tasked with more than the rote delivery of Shakespeare, vocabulary, grammar, and history. I am tasked with the duty of making teenagers care about the status of their minds and hearts. It is my duty to remind them, every day, that their claws and fangs, while small, are sharp and will become sharper still. I am burdened with the assignment of ensuring that they do not disconnect. I am warmed by the knowledge that, thus far, I have succeeded far more often than I have failed.

I am the drop of water falling from that high ceiling.

At dawn, the teachers rise. They go forth in hope, and hold high by their own personal example the belief that to care is to succeed. They toil against stony indifference, they wear away the rock one drip at a time. It does not matter that their political views do not always meld. In the end, it matters only that they rise.

If you need a hero, an example to emulate, look to my compatriots. They are the finest example of patience and endurance you will ever need to find. They care, and thus they prevail.

We are out here, we happy few. When you despair, remember us. When you wish to surrender, remember us. When you cannot imagine a way in which your voice or your desire for change will ever make a difference, remember us. We move out into the world, one drip at a time, and we make change with squared shoulders and hope ever on our lips. We say to you, tamed lion, that caring is an act of defiance which you are still capable of. Remember this at dawn when you rise.

I am not Robert Kennedy. I was not born to a family of American political royalty, guaranteeing that my voice be heard when I choose to speak. I have to spend a good deal of my time working, or sleeping in preparation for work, in order to keep the lights on and have food. I have very little in the way of disposable income.

Robert Kennedy said that one person could make a difference. From his Olympian height, he looked down upon all of us and saw individuals who could cut a swath through the injustice in the world, if only we would rouse ourselves. Down here on the ground, I stare up at Robert's marble bust on that mountain and think, 'Easy for you to say.'

There is so very much I want to do, and I am mortally sure that this nation is literally teeming with those who share my desire for action. But we work. We raise kids. We take care of aging parents. Speaking bluntly, we bust our asses all week long for that paycheck and for the few precious weekend hours that more often than not are spent sleeping, drinking, shopping, or watching sports on the television.

It takes a massive amount of one's mental capacities to do the mundane day-to-day activities that are required of the average American, if that American wishes to eat, be clothed, and live inside of doors. It is exhausting. There is that great line from the head of the Trade Services

Union about the 'boom' years of Clinton's administration: 'There have been eight million new jobs created, and I've got three of them.'

Where, then, do we find that space and time and energy needed to heal the wounds we see gaping in the body and soul of our nation? They are right there in front of us, red and bleeding, crying out for someone to do something. Too many of us, sadly, shoulder our various burdens and turn away with a prayer on our lips that somebody with the time will come along and address things.

I know a way for all of us to climb up on that Olympian perch with Robert. I know a way we can make that difference. It requires sacrifice from each of us, and thus is worthy of being called a Movement. It can be something you do every moment of the day if you do it right. If enough of us do this thing, and do it well, and do it faithfully, and turn others towards it, we will bring about such a massive change as has not been seen in this nation since the shot heard 'round the world.

Like so many great ideas and movements, this one is simplicity itself. Just boycott everything.

Take public transportation to work, or walk to the corner store, or figure out a way to leave your car in the garage for the weekend. If you own an SUV, sell it. If you are in the market for a car, look into the gas/electric hybrids that are available. Thus, you boycott the petroleum companies that rape our planet, soil our air, and dictate the foreign policy that makes our current War on Terror such a disastrous fraud. Recent television ads have claimed that drugs fund terrorists. This may well be true. But funding for terrorism is found in a far more common moment – the moment when you step on the accelerator in your gas-guzzling 12-miles-to-the-gallon behemoth automobile. When you tank up, where do you think that money is going?

Make your own coffee or buy your morning cup of brew from the mom 'n' pop joint you always walk by on your way to Starbucks or Dunkin' Donuts. Sure, it's a crummy brew. But you are boycotting corporate hegemony.

Turn off the God damned television. While it is on you are a vapid receptacle for all of the invasive nonsense that is our sad and deranged estate. By simply boycotting television, you are saying 'No' to all the advertisers and corporate hucksters and infotainment peddlers disguised as journalists who have sold us all down the river. If you are a news junkie, satisfy your jones with the dozens of print newspapers available on the Internet.

Go out this weekend without makeup, and do not purchase any. The cosmetics industry has perpetuated a massive crime against women by selling them a destructive myth of beauty that is utterly unattainable for 99% of human females. The vicious cycle of self-hatred begins at a very young age for women, brought on by images proffered by the cosmetics industry in the pages of glossy magazines. Do not allow one of your hard-earned dollars to line the pockets of those who profit by telling you that you are not beautiful enough.

Be aware of your purchases in the grocery store. Buy locally grown foods whenever possible. Using the remarkable research tools of the Internet, find out which agribusinesses are selling what and where. If you do not like what those massive corporations are doing, do not buy their products.

Turn off the lights. Live without air conditioning whenever you can. Make a project out of trimming your electricity bill as much as you can.

You are expected to be a consumer. Thus, you wear the yoke. Boycott the very idea. Take your yoke and plow a new field. Be mindful of that money you have so vigorously earned, and understand that when you buy gasoline or leave the lights on when you're not in the room, you enrich those whom you lust to defy and bring low. You work against yourself.

Boycott the idea that matters are beyond your control. They are not. This is capitalism, Jack. You have to play by the rules if you're going to carry the day. We are a nation of consumers, and this corporate control of our politics and our future is within our grasp to overthrow. We cannot vote them out, so we must nickel and dime them out. As long as we continue to enrich those who enslave us, all our hollering and marching will come to nothing. We are feeding ourselves to the beast.

Boycott everything. If you are a consumer, then so be it. But be a damned savvy consumer. Give not one shiny penny to those whom you would otherwise oppose. Figure out what you are spending your money on. You may fancy yourself as someone who is tuned into politics. Become tuned into your *alter ego*, the consumer you. Pay attention to where you spend your money.

The stakes in our democracy have been raised. No longer does 'one person, one vote' carry the day. We are surrounded by interests who sup upon our paychecks through our consumption of their goods. They take that money and fund politicians whom we abhor, they push policies that poison and kill us, they bankroll actions with our money that we would spend our lives opposing. This is another vicious cycle, one I am sure was never envisioned by the Framers.

We have in our wallets the power to break that cycle, and bring these dogs to heel.

This Movement will take sacrifice. A little bit here and there. Trim the lusher corners of your life. Discover some simplicity, a rare commodity indeed, one that is not sold in the aisles of Wal-Mart. If, in this simplicity, you discover that you have the time and energy and money to become more politically active, then so much the better. Boycott everything. Tell your friends. Begin to make that difference. I am sure Robert would approve.

The context for all this comes, of course, in the presence of the funeral shroud. The events of September 11 have been described in a number of ways. It has been called another Pearl Harbor. It has been called an act of war. It has been called a crime.

The new reality that has settled in since the attack has likewise been described in various ways. We have heard the burgeoning conflict described as a 'Crusade.' We have heard it explained as a battle against good and evil. Our society has been called a changed one, where rights are less important than safety.

Ask my mother what name to bestow upon everything that has happened, however, and she will use a term that has probably been in my family since the earliest Irish immigrants in my line beheld the Statue of Liberty for the first time. She would call it a gut-check.

Integrity has been described as the quality of the actions one takes when no one is looking. My mother worked to instill this lesson in me from the beginning of my life. Living according to that simple code has been a difficult struggle, one that virtually everyone can relate to in some form or another.

A gut-check, in my family, is the moment of deliberation when you decide what to think or do in the aftermath of a calamity or moral dilemma. That moment can last hours, days or weeks if need be. A gut-check is a test; if you pass it, it allows you to look into a mirror without fearing what you will see reflected in your eyes.

The attack upon New York City, upon Washington, D.C., upon every civilian and soldier, upon the entire country, is unquestionably the most frightening and unnerving and important gut-check this nation has ever faced. Everything depends upon our reaction to this.

If we, as ordinary citizens, are to gauge our own reaction, it is helpful to review how those visible in our society have reacted. We may measure ourselves by them.

Jerry Falwell failed the test in spectacular fashion. His first instinct was to turn upon those whose lifestyle or politics he finds distasteful and subject them to a withering verbal assault. In essence, he blamed his fellow Americans for the horror visited upon us. I am sure the gay New York City firefighters who rode Tower Two down to dusty death would have an opinion on this. Sadly, they have no voice now. Therein lies the essence of Falwell's failure.

The aforementioned firefighters, along with their comrades and those who answered the call within the New York City police and disaster rescue departments, cannot be lionized enough. Among the dead and the living within their ranks walks the pride of a nation. We hold them all in the light. In this test of tests, these men and women pass with all the flying colors of the rainbow.

Those within our nation who have turned their anger and fear upon our Muslim citizens have failed the test in truly bloody fashion. Falwell's attack was nauseating, to be sure, but in the end was only words. Fists, clubs, spittle, vitriol, and gunfire have rained down upon Americans who share cultural connections with those who attacked us. The immigrant is the easiest to blame, and doing so has been a wretched American parlor game passed from generation to generation like a malignant gene. Those who do this shame us all.

To our great misfortune, the entity most able to inform and heal has been once again perverted to more insidious purposes. The news-providing wing of the American media establishment has allowed coverage of this event to merely skim the surface of an important topic, and has likewise kept all but the narrowest of viewpoints from disbursement to the American public. The news outlets have told us the attack against us came because our enemies hate our freedoms. No more dangerous an obfuscation could be foisted.

Certainly, within the fundamentalist Islamic community, there are cultural gulfs. Imams of that wing of the Islamic faith deplore our ability to speak anything but orthodoxy. The freedoms American women enjoy jar against the traditions espoused by the Taliban and other fundamentalist sects.

This cultural divide is only a small part of the explanation for Tuesday, September 11 and does not do just service to the large majority within Islam who deplore the attacks. The rest of the truth lies in our long and often disreputable involvement in those regions, for purposes that are as simple as the numbers on the sign above your local gas station.

This nation must reexamine our priorities and our history, for we have at last been taught the horrible lesson that actions have consequences. The actions of tomorrow, under these new circumstances, do not escape this immutable law. The media could and should be assisting in this, but do not. They hide history behind rhetoric, dooming us to repeat what has befallen us.

Because the media has failed this test, it falls to the common citizens to seek that information and introspection for themselves. Perhaps the most common reaction to these attacks has been, 'My God, why did this happen?' The information is out there. This is but one aspect of the gut-check we as citizens face.

With only a fraction exempted, it can be said that the great body of the American citizenry have passed the test, and passed it well. We hold each other close. We gave so much money, food, and supplies that it became difficult for those collecting it to know what to do with it. They were over-whelmed with generosity.

Opportunistic politicians took advantage in the immediate aftermath of this crisis by wrapping new and fiscally dangerous tax-cuts in the flag, describing what would be yet another windfall for the rich as something desperately required for national and economic security. Some attempted to attach to the Defense Appropriations bill a rider that would open the Alaskan National Wildlife Reserve to plunder by the petroleum industry.

Actions like these were taken in stealth. This is still America, and such important decisions must be done before the ears and minds of the American people. Not everything changed, and actions that favor the few over the many should never have been advantageously attempted by leaders who know we were necessarily distracted.

Those among our leadership who stampede to restrict and shred our personal American liberties deserve loud condemnation. Many aspects of our American life must change in order to secure ourselves from further catastrophes, to be sure. This is not an excuse to recreate America into a fearful totalitarian state, something that appears to be happening one drip at a time. If we fall into this trap, those who attack us win, even if we should destroy them all.

At the end of the day, all of the confused, fearful, and greed-influenced failures described above must be laid at the feet of George W. Bush. As the plaque that once sat upon his desk clearly states, the buck stops there. Has he gone through a gut-check? Have we seen evidence to suggest this? No.

Over and over, he told us that we were attacked because our freedoms and liberties are hated, reinforcing the lie. This was a failure, a shout into our national echo chamber that resonates loudly, drowning out truths that require a full and complete airing.

Perhaps the greatest failure of Mr Bush has been to challenge other nations in such a bellicose manner. They are either with us or against us, we are told. Machiavelli spoke of this long ago and said that such a challenge inevitably causes all to be against the challenger. This ham-fisted diplomacy carries none of the delicacy required to face the threat.

This is not a conventional war. It will be a struggle whose ultimate outcome will be based upon diplomacy and the mutual sharing of information. Many nations will not do this at gunpoint. We lose possible sources of information that could aid us with our threats.

This leads to the last aspect of the test we as Americans face in this time of trial. It has been made quite clear in a variety of ways that dissent at this time is nearly tantamount to treason. Disagree with the leadership, disagree with Bush, and you are herded into the same corner with the terrorists. Nothing could be further from fact, and nothing could be more unhealthy to our nation. Now more than ever, the simple fact that the citizens are ultimately the essence of the government comes into play. We The People, that parchment reads.

If we dissent, we must speak. If we see a better way, we must speak. If we are being taken down a path dangerous to all we hold dear, we must speak. If we hear things that are not true, or see leaders who seek to hide the truth, we must speak to set the record straight. We have been told to keep to our American way as much as we can. We are told to spend money as an aid to our wounded economy. We are told to go out into our cities and sports arenas, juicy targets all, and live our lives with as much normalcy as possible.

In exactly the same vigorous manner, we must nurture and tend that flame of dissent, for it is the fire that first forged America and is the fire that has kept us warm for generations. Dissent is our birthright. Forfeit it and we forfeit everything.

Finally, we must not give in to our fears. Fear begets vengeance, and vengeance is a river of blood that has no end. We look forward to a day of justice, in the name of the lost. Justice, however, cannot be revenge. This, perhaps, is the most pressing aspect of the test. The status of our very souls are on the line.

I do not come to these assessments lightly, for I have faced my own gut-check.

One Thursday night a few days after September 11, I heard of a threat to my home city of Boston. The existence of that threat was confirmed Friday morning – Attorney-General Ashcroft had telephoned Boston mayor Thomas Menino and informed him that credible evidence was in hand describing a potential attack on the city, scheduled for the coming Saturday. I was faced with a decision. I could stay in the city with my loved ones, and have faith in those who defend it. Or I could leave with my loved ones, seek safety in distance, and wait to see what transpired. Within this decision lived so many of the dilemmas described above – fear, freedom, integrity, and measured response to a threat among them.

I remembered my years in San Francisco. Each day I went to work in offices housed high in skyscrapers. The threat of earthquake was ever-present, and images of 1906 loomed large. Despite this, my life continued. I went to work each day, walked passed buildings made of glass, and traveled across bridges whose structural strength was uncertain. I did this because I refused to live in fear.

If someone had told me that an earthquake was almost definitely coming tomorrow, however, I would not have planted myself on Market Street with my middle finger pointed at the ground. I would have left, sought safety, and not thought twice about it.

So it was the next Friday night, when I found myself in a Jeep with my people traveling west on Route 2. I spent the next night and day in New Hampshire, watching the news and slowly becoming convinced that the reports of danger had been badly overblown.

The Attorney-General, it seems, received a poorly translated bit of intelligence pointing a bloody finger at Boston. He called with the warning before consulting other sources, and the brushfire began. I am heartened that he is so ready to respond to threats, but am disturbed that such dire news was launched before due consideration. The Jose Padilla dirty-nuke threat was released months later in a similarly slipshod fashion, further eroding my threadbare confidence in the Top Cop.

I refuse to regret the fact that I sought shelter for myself and my family. Nevertheless, I will not forget watching the skyline of Boston recede into obscurity in my rear-view mirror that Friday night. I still wrestle with the fear that leaving Boston was an act of cowardice, that I too was cutting and running. I fear that I ceded a small victory to those who attacked us.

I am not finished with my gut-check, and my actions on that Friday are proof of this. There is much of my course I do not yet know. So it is with many of us.

I take courage in my test from something I saw while in New Hampshire. I walked the streets of Keene that day and came upon the town square. There were gathered about 20 people, who faced the traffic with American flags and signs which read, simply, 'Peace.' They had completed their gut-check and were acting upon principles invigorated by the test. They did not want bloodshed and they did not want war. They had not fallen into the awful quagmire that is the desire for vengeance.

Whether you agree or disagree with those people from Keene, you must respect them. They have reached a place we all must seek. They stood upon firm ground, and they spoke and acted without fear. They passed the test.

Self-assessment is only one part of the deal. After deciding to act, you must decide whom to act upon. All of America has been acted upon by a particularly virulent breed of conservative Republican for the last ten years. They are a great place to start, because they happen to control the conversation at this point. There are myriad reasons for this, but there is no getting around the fact. Bluntly, these are the people we must fight tooth and nail if we are to get anything done.

Indulge my desire to offer a brief history lesson. In 1988, in a hotel lobby near the New Orleans-hosted Republican National Convention, Tom DeLay gave a press conference to defend the military service record of George Herbert Walker Bush's vice presidential pick, J. Danforth Quayle. The press had begun to auger in on the fact that Quayle had apparently used family influence to avoid serving in the Vietnam War, and had instead defended the bucolic splendor of Indiana from being overrun by the Cong as a member of the National Guard.

DeLay did not bring up the awful confusion of those days. He did not speak of fear, nor did he mention loopholes created by influential family connections. Instead, he offered what could go down as perhaps the most novel excuse for draft-dodging ever spouted by an American in the entire history of the nation. Mr Quayle was prevented from military service, claimed DeLay, because of all the minorities who had volunteered ahead of him. All the spots were gone when patriots like Quayle sought to serve, taken by ethnics seeking the excellent pay to be found in a life within the armed services.

The members of the press who assembled to hear this remarkable explanation did not know that Mr DeLay felt the slings and arrows raining down on Quayle in a most personal way. DeLay came of service age in 1970, but somehow found his way into the bug-killing business instead. The assumption that the communist-killing business had no purchase within him, however, was put to rest in that lobby. DeLay and Quayle wanted to serve, but the Negroes were just too fast for them. Never mind that the *Houston Post* in 1988 printed a different excuse – DeLay avoided enlisting at the urging of his wife, yet another amazing dodge. For guys like Tom, it's always about the minorities at the head of the line.

If this is the first time you have heard this tale, do not castigate yourself for failing to pay attention. You did not know this because you never heard it repeated *ad nauseam* on a nationally syndicated radio show after DeLay became the Republican Majority Whip in the House. You did not know this because no senator or congress person on the Left took to the TV talking-head circuit to pound this nail in front of every camera they could find. You did not know this because no syndicated liberal columnist mentioned it on a weekly basis in every newspaper from sea to shining sea.

You did not know this because it was a sword left in its scabbard. If the situation were reversed and a Democrat had dared uttered such a farcical excuse, rest assured that the sword would have been drawn and would have found meat to cleave. Yet this rhetorical bumper crop given into the hands of Democrats has gone unreaped for 14 years, repeated only in the smallest of circles and never given the prime-time airing it deserves.

In this time of darkness and war, there has been much chest-thumping from some conservatives regarding the true definition of patriotism. When senators like Tom Daschle and John Kerry stand upon their constitutional duties and ask where this apparently rudderless war is headed, when they seek a definition of victory, when they wonder why Osama bin Laden has eluded capture, they are dunned as traitors by Republicans who claim to occupy the high moral ground.

John Kerry served in Vietnam. He earned a Silver Star, a Bronze Star, and was three times awarded the Purple Heart for wounds received in battle. His detractors – Trent Lott, Dick Cheney, Dick Armey, George W. Bush, to name a few – avoided service in that conflict through deferments and powerful family contacts. There is ample evidence that Bush himself didn't bother to show up for the final year of his stint guarding the coastline of Texas from Viet Cong invasion. That these men dare impugn the patriotism and honor of a man like John Kerry bends the definition of hypocrisy into bold new shapes.

Do not abuse yourself if some of this information is new to you. Do not let the fact that George W. Bush, Dick Armey, Dick Cheney, Bill Bennett, Pat Buchanan, Newt Gingrich, Tom DeLay, Phil Gramm, Jack Kemp, Dan Quayle, Trent Lott, Pat Robertson, Ken Starr, and George Will all managed to evade military duty, even if many of these men later lambasted Bill Clinton for the same offense. How could you know? These bullets were left mostly unfired in the last ten years of American political debate.

There is a war being fought across what Kerouac called the bulge of America. Like any war, it requires funding. Such has been provided to ideological conservatives by men like Richard Mellon Scaife, heir to the Mellon Bank fortune. Scaife has spent upwards of $300 million funding right-wing newspapers and think tanks, and was the principal source of funding for those engaged in the jihad against Bill Clinton.

Scaife is motivated by a deep and resounding hatred of all things Left, a hate that bloomed during the upheaval of the 1960s. In many ways, his influence within conservative circles today is a reminder that the bloody business of that bygone era is not yet finished. Scaife is still fighting the protesters who demanded civil rights and stood against the Vietnam War. The fact that many of his contemporary conservative avatars dodged service in that conflict is merely an accent in the hypocrisy which serves as the score to this decades-old battle.

Scaife's politics found purchase within the hearts of those ideological conservatives who conspired to take over the Republican Party in the wake of Barry Goldwater's defeat in 1964. By 1980 they had a champion in Ronald Reagan and the days of a moderate GOP were done. The conservative world became one where the rainbow shone only in black and white, where anyone not 100% dedicated to any cause that sought to engage communism, no matter how nefarious, was open to charges of treason.

The fall of the Soviet Union heralded a time of crisis among ideological conservative ranks. There was no longer an Evil Empire, no great enemy abroad to fight tooth and nail. That which defined this cadre had ceased to exist. Knives still drawn, these conservatives sought a new enemy. They found one soon enough. They found the American Left.

It began with the thwarting of Robert Bork's nomination to the Supreme Court and bloomed into a full-fledged Movement when Clarence Thomas faced a similar challenge. An army of conservatives, funded by men like Scaife, came to the conclusion that fighting fair was no longer an option. They would do whatever was necessary, distort whatever facts they could find, shriek whatever half-truth was available, all the while ignoring the flagrant hypocrisy represented by the yawning chasm between their words and their deeds, to further their political agenda and subvert the standing of any liberal within sight.

Consider the case of Rush Limbaugh, whose conservative radio show went national in 1988. Twice divorced with a reputation for extramarital dalliances, an avoider of church, Limbaugh nevertheless parlayed a career that began in comedy into a truly formidable force in American politics. Limbaugh, another victim of minority crowding in the lines headed for

Vietnam, presents himself as the moral voice for the nation. He has lied many times along the way, once claiming that no one was indicted in the Iran/Contra scandal (there were 14 indictments), and once stating that the Democratically controlled Congress had failed to support President Bush during the Gulf War (both Houses backed the president in the conflict).

Rush would be foolish if he were not so powerful – millions of people listen to his show daily on 450 different stations – and if weighty office-holders like Newt Gingrich (who, it should be noted, has smoked marijuana, dodged the Vietnam draft, and divorced his wife while she lay sick in bed with cancer) had not stolen pages from his playbook. Rush, Gingrich, and the cavalcade of conservative assassins who pollute the politics of the country do so from no moral high ground, but from a desire to win at any cost.

Gingrich, for example, made a point through his political action committee (GOPAC) to disseminate among the ranks of fellow conservatives an action memo instructing them to associate liberals with words like 'stupid,' 'corrupt,' 'anti-family,' and 'traitor.' Someone once said that politics was the art of compromise. In this war, such thoughts were left by the side of the road with the cigarette butts. Scaife, Limbaugh, Gingrich, and the rest of the officers in this conservative army have no use for compromise.

This war has been waged against the Left for well over a decade. Concepts such as environmentalism, women's rights, racial equality, and even the good use of government in the lives of the people have been denigrated almost unto dust. These ideas have not suffered because they are poor ideas in and of themselves; they have suffered because they are equated with liberals, and are therefore considered cannon fodder in this war. This makes the fight pertinent to the lives of every breathing American, because ideas that would vastly improve this American life are being gutted in a partisan war that has little to do with what is best for the people. It has become all about power, plain and simple.

In this fight, liberals have been woefully inadequate in pressing their side. Perhaps the Left considers itself above such prurient tactics. Perhaps the Left is too interested in an intellectual debate of the facts and cannot fathom an enemy that uses fact the way a cat uses litter. Simply blaming a corporate/conservative media is not sufficient; it took Limbaugh 14 years to gain his current standing. He got it because he let the sword find meat and did not fear the knife-fighting required of modern politics. There is a lesson here about media appetites the Left could well learn from.

America suffered a terrible blow on September 11, one that came after these same conservatives spent eight years cutting the legs out from under a sitting president in a $70 million effort that spent Federal energy better used in other areas. These same conservatives, after gaining power in an election that could be called questionable at best, an election in which they once again stooped to mob action and fact distortion to gain an edge against liberal rivals who did not seem to have the stomach for a fight, would now use the horror of September 11 to exterminate the standing of the American liberal for all time.

Given all that is at stake, the time has come for the American Left to rise up and finally, finally, engage in this war with full and complete commitment. For too long the Left has sought the intellectual high ground and has left the trenches to those who care little for well-crafted arguments. In ten short years, the Left has lost a generation's worth of ground. It must be taken back.

Never let a man like Tom DeLay get away with the lame excuses he offered for his absence during the Vietnam conflict, for it was proven that he will capitalize on similar actions taken by a Democrat for gain and be damned to the contradictions. Never let a mouthpiece like Limbaugh pretend to be the voice of morality in America when his lifestyle proves him a hypocrite. Never let a man like George W. Bush speak of patriotism while he pushes a conservative agenda cloaked in the fog of an ill-defined war.

If you have a liberal bone in your body, then you have a dog in this fight. These people, who have spent the last ten years shattering every rule of decency and truth in an effort to gain power for the sake of power itself, and to avenge grudges held since the days of Abbe Hoffman and Medgar Evers, cannot be trusted to shepherd this country through this time of trial. There is too much at stake for people of such thin moral fiber to be allowed to run unchecked anymore.

Scream at the top of your lungs until they burst. The soul of this nation is at stake, the culture war continues unabated, and it is time for the Left to storm the battlements. It is past time. If you are cowed by tall presidential ratings, you are of no use. If you have no stomach for a fight, you further the causes you despise. If you cannot take joy in the sound of a sword striking meat and drawing blood, step aside.

Believe that a liberal government can defend this nation while helping its citizens. Believe that a liberal president can be strong and sound. Believe that liberal policies foster a healthy economy. Believe these things because they are true. Believe that the conservatives who would call such truths lies do so for no other reason than to grasp, maintain, and augment their power, for this is true as well.

Let the word go forth in this time and place that there are some things worth fighting for. The Right has known this for years and has capitalized on it to our common woe. Unless we do the same, we shall indeed earn the title of traitor.

I speak of these things because I have made a personal decision to engage in this fight. I did so one afternoon while climbing to the summit of a bald bulb of a hill called Mt Monadnock, which rises incongruously from the level plains of southern New Hampshire. The day was bright and clear with little wind, a perfect day for a hike. I reached the top in under two hours and paused to absorb the view. New England lay before me to all points on the compass, brown and prepared for winter. Here and there were lakes and houses. In the distance something burned, sending a column of smoke into the air.

The hard blue November sky was stitched with white lines that crossed each other in every direction, as if a deranged skywriter had decided to paint the air repeatedly with the letter 'A.' It took me a moment to understand what I was seeing: contrails from combat aircraft arriving and departing from various bases across the region. Even here, some 4,000 feet above the world, the troubles that consume us hover above, close enough to touch.

The image was fitting. Once upon a time this nation seemed above the world, of it but beyond its scalding touch. We were protected by two oceans, vast treasure, armed guardians, and thousands of atom-tipped missiles buried in the earth. One day the sky fell in, and we found ourselves somewhere we had not been for generations. We found ourselves in the middle of things. We found ourselves to be vulnerable.

A fundamental shift of comprehension has been fermenting within the minds of American citizens since September 11. All of a sudden, the realization that each and every citizen has a stake in the actions and policies of this country has begun to take root. Simply, if justice fails, the common folk become targets. If economic privation goes unchecked, the common folk become targets. If extremism, American or otherwise, achieves too much power, the common folk become targets.

If a liberal, progressive agenda is to achieve purchase in today's climate, this basic truth must be seized upon and repeated over and over again. The fellow who only reads the sports page, who hasn't voted for 20 years, or who votes Republican because he likes his tax-cut, needs to have a finger thrust into his face. He needs to be made to understand that the next intelligence failure, the next proxy war, the next arms deal, the next corporate bailout, could result in his shattered corpse lying in the dust.

This is brutal and cruel. It is also the truth. We are all on the firing line. We are the targets in this war. There are reasons for this that have nothing to do with people who hate our freedoms.

This is the most dangerous idea in the world for those currently in power in America. It is an idea that has taken a slow burn through the populace. If it flares alight, people will not shop. They will not tolerate excessive tax-cuts for financially healthy corporations. They will demand solutions that do not involve carpet-bombing with B-52s. They will not stand for the dissolution of their constitutional rights. In short, they will demand actions that will reap actual results, instead of actions that give only the illusion of progress. They will want to move forward as progressives instead of backwards as conservatives. They will know that their very survival depends upon it.

Liberals and progressives must seize this time, pour kerosene on that slowly burning idea until it explodes into a pyre upon which will burn all of the sad, sorry, broken policies that brought us to this house of woe.

But who is to do it?

It has become an article of faith since January 20, 2001 that the Democratic chieftains who walk the halls of power in Washington, D.C. cannot be trusted to fight for this agenda. When the result of the scandalous 2000 election was ratified in Congress, only the Black Caucus had the courage to turn their backs in protest. When religious extremist John Ashcroft stood for nomination as Attorney-General, no true opposition was offered.

Today, as the First, Fourth, Sixth and Thirteenth Amendments to the Constitution are disposed of, as Posse Comitatus is replaced by clandestine military tribunals that know no civil authority, the Democrats stand almost completely silent. Only the timely defection of Senator James Jeffords temporarily allowed Democrats to thwart Republican thrusts into the Federal larder and our environmental inheritance. Had Jeffords not jumped, there would have been no stopping the neo-conservatives within the GOP.

Some Democratic senators worked night and day to craft the abominable PATRIOT Anti-Terrorism bill, possibly the most invasive bit of work to come out of Washington since Lincoln suspended habeas corpus. Perhaps they believed that we must destroy freedom in order to save it, but it is more likely that they succumbed to political cowardice and went along for the ride to ensure a safe trip to the primaries in 2004.

On any other day, the anthrax sent to Senators Daschle and Leahy would be called assassination attempts. Today, these attacks are shrouded in the threatening veil of international terrorism, despite the fact that they almost certainly originated from the Ashcroftian wing of the American Right. Even after this most dire of threats, the Democrats stood mute. For months after September 11, Bush enjoyed approval ratings that would make Jesus Christ Himself blush, a formidable obstacle for Democrats who may have felt in their guts that the nation is on the road to Hell. Their timidity is our catastrophe.

Thus, it falls to us. We must become the calcium in the withered Democratic backbone, and we must do it now.

Writing to these people is useless. Letters to the editor go unread. Emailing like-minded friends amounts to political masturbation. We are a people made too comfortable by pleasant arguments and debates. The day has arrived where action is demanded, else all that happens from here on out can be placed at our own feet. The document in question says We The People for a good reason.

Take heed of conservative successes. They ran for state representative positions, took over school boards, got jobs in local government and basically stormed the bulwarks of the Republican Party from the bottom of the walls. It took ten years, but they did it, and the presidency of George W. Bush is but one reward they have reaped by their labors. The media is awash with the conservative viewpoint because they commandeered the dialogue after years of grass-roots work. This is another reward, one that ensures their continued success.

To overcome this, we must become it.

The only reason the Democrats moved to the Right is because of the aforementioned conservative grass-roots revolution. The Party had nothing to counteract the surge of conservatism that blasted through Washington with Gingrich in 1994, no shock troops of their own, so they swung rightward in order to survive. Now, the Parties are slowly becoming indistinguishable. They are not yet there, no matter what Ralph Nader says, but they are on their way and this can not be denied.

It has been argued that true progressives will never find a home in the Democratic Party, because it has sold too much of its soul in a hard tack to the right born of defensive strategy and political expediency. This leaves two alternatives: either abandon the Party completely or roll up some sleeves and clean out the Augean stables.

Despite its flaws, the Democratic Party is the best tool we have available for the propagation of the liberal, progressive agenda. The Party has faithful followers in every state and unconquerable strongholds on both coasts. The Democratic political machine stands in every county in every state in the Union. There are doubtless men and women in the House of Representatives who would savor the chance to act upon principle instead of from a core of self-defense, a chance we can give them if we get to work now.

The time has come to invade this Party, to storm it from the ground up. The Democratic Party can again become an effective voice for the people, as the Republican Party has become a bastion of ultra-conservatism, if American progressives take it over from pillar to post. If we take back the Party, if we change the dialogue coming from the media through the brute reality of our strident and unyielding voices, if we tend and nurture that flame of new comprehension blazing in every American breast, we can achieve all that our dreams have whispered.

Most within the Party will welcome this, I believe. Those who do not can be reminded of the wisdom spoken by an old politico named James H. Rowe: 'The old bulls never quit until the young bulls run them out.'

Master the issues. Walk down to your local Democratic Party office and find work. Don't let anyone there tell you they have nothing for you. Take as much responsibility as you can and make it your office. Start a local Democratic Party club and beat your local officers over the head with it if they don't let you in.

Run for positions on your school board, or within your local government, or stand for election to your state congress. If you cannot do these things, find someone who is doing them and dedicate your energies to their success. Run the old bulls out and harness the young bulls to plow new fields. Make the Party a home for everyone who knows in their heart that things must change in this country before the targets can be stripped from our backs.

It will take time and patience. The target is 2004. Don't look to the Oval Office, for working from the top down has bred a dizzying array of recent failures. Go from the ground up, one step at a time.

What a paradise we can make of this world if given the chance. The chance will not come on its own. We must make it, take it, demand it, fight for it tooth and nail.

The next question, of course, is simple: What should you be working towards? What are the goals we need to gain? Where shall we direct our energies? It is not enough to complain. If we cannot offer solutions to that which we would deride, we are useless.

The attacks of September 11 were the defining events within a year that saw so very much go wrong. The reaction of the current administration has exacerbated the fallout from that traumatic day to such an incredible degree that one is forced to wonder if the terrorists have not already won this undeclared war. This is not the same America that saw the dawn on September 10, a fact that is sure to bring smiles to the faces of Al Qaeda warriors from horizon to horizon.

So be it. The past cannot be changed. The future, however, is another matter.

The world was born again by fire on the morning of September 11, 2001. In its wake lies the tattered remains of a nation that once was considered a beacon of freedom that illuminated the world. We are tasked to live on in the wreckage and are faced with a defining realization: at the bottom, the passivity of the American people invited the catastrophes of 2001. We were unconcerned, unprepared, disinformed, disinterested, willfully blind.

September 11 jarred us into comprehending a fundamental truth that had for too long been obscured. In the final analysis, each and every American has a personal stake in the dispensation and cultivation of true justice and equality within our borders and around the world. When there is economic disenfranchisement, grinding poverty, political suppression, and abridged freedom, we American civilians become the targets of murderous hate and violence. Religiously extremist fundamentalism breeds like a virus in such circumstances, both here and abroad, and is the last bastion of the desperate and the disenfranchised.

If we are to survive and flourish in this brave new world, we must acknowledge the hand we have played in the flourishing of these circumstances. Our addiction to oil, our propensity for diplomatic expediency for the sake of that poisonous ooze, the globalization of the vicious immoralities and inequities found within the gears of unrestrained capitalism, and the profound ignorance of our populace regarding all matters pertaining to the aforementioned, have led us inexorably to the realities presented in the wake of 2001.

We must not let it happen again. What follows is a petition of grievances. Our will and ability to address them in a comprehensive fashion will determine the fate of this nation and this world. There can be no more compromise, no more patience, no more passivity. We cannot survive another year like 2001.

A constitutional amendment: the right to vote

Americans make much of their rights, but few are aware that technically there is no right to vote in this country. We are allowed to vote by our legislators and our leaders but, if they feel the need, those votes can easily be taken away. This was outlined succinctly in the Supreme Court Opinion from *Bush* v. *Gore*.

The Fifteenth and Nineteenth Amendments to the Constitution do not grant an affirmative right to vote. Rather, they seek to thwart any actions that may keep certain groups – women, minorities, immigrants – from casting a ballot. At the end of the day, the right to vote lies with the largesse of those who hold elective office in whatever state you vote in.

When drawing the first dim outlines of our national charter, the Founders specifically left off a constitutional right to vote. At the time, each state had its own set of voting standards, and it was feared that an all-encompassing Federal rule pertaining to voting rights would impede ratification and scuttle the deal. The existence of slavery in some states played a central role in this decision.

As time passed, more and more freedoms were outlined within the voting charter: women, then immigrants, and then minorities were given constitutional voting protections by the courts, but none were given the specific right to cast a ballot. Many of these leaps forward came in the aftermath of war – women gained suffrage after World War I, the poll tax was eliminated after World War II, the voting age was dropped after Vietnam, and minorities were given protections slowly but surely throughout the Cold War.

A constitutional amendment guaranteeing the right to vote for all citizens is essential as we approach a new election season in 2004. The catastrophes of Florida in 2000 must not be repeated; indeed, many of the problems from that election would have been much more easily handled if Americans had the solid right to vote, instead of merely the opportunity.

The mistakes made by ChoicePoint in the compilation of Florida voter rolls, mistakes that stripped voting privileges from tens of thousands of minorities, would have been a constitutional issue instead of an example of corporate malfeasance. Secretary of State Harris and Governor Jeb Bush would not have dared to act as they did had voting been a constitutionally protected activity. The Republican-dominated Florida legislature would have been unable to muddy the waters by threatening to choose their own electors. The Supreme Court would likely have not been able to toss aside 50 million votes in their decision.

The point cannot be made often enough: The document says We The People for a reason. If Americans are truly supposed to decide their own fate, if We The People are meant to rule, our right to exercise power at the voting booth must be Constitutionally protected. An amendment to the

Constitution guaranteeing the right to vote for every American citizen must be introduced, and passed, with all haste.

No more tax giveaways to corporations and the rich

When George W. Bush took office in 2001, his first priority was the passage of a massive tax-cut that overwhelmingly benefited corporations and the wealthy. Nearly half of the trillion-plus dollars he stripped from the Federal budget went to these two groups, leaving average Americans to collect a paltry $300 per person. The geometry of this action was determined in no small part by wealthy donors who, using financial influence described above, were able to lobby Bush and Congress to great effect.

The tax laws in this country already enormously benefit corporations and rich people. They did not need this tax-break. Rather, they are offended by the very idea that they are required to pay taxes at all. Bush, clearly under their sway, resolved to give them their money back. The result of this decision has been disastrous.

With the slowdown of the economy, the vast Clinton surplus projections became depleted. The tax-cut further stripped money from the Treasury. The events of September 11 required massive spending by the Federal government for clean-up operations, investigations, and military preparations. Today, because of these factors, the United States has returned to the ruinous days of deficit spending. Had George W. Bush not denuded the Treasury with his tax giveaway, the Federal government would not be spending in the red.

The ultimate motivation for the tax-cut is clear: Bush is influenced by those who believe the Federal government is too large, and should be, in the words of one hardcore anti-tax advocate, shrunk to a size where it can be drowned in a bathtub. The attacks on September 11, and subsequent reactions, have proved beyond the shadow of a doubt that Republican rhetoric regarding the size of government has been terribly misplaced. Had the Federal government not been as large as it is, had it not been equipped to deal with the fallout from those attacks, thousands more may have died and the republic may well have fallen into total disarray.

Even with these facts staring him in the face, Bush and his Republican cohorts tried to pass yet another tax giveaway package, disguised patriotically as a 'stimulus package' for the economy and the people. In truth, the package would have been an early Christmas present: billions of our dollars for corporations already operating in the black.

Only the determination of Senator Tom Daschle, who refused to allow passage of the House bill in the Senate unless protections for the million or so newly unemployed Americans were included, kept this farcical 'stimulus package' from passing. In an astounding example of aerobic backpedaling, Bush responded by claiming that, in reality, he wasn't sure if the stimulus package was actually necessary.

It is worth noting the thin margin Daschle had in his decision. Had James Jeffords not switched parties, the ruinous House bill would have likely passed through the Senate with ease.

Twenty-three years ago, George H.W. Bush referred to Reagan's trickle-down economic theory as 'voodoo economics.' He was more right than he knew. Reagan's folly left millions of the living dead walking the earth: AIDS victims, crack addicts, millions of Americans suffering the deprivations of recession, all left exposed by a plundering of the Treasury that fed wealthy corporations at the expense of vital social programs. George W. Bush would see this flawed trickle-down concept returned to government. It must not be allowed to happen.

Congressional Democrats, as well as Republicans of good conscience, must at all costs continue to thwart any move Bush makes to undermine further the ability of government to aid the people in these trying times by giving more of our needed money away to those who do not need it. Furthermore, they must revisit the tax plan already passed and restructure it accordingly, with the current circumstances clearly in mind. 2001 was a bad year for the average American, but a boon for the rich. The next few years will be worse if our government is too poor to help us.

Accountability for the airline industry

Many factors allowed terrorists to commandeer those commercial airplanes on September 11. One factor that has been largely ignored is the criminal negligence of the airline industry, whose security precautions were and continue to be so weak as to be nonexistent. This is a failure of catastrophic proportions and is responsible to no small degree for the death and ruin we have experienced.

For years now, the airline industry has lobbied Congress through the unregulated use of soft money contributions in an effort to keep any laws demanding that they beef up security off the books. On September 11, the terrorists passed through security checkpoints manned by people with little or no security training and who earn only the minimum wage. These security personnel were employed by companies under contract with the airline industry, such as Argenbright in Boston's Logan airport, whose safety records are nothing short of abysmal.

The subsequent passage of a bill Federalizing airline security has shored up the security failures to some degree, but nothing has been done to address the accountability of the airline industry in the attacks of September 11. Instead, $15 billion of our tax money was given to the industry as a bailout, with no strings attached. This must not stand. The capture of an airline passenger with explosives in his shoes demonstrates that security on passenger airlines is still less than adequate; the suspect raised suspicions because of a questionable passport, but was still allowed to board an airplane.

The airline industry's negligence, years in the making, came about because they did not want to spend money on security. They must be called to task for it. Congress must instigate a penetrating investigation into the vast array of failures and greed-motivated negligence that permeate this industry. We The People must exert market pressures upon these companies by instigating a nationwide boycott of their services. They will do nothing on their own, as has been demonstrated, unless we compel them to.

Repair the Constitution and the Bill of Rights

The response of this administration to the events of September 11 has been to curtail some of the most essential American rights in the name of security. In short, they have destroyed freedom in order to save it. With the passage of the PATRIOT Anti-Terrorism bill and Bush's signature on an Executive Order mandating secret military tribunals for anyone suspected of being a terrorist, there are precious few constitutional protections left. These acts violate the right to a speedy trial, the right to speak privately with an attorney, the right to avoid cruel and unusual punishment, and the right to be secure against government invasion of a private home.

The creeping oppression of our right to free speech began when we censored ourselves in the aftermath of September 11. It was furthered when presidential spokesman Ari Fleischer warned Americans to 'watch what we say.' It took a great leap forward when Attorney-General John Ashcroft proclaimed in the well of the Senate that anyone who questions his methods is aiding terrorism or is a terrorist themselves. Where shall it go tomorrow?

Supreme Court Justice William O. Douglass once said, 'As nightfall does not come at once, neither does oppression. In both instances, there's a twilight where everything remains seemingly unchanged, and it is in such twilight that we must be aware of change in the air, however slight, lest we become unwitting victims of the darkness.'

The terrorists have already scored a mighty victory because of the actions of this administration. Bush told us the terrorists attacked us because they hate our freedoms, and then turned around to shred those freedoms in an audacious manner. Osama bin Laden and his cohorts could not have asked for a more felicitous outcome. Oppression comes like Douglass's darkness, creeping unnoticed through the American body politic. It must be stopped.

As with his tax giveaway, as with the attempts to drill for oil in the Alaskan National Wildlife Preserve, as with so much else, Bush is using this crisis to further an agenda that had already been formulated before September 11. It is cynical opportunism of the worst kind, one that has been aided and abetted by the cowardice of Congress, who trembled in fear at Bush's overinflated approval ratings. These last acts, the suppression of dissident voices and the curtailing of essential freedoms in the name of patriotism, must not be allowed to stand.

Congress must act decisively to undo this damage. Waiting for the 'sunset provisions' in these bills is not sufficient. If we are to believe that this Congress stands for freedom and liberty, they must act soon and snatch this victory from the hands of those who attacked us.

Find the answers to unresolved questions

No avenue of questioning must be spared in Congress's search for answers regarding what happened on September 11. The preparedness and capability of the FBI, CIA, and NSA must be investigated, as must the multiple claims that a variety of hints and reports were out there for months indicating an attack was imminent.

This investigation must also undertake to parse the relationship between the Bush family connections to the business giant Carlyle Group and the oil barons of Saudi Arabia. Most of the terrorists involved in the attacks came from that nation, and it is no small leap to consider that a blind spot developed in our anti-terror preparations out of deference to these business connections. If this is true, the results were catastrophic and must be addressed, for that loophole still exists.

For months, Americans were terrorized by reports of letters filled with anthrax entering the mail system. These letters, it turns out, were nothing less than assassination attempts aimed at leading Senate Democrats such as Daschle and Leahy. Several civilians, including mail carriers, died as a result. Reports indicate that the anthrax was a strain developed by the US military and the CIA, leaving open the possibility that the attacks came from a rogue element within our government. It is more than likely that the assassination attempts emanated from someone steeped in the ideology of the Far Right, which has dabbled with anthrax in the past.

Attorney-General Ashcroft and his Justice Department failed in spectacular fashion to make even the slightest dent in this case, despite the fact that whoever sent the anthrax represents a clear and present danger to government officials and civilians. The arrest of anti-abortion extremist Clayton Lee Waagner, who sent hoax anthrax threats to hundreds of family planning clinics, does nothing to address the true threat. Is Ashcroft afraid of what will be uncovered if he breaks the case? Do his ideological underpinnings make him hesitate to pursue a suspect whose views might be in agreement with his? Whatever the case may be, the handling of this investigation has been deplorable in its utter lack of progress. It is time for the Senate to invite him in for another visit.

Another investigation that has collapsed into ignominious silence is the one surrounding the crash of Flight 587 into the New York neighborhood of Rockaway. The last words we heard on the subject stretch the outer edges of credibility: a jumbo jet which had taken off a full two minutes ahead of Flight 587 left behind enough wake turbulence to tear both engines and the tail off the doomed airbus.

If turbulence left in the wake of an airplane that took off two full minutes previous is strong enough to rip an airbus to pieces in midair, the land around dozens of airports would be piled high with the shattered remains of crashed airplanes. There is something else happening here, and we are not being told of it. Yet we were exhorted by patriotic commercials starring Bush to fly, fly, fly. It is likely that this airbus was in shoddy repair, or was tampered with, but the story is being suppressed by the government out of deference to airline lobbyists who have not yet finished counting the money they got in their Federal bailout payment. Break out those subpoenas, senators. It is time to know the truth.

Finally, the collapse of the giant energy corporation Enron has left enough questions to fill the agendas of a dozen Senate hearings. Enron's ties to Bush run deep, both within his staff and in his long personal relationship to disgraced Enron chief Kenneth Lay. Former SEC Chairman Harvey Pitt was selected by Enron because of his regulation-friendly policies, presidential advisor Karl Rove was once an Enron employee, and those secret energy policy meetings Cheney held and subsequently refused to describe were dominated by the needs and desires of Enron. The list goes on and on.

Some 4,000 Enron employees were left with nothing in the aftermath of this collapse. In their name, the Senate must act. They must determine why Enron fell apart, who knew it was coming, and which government officials had a hand in it. Bush would have us believe that capitalism free of governmental oversight is the proper way to do business in America and around the world. The debacle surrounding Enron gives great lie to these beliefs, and the Senate must step in with their oversight powers to make sure it never happens again. The subsequent collapse of WorldCom and Arthur Andersen, and the teetering state of the Stock Market, make this issue all the more pressing.

Media reform and the fairness doctrine

In 1996, President Clinton signed into law the Telecommunications Act in an effort to shore up his flank against ceaseless attacks by the GOP. This Act, among other things, did away with the backbone of journalistic integrity: the Fairness Doctrine. This Doctrine ensured that no one person or entity could control too much of the media. For example, if a corporation owned a newspaper within a city, they were not allowed to own a television station as well.

The magazine *The Nation* recently reported that ten corporations now control virtually all media, including the news. Once upon a time, journalism worked to curtail and control the worst excesses of these powerful entities. Now that the news is owned by these interests, the people are no longer informed about their activities and the impact these activities have upon their lives. Because of the deep connections between business and government, the media can no longer be trusted to report fairly and accurately on what is being done by our leaders in our name. This must stop.

The response from most Americans in the aftermath of September 11 was a numb shock. How did this happen? Why do they hate us? Once upon a time, journalism worked to inform Americans about what was happening around the world and what our government was doing abroad. This practice began to dissolve after the end of the Cold War, and was almost completely ignored after 1996. Because the American people went uninformed, they were not able to act in their own best interests. At the minimum, Americans should know what is happening, so when events like September 11 do come, we are not left in confused disarray.

Congress must step forward and reinstate the Fairness Doctrine as a matter of national security. We The People must know what is happening at home and abroad if we are to govern effectively. This responsibility cannot become the sole purview of multinational corporations, because they have proven themselves to be actively disinterested in the needs of the populace. If this nation is to remain healthy and free, the open exchange of information must be impeded by nothing and no one.

End our addiction to oil

At the end of the day, the American addiction to petroleum has led us inexorably to this nightmare. As our dependence upon foreign oil has grown, so have the entanglements. Our involvement in Saudi Arabia, our waging the Gulf War to protect the Saudi oil fields, our political involvement in that most complex of regions, all have been contributing factors in the arrival of this war to our shores.

There are two courses of action we can take. We can continue to be involved both politically and militarily in these regions to ensure the constant flow of oil into our economic veins. This will simply guarantee more terrorism, more war, and an increased weakening of our economic stability as oil becomes more and more scarce. Drilling in Alaskan National Wildlife Reserve and elsewhere will not suffice, as there is not nearly enough oil in America to sustain us. Involvement with the burgeoning oil industry in Russia presents similar complications.

Our other option is far more logical. The time has come to begin an energetic and well-funded exploration of alternative sources of energy that can be harvested and exploited at home, free from international entanglements. This will release us from the crucible of the Middle East and will herald the beginning of a new industrialization that is far kinder to our environment. The time is upon us. Either we shall have oil, war, and pollution, or we shall have alternative energy sources, peace, and clean air.

The decision appears to be simplicity itself, until the lobbying power of the petroleum industry comes into play. Congress must at all costs resist their appeals, deny their funds, and ignore their threats. Nothing less than the future of the planet depends upon our ability to wean ourselves from the oil addiction that has for so long poisoned our bodies and threatened our safety. The time is now.

We The People

None of the necessary reforms outlined above, not one, will see the light of day without the active and dynamic participation of the American people. Perhaps the most common emotion we felt in the aftermath of September 11 was a sensation of utter helplessness. We were caught unaware, and before we had our feet back under us, those in control of the government had changed the nation from top to bottom. Today, matters appear even farther out of our reach than before.

This is far from the truth. The American people have not been minding the store for decades – jaded by corruption, preoccupied with the complexity of normal life, content to let others do the work, we have allowed the machinery of government and media to slip farther and farther from our grasp. In reality, however, it would not require much of an effort to reclaim it all. If every American made an effort, we could take back the country from the hands of those who have been running it so very poorly for so very long.

Become informed about the issues. Contact your congressional representatives and let them know you are minding the store, or show up at their offices if you must. Become present in the daily civic life of your nation. Demand better information from the media. March in protest when you are denied what you want. Organize voter registration drives. Boycott industries that would have you take a back seat in the maintenance of your country. Run for office, or work for someone whose views are in agreement with yours.

Nothing will be changed by complacency, and it was complacency that gave us the dismal year 2001. If the future is to be any better, it will be up to us to make it so. We must fight for it. The alternative is to have no future at all.

Notes

The dream that was America

Data on the Stuart monarchy are found in *World History: Perspectives on the Past*, published by McDougal Littell. Jerry Vines' comments on Islam can be found in the *Florida Times-Union* in 'Vines Condems Islam,' dated June 12, 2002. Information on the status of Jose Padilla is found in a Cato Institute essay, 'Citizen Padilla: Dangerous Precedents,' dated July 1, 2002. Information on the OSU protest was gained from a friend and associate; further data can be found on a website created by OSU student activists: www.turnyourbackonbush.com. Information on the September 11 families rally is found in 'Lawmakers Join 9/11 Families in Calling for Independent Commission,' on CNSNews.com. Ashcroft's appearance before Congress was described in an article on CNN.com, 'Ashcroft: Critics of New Terror Measures Undermine Effort,' dated December 7, 2002. Bush's Executive Order codifying military tribunals was released on November 13, 2001, and can be found at www.WhiteHouse.gov. The USA PATRIOT Act is also entitled H.R. 3162, and can be found here: http://www.ins.usdoj.gov/graphics/lawsregs/patriot.pdf (Adobe Acrobat required). Analysis of Bush's stimulus package is found in a *BusinessWeek* article, 'Why Bush's Stimulus Package will Leave the U.S. Weaker,' dated October 29, 2001. Information on the airline security bill is found on CNN.com in 'Democrats: Bush Airline Security Plan Falls Short,' dated September 27, 2002. Data on Bush's decision to withhold the Reagan papers can be found in the National Security Archive, 'Historians, Public Interest Groups Sue to Stop Bush Order,' dated November 28, 2001.

Twenty pounds of bullshit in a ten pound bag

Falwell and Robertson's comments about September 11 are described in an ABCNews.com article, 'I'm Sorry: Falwell Now Says Gays and Feminists Not at Fault for Attacks,' dated September 20, 2002. Bush's comments on tax cuts for gas are found on CNN.com in 'Bush, in Impromptu Press Conference, Links Tax Cuts to Gasoline Prices', dated May 11, 2001. Data on petroleum company contributions to Bush were gathered by the Center for Public Integrity. Anthony York's *Salon* article about Chuy's ran on June

6, 2001. Data on FDR are found in *FDR* by Ted Morgan. McCain's campaign finance reform victory is described in a *Washington Post* editorial, 'Victory for Reform,' dated March 21, 2002. Information on *Buckley* v. *Valeo* can be found in Cornell's law database on the web; the case is also titled 424 U.S. 1 (1976). Rush Limbaugh's comments are found in his article, 'Tarnished Legacy,' dated March 20, 2002. Hughes' departure is decribed on CNN.com in 'Karen Hughes leaving White House for Texas.' Biographical background on Hughes is provided by CNN.com in 'Bush Aide Karen Hughes to leave White House,' dated April 23, 2002. IowaPulse.com describes Bush's mockery of Karla Faye Tucker in 'Bauer Slams Bush for "Disgusting" Comments to *Talk Magazine*,' dated August 10, 1999. The trifecta joke is described in an MSNBC.com article, 'Hitting the Trifecta,' dated June 27, 2002. Data on his absence from service can be found in a *Boston Globe* exposé, 'One Year Gap in Bush's Guard Duty,' dated May 23, 2002.

Enronomics

Zogby polling data can be found at www.Zogby.com. Market reaction to Bush's corporate responsibility speech is described in a *BusinessWeek* article, 'Wall Street Turns Thumbs Down on Bush Speech,' dated July 9, 2002. Market reaction to Bush's second speech on July 16, 2002 is described in another *BusinessWeek* article, 'Stocks Lose Grip amid Ongoing Jitters,' dated July 16, 2002. Data on PSLRA are provided by Consumers Union, owned by Consumer Reports, here: http://www.consumersunion.org/finance/securdc202.htm. Data on Cheney and Halliburton are described in an ABCNews.com article, 'Cheney's Corporate Liability,' dated July 19, 2002. Data on Bush and Harken can be found in a variety of places, but two good sources are: Molly Ivins' *Shrub* published by Random House, and in a *Washington Post* article 'Files: Bush Knew Firm's Plight Before Stock Sale,' dated July 21, 2002. The *New York Times* report on civilian casualties in Afghanistan ran on July 21, 2002, and was titled 'Flaws in U.S. Air War Left Hundreds of Civilians Dead.' Tom Ridge's proposal for using military forces in American police actions is described in a CBSNews.com article, 'Domestic Military Role Under Review,' dated July 21, 2002. Posse Comitatus is well described by the *Washington University Law Quarterly* here: http://law.wustl.edu/WULQ/75–2/752–10.html. The *Nation Magazine* has an amazing catalogue of Enron data here: http://www.thenation.com/special/2002enron.mhtml. Data on Enron contributions to elected officials were gathered by the Center for Public Integrity. James Greenwood's comments can be found in a BBC article, 'Investigator Fears Dozens of Enrons,' dated February 24, 2002. NarcoNews.com covered the coup in Venezuela in detail, but further data are found in a *Guardian* (UK) article 'Venezuela Coup Linked to Bush Team,' dated April 21, 2002.

A bright September morning

A frightening in-depth analysis of Bush's dealings with the Taliban over a natural gas pipeline prior to September 11 is provided by Jean-Charles Brisard, Wayne Madsen, and Guillaume Dasquie in their book, *Forbidden Truth*. The book is easily ordered on Barnes & Noble's website and also deals specifically with deceased FBI Deputy Director John O'Neill. Robert Wright's press conference is described by CNSNews.com in an article, 'Tearful FBI Agent Apologizes to Sept. 11 Families and Victims,' dated May 30, 2002. The press conference was carried live on C-SPAN. Bush Sr's involvement with the Carlyle Group and Saudi Arabia is described in a *Nation* article, 'Bush of Arabia,' dated March 27, 2002. WSWS.org describes the warnings we received prior to September 11 in an article, 'Was the US Government Alerted to September 11 Attack?' dated January 16, 2002. Khalilzad's involvement with Unocal is described in a *Boston Herald* report, 'US Ties to Saudi Elite May be Hurting War on Terrorism,' dated December 10, 2001. Karzai's Unocal connections are described in an article by the Pakistani news service PakWatan, 'US Seeks Pakistan's Oil Nod,' dated January 26, 2002. Stanley Hilton's lawsuit is described in a *San Francisco Examiner* article, 'S.F. Attorney: Bush Allowed 9/11,' dated June 11, 2002. Data on Operation Northwoods can be found in James Bamford's excellent book on the NSA entitled *Body of Secrets*, published by Doubleday. The actual Northwoods documents, now declassified, can be read here: http://www.fromthewilderness.com/free/ww3/11_20_01_northwoods.pdf (Adobe Acrobat required).

The light of the world

Joe Conason describes the warnings from Bush and Cheney to Daschle about the September 11 inquiry in an article, 'The 9/11 Coverup,' dated May 17, 2002. Lieutenant-Colonel Lester W. Grau and retired Afghanistan General Mohammad Yahya Nawroz wrote of the Soviet Union's history in Afghanistan in an essay published by the US Army's Foreign Military Studies Office entitled 'The Soviet War in Afghanistan: History and Harbinger of Future War?' The military service history of many prominent conservatives can be found in a database compiled by the *New Hampshire Gazette*, here: http://www.nhgazette.com/chickenhawks.html. The mother whom I quoted after her family was destroyed was interviewed for a BBC article, 'US Bomb Kills Ten in Kabul', dated October 28, 2002. The strafing of a wedding party in Afghanistan is described in an article in the *Independent* (UK), 'UN keeps Damning Report on Afghan Massacre Secret,' dated July 31, 2002. Descriptions of the humanitarian crisis in Afghanistan were compiled by the UN relief officials, and can be found here: http://www.un.org/News/dh/20010925.htm#26. The Associated Press reported on the massive influx of Pakistani fighters joining the Taliban in 'Pakistanis Leave for Holy War,' dated October 27, 2001. The bungling of the anthrax situation was described in an article in the *International Herald-Tribune*, 'FBI Lethargy Lets the Anthrax Killer Go Free,' dated July 3, 2002. Efforts by Clinton to deal with terrorism are described in the following articles: 'US Was Foiled Multiple Times in Efforts to Capture bin Laden or Have Him Killed' (*Washington Post*, October 3, 2001); 'Roadblocks Cited in Effort to Trace bin Laden's Money' (*New York Times*, September 20, 2001); 'President Wants Senate to Hurry with New Anti-terrorism Laws' (CNN.com, July 30, 1996). The White House Commission on Aviation Safety and Security can be found here: http://www.fas.org/irp/threat/212fin~1.html. The Hart–Rudman National Security Report can be found here: http://usinfo.state.gov/topical/pol/terror/01013102.htm. Everything you need to know about the airline industry is found in a *Boston Globe* article, 'Airlines Fought Security Changes,' dated September 20, 2001. The passage of the airline security bill is described by *USA Today*, 'Congress Passes Airline Security Bill,' dated November 16, 2001. The *Toronto Globe and Mail* article describing political motivations behind terror warnings is 'US Issues New Warnings on Terror,' dated May 21, 2002.

One crazy summer: the media before and after September 11

The *Times-Herald Record* of New Paltz describes Bozydaj's acts in 'No Plea for Accused New Paltz Shooter,' dated July 28, 2001. The running diary regarding Fox News was compiled on August 7, 2001. I pointedly refuse to endnote anything about Gary Condit – you can find it all pretty easily if you're a glutton for punishment. Information on which corporations own what news media was compiled by the *Columbia Journalism Review*. Their database is here: http://www.cjr.org/owners. Data on the Saudi nationality of the September 11 terrorists are described by CBSNews.com, 'First Saudi Terror Arrests,' dated June 18, 2002. Financial and intelligence ties between America and bin Laden are described by MSNBC.com, 'Bin Laden Comes Home to Roost,' dated August 24, 1998.

American elections: 2000 and beyond

Data on ChoicePoint and the Florida election were meticulously researched by Greg Palast of the BBC and published in his book *The Best Democracy Money Can Buy*, published by Pluto Press. My running diary of the debate was compiled on October 3, 2000. The Supreme Court Decision *Bush* v. *Gore* is here: http://www.usatoday.com/news/vote2000/ pres244.htm. Data on the French elections can be found in the following articles: 'Extreme Rightist Eclipses Socialist to Qualify for Runoff' (*New York Times*, April 22, 2002); 'France's Disgruntled Voters' (*New York Times*, April 23, 2002): 'Jospin Reveals a Left that is Losing its Platform' (*New York Times*, April 22, 2002).

'We The People' means you

The Santee shooting is described by CNN.com in 'An Epidemic of Violence,' dated March 8, 2001. The story of Betty Ann Waters is described by MSNBC in, 'Sibling Sovereignty,' dated March 15, 2001. Tom DeLay's remarkable explanation for missing Vietnam is described in a *Houston Press* article, 'Which Bug Gets the Gas,' dated January 7, 1999. Information on Richard Mellon Scaife and the ongoing Culture War in America can be found in several excellent books: *The Hunting of the President* by Joe Conason and Gene Lyons; *Blinded by the Right* by David Brock; *A Vast Conspiracy* by Jeffrey Toobin. Gingrich's GOPAC memo is entitled 'Language: A Key Mechanism of Control.'

The title of this book was taken from a speech given by Bill Moyers on October 16, 2001 to the Environmental Grantmakers Association. My two running diaries are formatted on a model I first saw used by ESPN sportswriter Bill Simmons. The term 'Enronomics' was first used, not in the mainstream media, but by a member of the DemocraticUnderground.com internet forums named Walt Starr.

Acknowledgements

This book would not exist but for the help and dedication of many people. Robert Arnold of San Francisco gave me my first shot as a writer. The editors of BuzzFlash.com, OnlineJournal.com, LiberalSlant.com, BushWatch.com, Citizens for Legitimate Government (LegitGov.org), SmirkingChimp.com, BartCop.com among many others gave me the opportunity to spread my writing across the progressive corners of the Internet. Radio commentators Meria Heller and Mike Malloy invited me to speak on the air and used their programs to spread the word of my work. Without the friendship and opportunity provided by all of these people, I would still only be sending outraged emails to a small circle of friends.

The editors and publishers at Pluto Press deserve my special thanks. They chose to take a chance on an unknown Internet screeder, and I am eternally in their debt. Likewise, I owe vast thanks to Fredda Weinberg, researcher for investigative journalist Greg Palast, for putting me in touch with Pluto and for arguing my case with them. Fredda is currently riding herd over an alternative media project called Webbis that everyone should pay great heed of. Without Fredda, this book would not be.

There are three political websites that deserve to be highlighted, both for their relevance to current American politics and for the information, community, and opportunity I have received from them. The first is Truthout.org, run by editor Marc Ash. Truthout is produced daily, capturing both national and international news stories of vital import to this country and the world. Marc and I, along with a host of writers, provide original content and analysis to Truthout that make it a must-see on your tour of political sites on the net.

The second is the colorfully titled MediaWhoresOnline.com, a site run by journalists who have become horrified at the manner in which news and information is subverted and perverted by this neo-conservative government and the corporate media that sit snugly in their lap. If you believe that the free and fair exchange of information is vital to the existence of a democracy, as Thomas Jefferson did, then MWO.com must stand prominently on your list. The existence of liberal media is a myth too often repeated, and MWO.com works overtime to demonstrate the lethal cracks in our news system.

Finally, and most importantly, there is DemocraticUnderground.com, created on January 20, 2001 by three young men in Washington, D.C. in the shadow of the Bush inauguration. This website offers daily commentary and analysis on all that is important to this democracy. Furthermore, DU is a community made up of tens of thousands of progressives who visit its many forums. DU has become nothing less than an electronic institution of memory for this republic. Every day DUers find the stories that matter to us all, post them in the forums, and thus provide information, analysis, and debate.

I would not have a tenth of the information currently at my command were it not for those who make it their business to enrich this news-junkie community. DU members span the entire ideological perspective of the Left – conservative Democrats to Social Democrats, Greens to anarchists to Socialists, and all the great body of progressives in between are represented on this dynamic site. It is a place where activism has taken root, where change has been forged, where inspiration can be found, and where those who feel as though their nation has left them behind can find true friends and allies.

I owe these people every praise and thanks. They are the burning heart of the American dream. Come and visit them, if you find the chance. I'll be there. WilliamPitt is my screen name. Let me buy you a drink in the Lounge.

Index